DAUGHTERS OF EDWARD I

DAUGHTERS OF EDWARD I

Kathryn Warner

First published in Great Britain in 2021 by
PEN AND SWORD HISTORY
An imprint of
Pen & Sword Books Ltd
Yorkshire – Philadelphia

ISBN 978 1 52675 027 3

A CIP catalogue record for this book is available from the British Library.

Typeset in Times New Roman 11.5/14 by
SJmagic DESIGN SERVICES, India.

Printed and bound by CPI Group (UK) Ltd, Croydon, CR0 4YY

Pen & Sword Books Limited incorporates the imprints of Atlas, Archaeology, Aviation, Discovery, Family History, Fiction, History, Maritime, Military, Military Classics, Politics, Select, Transport, True Crime, Air World, Frontline Publishing, Leo Cooper, Remember When, Seaforth Publishing, The Praetorian Press, Wharncliffe Local History, Wharncliffe Transport, Wharncliffe True Crime and White Owl.

For a complete list of Pen & Sword titles please contact
PEN & SWORD BOOKS LIMITED
47 Church Street, Barnsley, South Yorkshire, S70 2AS, England
E-mail: enquiries@pen-and-sword.co.uk
Website: www.pen-and-sword.co.uk

Or
PEN AND SWORD BOOKS
1950 Lawrence Rd, Havertown, PA 19083, USA
E-mail: Uspen-and-sword@casematepublishers.com
Website: www.penandswordbooks.com

Contents

Family Trees

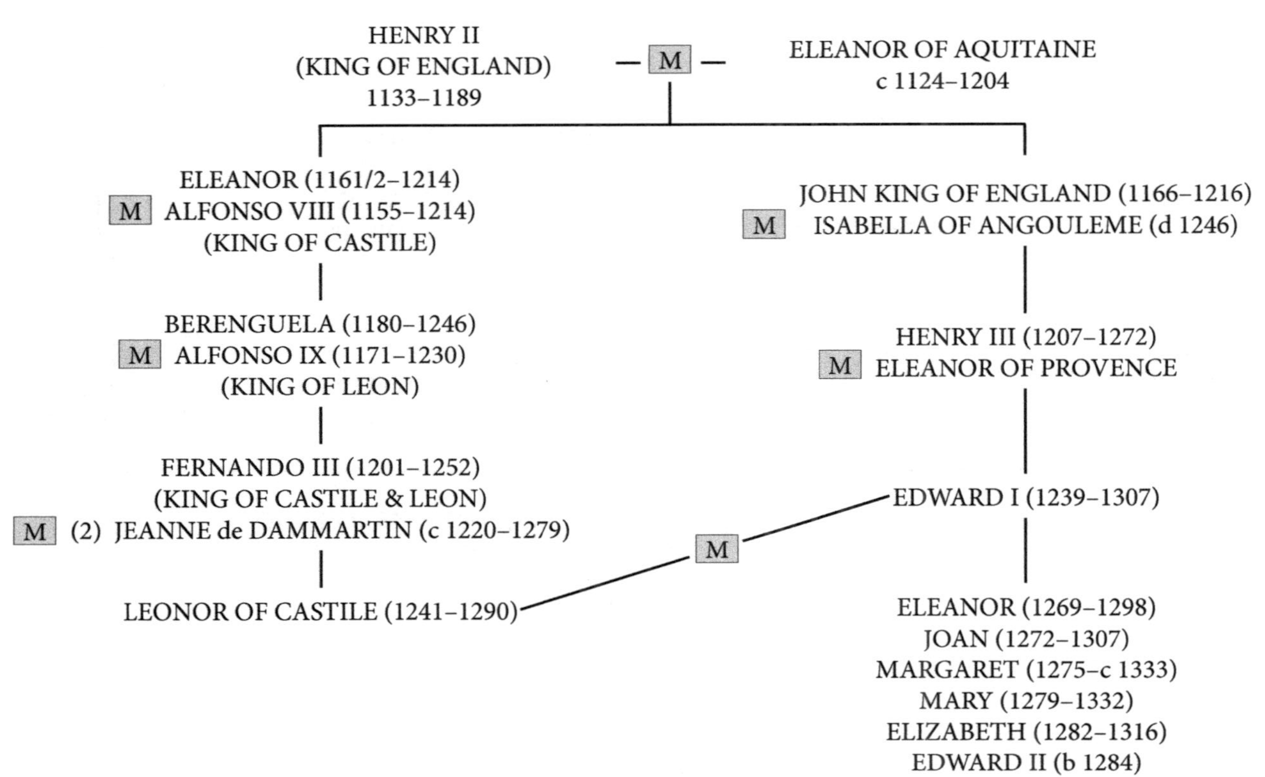

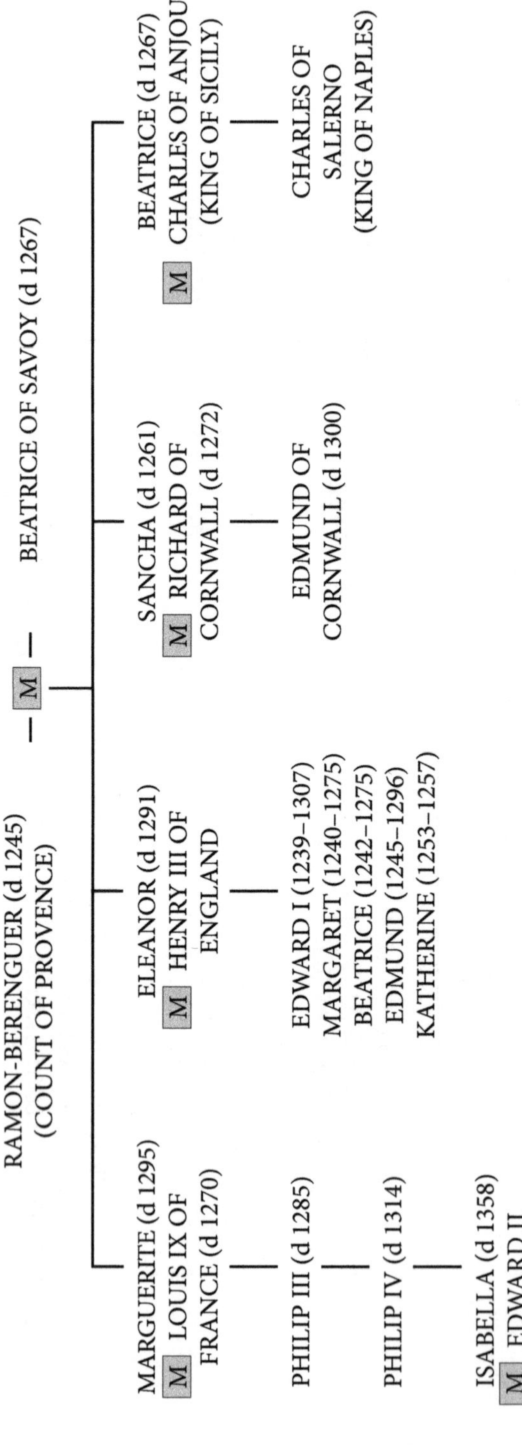

RAMON-BERENGUER (d 1245)
(COUNT OF PROVENCE)
M
BEATRICE OF SAVOY (d 1267)
MARGUERITE (d 1295)
M LOUIS IX OF
FRANCE (d 1270)
PHILIP III (d 1285)
PHILIP IV (d 1314)
ISABELLA (d 1358)
M EDWARD II
ELEANOR (d 1291)
M HENRY III OF
ENGLAND
EDWARD I (1239–1307)
MARGARET (1240–1275)
BEATRICE (1242–1275)
EDMUND (1245–1296)
KATHERINE (1253–1257)
SANCHA (d 1261)
M RICHARD OF
CORNWALL (d 1272)
EDMUND OF
CORNWALL (d 1300)
BEATRICE (d 1267)
M CHARLES OF ANJOU
(KING OF SICILY)
CHARLES OF
SALERNO
(KING OF NAPLES)

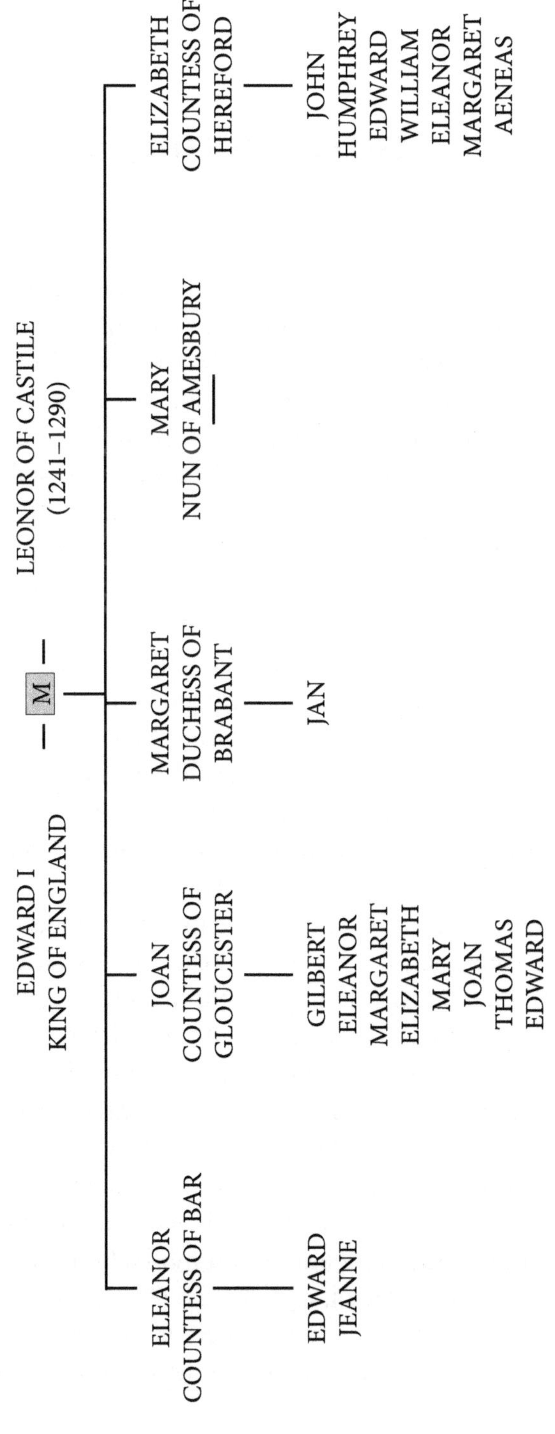
EDWARD I
KING OF ENGLAND
M
LEONOR OF CASTILE
(1241–1290)
ELEANOR
COUNTESS OF BAR
EDWARD
JEANNE
JOAN
COUNTESS OF
GLOUCESTER
GILBERT
ELEANOR
MARGARET
ELIZABETH
MARY
JOAN
THOMAS
EDWARD
MARGARET
DUCHESS OF
BRABANT
JAN
MARY
NUN OF AMESBURY
ELIZABETH
COUNTESS OF
HEREFORD
JOHN
HUMPHREY
EDWARD
WILLIAM
ELEANOR
MARGARET
AENEAS

Introduction

The five daughters of Edward I and his first wife Queen Leonor were born between 1269 and 1282, and although they have often been ignored or neglected, this is changing: they are the subjects of a joint biography published in 2019, and of an article in an academic essay collection about their father, published in 2020.[1] Louise Wilkinson, author of the academic essay, has pointed out how Edward I immersed his daughters in court ceremony, and both he and his son and successor allowed them to intercede on others' behalf and to wield influence at court. Despite his reputation as a stern and ruthless leader, it is apparent that Edward I loved his daughters dearly, and recognised their value. One of them might even, if her youngest brother had died in childhood as her three other brothers did, have become queen-regnant of England. Edward I considered this possibility in 1290, and rather than stating that he wished his throne to pass one day to his younger brother and nephews, declared that his eldest daughter should inherit his kingdom after him.

It is often very difficult to write about medieval women, who tend to disappear from the written record when married, and even when not married only rarely hove into view in extant documents. None of the five royal sisters left a will, or at least, a will which still survives. For one of the daughters, it is impossible even to ascertain the date of her death, though we are lucky that with all of the five daughters of Edward I who survived into adulthood, we know their dates of birth, at least approximately. Personal letters were practically non-existent in the late thirteenth and early fourteenth centuries; diaries had not yet been invented; and even surviving household accounts are few and far between. It can, therefore, be very difficult, even impossible, to ascertain medieval people's thoughts, feelings and motivations, and as is usually the case with medieval women, even kings' daughters, the list of things we do not know about the five royal sisters is far longer than the things we do know. For example, we cannot know for certain what any of the women looked like, as no source recorded their appearance. Possibly they were tall, as an eighteenth-century examination of their father's remains revealed that he had stood 6 feet 2 inches, and their brother Edward II was also described as tall by several chroniclers. In childhood, their father had curly fair hair, which darkened as he grew into adulthood, and had a drooping left eyelid inherited from his father and a lisp. Their Castilian mother Queen Leonor's colouring is not recorded, though her modern biographer believes she is likely to have had dark, thick, wavy hair.[2] On the other hand, the fourteenth-century Castilian descendants of Leonor's half-brother had light blond hair, pale skin and blue eyes, and her son Edward II was often depicted in his own lifetime and afterwards with fair hair, and it is probably impossible to say for certain what Leonor and her daughters might have looked like.[3]

The five royal sisters lived in a world that was far more international and cosmopolitan than we might imagine. The women are, with their younger brother Edward II and Queen Mary I (b. 1516, r. 1553–58), the only English royals in history who had a Spanish parent.[4] Their Spanish grandfather was canonised as a saint of the Catholic Church and is the patron saint of the city of Seville, and their parents' wedding took place near Burgos in the north of Spain. Three of the five sisters married overseas, one into eastern France and the others into the patchwork of counties and duchies which is now Belgium, the Netherlands, northern France and western Germany. As well as the royal marriages which took place, several of the sisters were betrothed, ultimately unsuccessfully, into Spain, Germany, and the county of Savoy, which lies in modern-day France, Italy and Switzerland.

One of their brothers was born in Bayonne, south-west France, and another in North Wales. Their father Edward I, accompanied by their mother, led the last great Christian crusade to the Holy Land, and Joan, second of the five daughters, was born in the port of Acre, which is now called Akko and is situated in northern Israel, and is one of the oldest settlements in the world, first mentioned around 2000 BC. Nineteen years after Joan was born, her birthplace fell to the Mamluks, a Muslim dynasty of former slaves who ruled much of Egypt and Syria for centuries until overthrown by the Ottomans in 1517. Edward I was lord of Ireland and duke of Aquitaine in south-west France as well as king of England, and the sisters' younger brother Edward II was the first heir to the English throne to be made prince of Wales. He also inherited their mother's county of Ponthieu in northern France; the fact that a king of England was born in Wales and inherited a county in France from his Spanish mother takes some unpacking. One of Edward I's uncles was king of Germany, and his aunts included the Holy Roman Empress and queen of Sicily, another queen of Sicily, the queen of Scotland, and the queen of France. Edward was a first cousin of the kings of France and Naples, the queen of Hungary, the empress of Constantinople, the duchess of Burgundy, and the Italian-born countess palatine of Saxony and landgravine of Thuringia; his sister-in-law was queen of Navarre in northern Spain and countess of Brie and Champagne in France; and his brothers-in-law included the king of Scotland, the duke of Brittany, the king of Castile and Leon, the archbishop of Toledo, the archbishop-elect of Seville, and a senator of Rome. One of his nieces was queen of Norway, and a nephew, the lord of Villena and duke of Peñafiel, is considered one of the greatest Spanish writers of the Middle Ages. The daughters of Edward I were, therefore, born into a powerful network of relatives which stretched far across Europe.

Chapter 1

A Spanish Wedding

Lord Edward, 15-year-old son and heir of the king of England, met Doña Leonor, half-sister of the king of Castile and Leon and aged almost 13, a few days before their wedding on 1 November 1254. The venue was the magnificent abbey of Santa María la Real de Las Huelgas just outside the city of Burgos in northern Spain, founded sixty-three years earlier in 1187 by King Alfonso VIII of Castile (r. 1158–1214) and his wife Eleanor of England, Doña Leonor's great-grandparents.[1]

Edward's great-uncle Richard Lionheart, king of England from 1189 to 1199, had also married a Spanish bride, Berengaria of Navarre, in 1191, because her brother King Sancho VII of Navarre was believed to be a useful ally for the king of England in his capacity as duke of Aquitaine in southern France. Sancho's kingdom lay next to Richard's duchy, which would help to protect Richard's borders, and Navarre was usefully located for trade routes across the Pyrenees. The reasons behind Lord Edward and Doña Leonor's union were somewhat different. For more than 500 years, since 711, a large part of the Iberian Peninsula had been ruled by Muslims from Arabia and North Africa, firstly the Umayyad caliphate then the Nasrid dynasty, and, beginning in the second half of the twelfth century, the Almohad caliphate of Morocco. The area of Spain and Portugal conquered in and after 711 was called al-Andalus. The Christian rulers of the much-diminished Iberian kingdoms – Portugal, Castile, Leon, Aragon and Navarre – waged war against the Muslim rulers of al-Andalus for centuries, and their decisive victory over the Almohad caliphate at the battle of Las Navas de Tolosa in July 1212 proved a decisive turning-point in the centuries-long *Reconquista* or 'Reconquest' of Spain. The Almohads were severely weakened, and their opponents saw their chance.

Fernando III, born probably in 1201, was the grandson and heir of Alfonso VIII of Castile, one of the victors of Las Navas de Tolosa. Fernando became the ruler of the powerful kingdom of Castile as a

16-year-old in 1217 when his mother Queen Berenguela, Alfonso VIII's eldest daughter, surrendered her rights to the throne in his favour, and he also inherited the much smaller kingdom of Leon in northern Spain when his father died in 1230. From the early 1220s to the late 1240s, Fernando and his armies swept through al-Andalus, and his fellow Christian kings also took the opportunity to expand their territories at the expense of the weakened Almohads until all that remained to them was a small vassal state known as the Emirate of Granada (which finally fell to King Ferdinand of Aragon and Queen Isabella of Castile, the 'Catholic Monarchs', in 1492). Fernando III captured town after town during his brilliantly successful campaigns in al-Andalus over more than a quarter of a century, including Jaén, Córdoba, Murcia, Badajoz, Cartagena and Alicante. In November 1248, he captured the finest prize of all: the great city of Seville, in the twenty-first century still the largest city in southern Spain and the fourth largest in the country. Fernando III died in Seville on 30 May 1252, leaving his eldest son Alfonso X (b. 1221), from his first marriage to Beatriz of Swabia, as his successor. He was outlived by his much younger second wife, the French noblewoman Jeanne de Dammartin, who had become countess of Aumale and Ponthieu in her own right on the deaths of her parents Simon and Marie in 1239 and 1250.

King Fernando and Queen Jeanne married in September or October 1237, when Fernando was a 36-year-old widower with ten children and Jeanne was an heiress of about 17 or 18 who had made the long journey south to Spain from her home in northern France. Jeanne had in fact been married by proxy to King Henry III of England (r. 1216–72) in 1235, and Henry wrote to her father Simon de Dammartin, Count of Aumale, to arrange a date for her to arrive in England and to be crowned its queen.[2] The powerful Blanche (née Blanca) of Castile, however, regent of France for her son Louis IX (r. 1226–70) and Louis's chief adviser for many years, did not wish the English king to gain a foothold in the county of Ponthieu, which lay next to the rich duchy of Normandy and was held by Jeanne's mother Marie. Henry III's father King John had lost possession of Normandy to Queen Blanche's father-in-law Philip II Augustus of France in 1204, and Blanche had no mind for Henry to attempt to take it back. She threatened Simon and Marie that a French army would invade Ponthieu if they married their daughter and heir to the king of England, and, on the advice of her eldest sister Queen

Berenguela, suggested Berenguela's recently-widowed son Fernando III of Castile and Leon as a husband for the young woman instead.

Although she was heir merely to two fairly small French counties, Jeanne de Dammartin was, via her maternal grandmother Alix, countess of Vexin and Ponthieu, a great-granddaughter of Louis VII of France and a great-great-granddaughter of Alfonso VII of Castile and Leon, and hence was both a distant cousin of Fernando III and of suitably illustrious birth to marry him.[3] Deprived of his bride, meanwhile, Henry III of England married Eleanor of Provence, whose elder sister Marguerite was already married to Blanche of Castile's son Louis IX of France, in January 1236. Their eldest child Lord Edward was born at Westminster on 17 June 1239, and was heir to the English throne from the moment of his birth. Henry III and Eleanor of Provence's son would marry the daughter of Henry's former fiancée in 1254.

King Fernando III and Queen Jeanne's first child, Infante Don Fernando, was probably born in the winter of 1238/39, and their second, Infanta Doña Leonor, almost certainly in November 1241. Leonor's biographer Sara Cockerill has suggested 23 November 1241, a date which would make Leonor exactly twenty years, to the day, younger than her eldest half-brother King Alfonso X. Doña Leonor was probably conceived in Toledo in central Spain in late February or early March 1241 after her parents were reunited following King Fernando's long sojourn in the far south of Spain, and she may have been born in Valladolid, where her father was based in the winter of 1241/42. Leonor was most probably named in honour of her great-grandmother Eleanor of England, Queen of Castile. Infante Don Luis, the third child of King Fernando and Queen Jeanne, was born before the end of March 1243, and their fourth and fifth children, Don Ximen and Don Juan, followed in 1244 and 1245.[4] Ximen, named after his maternal grandfather Simon de Dammartin, and Juan both died in infancy; Ximen was buried in Toledo and Juan in Córdoba.[5] In total, from his two marriages, King Fernando III had eleven sons and four daughters.

Infanta Doña Leonor of Castile was 10 years old when her father died at the end of May 1252 and her half-brother Alfonso X succeeded him as king. Leonor was present at King Fernando's deathbed in Seville, and until 1254 lived with her mother, the dowager queen, but Jeanne de Dammartin quarrelled with her stepson Alfonso over her dower, and decided to leave Spain for good and return to her native Ponthieu.

This was a county which no longer exists on the political map of France, but which covered much of the modern departments of Somme and Pas de Calais in the far north of the country (the tiny county of Aumale which Jeanne also held now lies in the Seine-Maritime department, also in the far north of France). Some years after her return to her homeland, Queen Jeanne married her second husband, Jean de Nesle, lord of Falvy. Her two eldest Spanish children also left their homeland: Leonor married and moved to England, and Don Fernando succeeded his mother as count of Aumale and married a French noblewoman called Laure de Montfort. Don Luis, Fernando III's youngest surviving child, spent all his life in Spain and became lord of Marchena, but he and his children were all already dead when Queen Jeanne died in 1279. Don Fernando also died before his mother and Doña Leonor was the only one of Jeanne's five children who outlived her, and from her French mother and her grandmother Marie inherited the county of Ponthieu, which passed to her English son after her own death.[6]

On the northern border of the large Spanish territories inherited by Alfonso X stood the great duchy of Aquitaine, and Alfonso began casting a covetous eye on it within months of his accession. He claimed that Aquitaine had been the dowry which his great-grandmother Eleanor of England brought with her on marriage to Alfonso VIII of Castile in 1177. Alfonso VIII had invaded and occupied much of the duchy in and after 1204 following the death of his mother-in-law Eleanor of Aquitaine, dowager queen of England, though his grandson and successor Fernando III had been too preoccupied with his decades-long and highly successful campaigns against the Almohads to pay much attention to the Castilian claims to the duchy.[7] Freed from the Almohad threat, Alfonso X decided to promote a rebellion in Aquitaine in 1252/53 with a view to invading, occupying and taking over the duchy as his ancestor had done nearly half a century earlier, and this decision was to bring about the English-Castilian royal marriage.

Far away in England, Henry III, who had inherited the duchy of Aquitaine from his father King John (r. 1199–1216, Eleanor of Aquitaine's youngest child and heir, and Richard Lionheart's brother), watched events with alarm. To avoid going to war against a powerful king and to avert the risk of losing his large French territory, Henry proposed a solution in May 1253: a marriage between his elder son and heir Lord Edward, then coming up 14, and a female relative of Alfonso

X. By May 1253, Alfonso's 11-year-old half-sister Leonor was the only daughter of Fernando III left available; her older half-sisters Leonor the elder and María had died young, and her other half-sister Berenguela had become a nun at the abbey of Las Huelgas. Alfonso X married Violante of Aragon in January 1249, but she was many years his junior and not yet old enough to bear children, and their eldest child (another Berenguela) was not born until October or November 1253. Leonor was, therefore, the only real option as a bride for King Henry's son, and conveniently, she and Edward were close to the same age. Leonor would become queen-consort of England and duchess of Aquitaine when her father-in-law died and her half-Castilian son would be the next king of England and duke of Aquitaine, and Henry III hoped that this would persuade Alfonso to give up his claims to the duchy.

Fortunately, Alfonso X decided that the arrangement made good sense, agreed to the English marriage, and withdrew his claim to the duchy of Aquitaine. Henry III's fury at the Castilian ruler's behaviour is, however, apparent in his comments that Alfonso had encouraged Henry's subjects in Gascony to 'set up the horns of their pride against' him, and that they had 'made a crafty treaty' with Alfonso. He further stated that 'the enemy grows madder every day and opposes the king [Henry] and his [people] more often and more bitterly than before'. Whether correctly or not, Henry suspected Alfonso of wishing to invade England and Ireland 'with an army of Christians and Saracens', i.e. Muslims, as well, once he was done with Aquitaine. For all his undoubted satisfaction at the success of his diplomatic strategy, on a personal level Henry III had no great reason to feel much affection for Alfonso X, and furthermore, his son's impending marriage into the royal family of Castile caused envy and suspicion in the powerful kingdom of France. According to the Westminster Abbey chronicler, Louis IX 'demanded that a daughter of the same king of Castile should be given as a wife to his son, in order that he might thus place himself in a better condition, inasmuch as he obtained a daughter, while the king of England had only obtained a sister'.[8] Alfonso X and Queen Violante's eldest child Doña Berenguela was duly betrothed to Louis and Queen Marguerite's eldest son Louis of France (b. 1244), though he died in 1260 before the wedding took place and did not succeed his father as king.

The bridegroom, Lord Edward, left England with his mother Eleanor of Provence on 29 May 1254, and 300 ships were required to carry the royal party from Portsmouth to Bordeaux. Henry III gave his son, who turned 15 three weeks after his departure from England, the duchy of Aquitaine (or rather, the part of it still ruled by the English kings and called Gascony or Guienne) and lands in England, Wales and Ireland to a total value of £10,000 annually.[9] This gave Edward the landed endowment and the gravitas deemed necessary to marry a Castilian infanta. Edward and his retinue arrived in the city of Burgos on or about 18 October, and Edward was knighted personally by his soon-to-be brother-in-law Alfonso X before he married Leonor. King Alfonso had insisted on being allowed to perform this important and meaningful ceremony as a condition for the wedding to go ahead, and Edward's father paid a messenger 100 shillings (£5) for bringing him the 'happy report' of the young man's recent knighting.[10]

The St Albans chronicler Matthew Paris gives a long account of the Spanish royal wedding and says that the people of Burgos were impressed by the tall, handsome young Englishman – Edward in adulthood was (and still is) known by the nickname Longshanks, 'long legs' – who married Doña Leonor.[11] (How Matthew, in distant St Albans, was able to ascertain the feelings of the townspeople of Burgos on the matter is not clear; perhaps one of the wedding guests told him.) On 1 November 1254, the day of Edward and Leonor's wedding, Alfonso officially ceded all his rights in the duchy of Aquitaine to his new English brother-in-law.[12] None of the bridal couple's parents attended the wedding in Burgos. Fernando III was dead, Queen Jeanne had returned to her native Ponthieu some months before, and Henry III and Queen Eleanor stayed in the south of France and did not travel over the border into Castile. Jeanne spent some time with her former fiancé Henry and his wife, and her future son-in-law Edward, in Bordeaux in August 1254, on her way home to the north. Her eldest child, Don Fernando, now about 15 and heir to Jeanne's French lands, travelled with her, and permanently moved himself and his household to the north of France at this time.[13]

King Alfonso X did attend Edward and Leonor's wedding, however. He issued a charter while he was at the monastery of Las Huelgas, and wrote:

> I, Don Alfonso … the first time I came to Burgos after I acceded to the throne, there also came here Don Eduardo, the first son and heir of King Enrique of England,

> and was knighted by me in the monastery of Santa María la Real of Burgos, and married my sister, the infanta Doña Leonor, and received the blessing there with her.

Evidently impressed with his adolescent brother-in-law and proud to have been the man who dubbed him a knight, for more than a year the Castilian king dated all the documents issued by his chancellery with the phrase 'The year that Don Eduardo, first son and heir of King Enrique of England, was knighted at Burgos by the King Alfonso mentioned above.'[14]

Alfonso X and Leonor's father Fernando III was canonised as a saint of the Catholic Church in 1671 as San Fernando (Saint Ferdinand) and is now the patron saint of the city of Seville; his feast day is 30 May, the date of his death in Seville in 1252. A valley and a city in California are just two of the many places around the world named after him. Fernando was praised for his role in maintaining the *Convivencia*, the peaceful co-existence of Christians, Jews and Muslims in medieval Spain, and his son and successor continued this tradition. Alfonso is known to posterity as *el Sabio*, 'the Wise' or 'the Learned', and was a polymath: a lawgiver, musician, writer, translator, and amateur scientist who took a particular interest in astronomy. The Alphonsus Crater on the Moon is named after him. He is still well-known today for his composition of more than 400 poems with musical notation which he called the 'Cantigas de Santa María'; he wrote, edited and sponsored books including one about astronomy and one titled *Estoria de España* ('History of Spain'); and he devised a massive and influential law code named the *Siete Partidas*, which Spanish explorers introduced to the New World centuries later. At least two of his brothers, Don Felipe and Don Enrique, were educated at the University of Paris. One of Alfonso's closest friends was the Englishman Geoffrey of Eversley, who was not only the king's ambassador to Edward and Leonor in Geoffrey's native England, but a master of rhetoric who dedicated a treatise on the art of letter-writing to Alfonso. Fernando III and Alfonso X's glittering, intellectual and multicultural court was the world in which the future queen of England, Doña Leonor de Castilla, was raised.[15]

While in and near Burgos for their wedding in early November 1254, Edward and Leonor must have seen the great cathedral under construction there. Leonor's then 20-year-old father Fernando placed the foundation stone of the cathedral on 20 June 1221, at a time when his 16-year-old first wife, Beatriz of Swabia, was four months pregnant with their eldest child Alfonso X. A sculpture which still exists today in the cloister of Burgos Cathedral shows King Fernando giving Beatriz her wedding ring; the young couple married in the city on 30 November 1219. Fernando also married his second wife Jeanne of Ponthieu in Burgos in the autumn of 1237, a fact which their daughter must have been aware of when her own wedding took place in the nearby monastery of Santa María la Real seventeen years later.[16]

As well as King Alfonso, Lord Edward must have met some of Leonor's other older half-brothers in Burgos: Don Sancho, shortly to become archbishop of Toledo though only in his twenties; Don Felipe, the Paris-educated archbishop-elect of Seville, who in 1258 was to give up a promising career in the Church to marry Kristina, daughter of King Haakon of Norway; Don Fadrique, who decades later would be secretly executed by his own brother Alfonso X; Don Manuel, whose son Don Juan Manuel (1282–1348), lord of Villena and duke of Peñafiel, is considered one of the greatest Spanish writers of the Middle Ages; and the colourful Don Enrique, who was 24 years old in 1254 and was the fourth of Fernando III's numerous sons, and had also studied in Paris. Rumour had it, probably incorrectly, that Enrique was the lover of his stepmother, Leonor's mother Queen Jeanne, and he had to leave Castile soon after Edward and Leonor's wedding after leading a rebellion against King Alfonso. Enrique would spend several years at the court of Henry III in England, cheerfully sponging off his sister Leonor's father-in-law, and later in life would become a mercenary in North Africa, a senator in Rome, and a prisoner for more than twenty years in Naples.

Chapter 2

Arrival in England

The marriage of Lord Edward and Doña Leonor would last for thirty-six years until Leonor's death in late November 1290 just past her forty-ninth birthday, and would prove to be one of the great royal love stories of the English Middle Ages. Edward I is not known to have fathered any illegitimate children and perhaps did not even have mistresses, and, like his father Henry III, was a devoted husband. Their marriage was an astonishingly fertile one: Leonor gave birth to at least fourteen children, perhaps as many as fifteen or sixteen, four or perhaps five sons and ten or eleven daughters. Presumably Leonor spoke French, the lingua franca of European royalty in the thirteenth and fourteenth centuries and the native language of both her mother Queen Jeanne and her new husband (though Edward could speak English as well). Both Leonor and Edward probably knew Latin. Communication between the couple is not likely to have been a major problem.

After their Burgos wedding, Leonor and Edward travelled to Aquitaine, though Leonor did not yet have a chance to meet her parents-in-law King Henry and Queen Eleanor, the royal English couple having travelled to Paris to spend time with Eleanor's elder sister Marguerite of Provence and her husband King Louis IX. Louis gave Henry III a gift of an elephant on the English party's departure, and in February 1255 Henry ordered the sheriffs of London to make an enclosure for the animal 40 feet long and 20 feet wide within the Tower of London, where it joined the rest of his menagerie.[1] Chronicler Matthew Paris travelled from St Albans to London to see and marvel at the elephant, and drew pictures of it in his *Chronica Maiora* and his *Liber Additamentorum*. The impressed annalist of St Paul's also mentioned the animal.[2]

It is possible that Leonor bore a daughter in Bordeaux in the duchy of Aquitaine on 29 May 1255 when she was still only 13 ½ years old. In 1286/87, she provided a gold cloth to mark the obituary of her daughter who died on 29 May in an unstated year and was buried at the Dominican priory in Bordeaux, and it is difficult to identify another year when Leonor was in Bordeaux on 29 May, except in 1255.[3] This was just under seven months after her wedding, so if she did indeed give birth on that date, she and 15-year-old Edward must have immediately consummated their marriage even though Leonor was almost certainly not yet 13, and obviously the pregnancy cannot have gone to term. The child's name was not recorded, assuming she ever had one; as it was not a full-term pregnancy, the infant might not have lived long enough to be baptised. This too-early consummation was perhaps a result of a lack of adult supervision, all three of Edward and Leonor's living parents being far away in France when the young couple wed and for a while afterwards. Alfonso X's wife Queen Violante gave birth to their second child Beatriz around 5 November 1254 just after Edward and Leonor's wedding, so perhaps he was too distracted to notice what his young half-sister and her new husband were up to.[4]

Although Leonor never set foot in Spain again, there is much evidence that her homeland remained important to her for the rest of her life. At her favourite residence of Langley (now Kings Langley) in Hertfordshire, she hired Spanish gardeners and seems to have created typically Spanish water gardens there, and frequently ordered fruits such as pomegranates, figs, lemons and oranges, as well as olive oil, for which she had evidently gained a taste in childhood. All her life, she preserved the Castilian fashion for tapestries, carpets and wall hangings, and purchased four green and three red carpets in 1278.[5] Leonor saw her half-brother Alfonso X again in the south of France in 1273, and kept in touch with him and with at least some of her other brothers and half-brothers, certainly with Don Enrique, who lived into the 1300s.

It is impossible to know for sure what Leonor's English daughters heard about her early life in Castile, but perhaps she told them about her father's triumphal entry into Seville in December 1248 once it fell to him following a thirteen-month siege, after 536 years of Muslim rule over the city they called Ishbiliya. Leonor was 7 years old in December 1248 and was surely present during her father's procession into Seville, and her mother Jeanne is known to have lived in Fernando's army camp during the siege.[6] Leonor might therefore have seen Fernando ride his horse up the Giralda Tower after his arrival in the city he had conquered. The Giralda was then the minaret of Seville's Great Mosque, later rebuilt as Seville Cathedral and the second largest church in Europe after St Peter's Basilica in Rome, and the tower is now an important symbol of the city.

Leonor of Castile was not the first Spanish queen of England, nor the last, but she was the first to live there; Richard Lionheart's wife Berengaria of Navarre famously never set foot in England while she was its queen between 1191 and 1199, and she and Richard had no children and his successor was his brother, King John. Leonor's son Edward II, who reigned from 1307 to 1327, was England's first half-Spanish monarch. Edward II's great-grandson Henry IV (r. 1399–1413) married Juana of Navarre in 1403 as his second wife, but she was not the mother of any of his children, and his son and successor Henry V (r. 1413–22) was not of Spanish descent. It was not until Tudor times that the country had its next half-Spanish ruler: Queen Mary I, born in 1516 as the daughter of Henry VIII and his first queen, Katherine of Aragon (Mary also had a Spanish consort, her cousin Philip II, though the couple had no children). The Spanish origin of Doña Leonor and Lord Edward's children was a novelty, and therefore of interest to contemporaries. An English writer referred to Leonor as *Alienor Despayne* or 'Leonor of Castile' ('Spain' almost always meant Castile in medieval English usage), and an English clerk who wrote a chronicle called 'The Life of Edward II' about the disastrous reign of Leonor's son points out his Spanish background as one of the few positives to be noted about him. When a Castilian cardinal and envoy, Petrus Hispanus, visited England in 1306/07 and met Leonor's widower King Edward, the king commented to Petrus that he should look forward to meeting his and Leonor's son the younger Edward, 'as he is of Spanish descent'.[7] This statement applied equally, of course, to Edward and Leonor's daughters.

Doña Leonor arrived in England for the first time in October 1255, the month before her fourteenth birthday, landing at Dover. Her half-brother Don Sancho, archbishop-elect of Toledo, came with her and spent several weeks in England, and Don Enrique, another of her seven older half-brothers, was also there. A clerk and a messenger of yet another of her half-brothers, Don Felipe, archbishop-elect of Seville and the future husband of Kristina of Norway, also came with her, and Alfonso X sent two minstrels to England with Leonor; they returned to Castile in early December 1255 with a gift of 20 shillings each from Henry III. Chronicler Matthew Paris in St Albans, who sometimes expressed a xenophobic dislike of foreigners, declared that so many

Spaniards arrived in England with the young infanta that some English people believed that the country would be 'violently occupied by them'.[8] From Dover, the retinue travelled to the largest city in the realm, London. The *Chronicles of the Mayors and Sheriffs of London* states that 'a countless multitude of bishops, earls, barons and knights' went to the city to greet Leonor, 'the sister of the king of Spain' (as noted above, Castile was almost always called 'Spain' in England in the thirteenth and fourteenth centuries, rather confusingly, given that the country of Spain in the Middle Ages consisted of four kingdoms, Castile, Leon, Aragon and Navarre).[9]

Leonor and her retinue made their way the couple of miles from London to Westminster, where she offered a gold buckle at the shrine of Saint Edward in Westminster Abbey shortly after her arrival. Her husband was named after this particular royal saint, known to posterity as Edward the Confessor, the king of England who died in early 1066 and was canonised a century later. Her father-in-law King Henry, who revered the Confessor, was presently having a chapel dedicated to him built in Westminster Abbey; it would be completed and dedicated in 1269, and Henry himself, Edward and Leonor would all one day be buried there. Leonor's steward William Chenney received 50 marks (£33) for her expenses, and Henry III spent 20 marks on a silver alms-dish for her. Lord Edward himself returned to England a few weeks after his wife and also landed at Dover, where his only brother, Edmund, born in January 1245 and five and a half years his junior, went to meet him.[10]

As well as the almost 10-year-old Edmund, Leonor met two of her husband's three other younger siblings: his sister Beatrice, born in June 1242, and their tiny sister Katherine, born in November 1253 and not quite 2 years old when Leonor arrived in her husband's homeland. Edward and Edmund's other sister Margaret, born in September 1240, lived in Scotland, where she was the wife of the young King Alexander III, a year her junior. Sadly, Katherine, who was deaf and mute, died in May 1257, aged 3 and a half. Henry III and Eleanor of Provence, loving and caring parents for many years to all their children, grieved so much for their daughter that they both became seriously ill, and Henry paid for a lavish funeral for the little girl in Westminster Abbey.[11]

Leonor had the good fortune to marry into a very close-knit family, and to have parents-in-law who were, by the standards of medieval royalty, unusually closely involved in the lives of their children.

When Edward was seriously ill in 1246, his mother insisted on staying at Beaulieu Abbey in Hampshire with him for three weeks even though women were not allowed to spend the night in Cistercian houses. Henry III subsequently spent over £30 feeding the poor in his great hall at Westminster 'for the love of him who made the king's son safe and sound'. The king and queen of England themselves rode all the way to Edinburgh when they heard that their eldest daughter Margaret was unhappy and was being kept apart from her husband Alexander, rather than sending someone else to check on her.[12] In September 1244, when she was 2 years old, Henry III affectionately called his second daughter Beatrice 'Bella B', meaning 'Beautiful B', and Beatrice's second son John of Brittany (b. *c.* 1266), who grew up in England with his mother's family, was jocularly known as 'Briton' to his English relatives. Beatrice and her husband spent much of their adult lives at the court of King Henry and Queen Eleanor, and Beatrice's older sister Queen Margaret of Scotland was evidently also very keen to spend as much time in England with her parents as possible, and gave birth to her first child at Windsor Castle in 1261.[13]

King Henry's only full brother was Richard (b. 1209), earl of Cornwall, and elected King of the Romans, i.e. king of Germany, in 1257. After falling out badly with Henry in 1238 to the point of rising in rebellion against him, Richard remained staunchly loyal to his brother for the rest of their lives, and even neglected the affairs of his own German kingdom in order to support Henry through the political crises of the early to mid-1260s. Richard's only real rival for the German throne in 1257 was Alfonso X of Castile, and Henry III's support for his brother over his son Edward's brother-in-law was another major factor, along with Henry's warm reception of Alfonso's brother and enemy Don Enrique, which led to a rapid cooling of the relationship between England and Castile after the mid-1250s. Other members of the extended English royal family in the 1250s were the Lusignans, younger half-siblings of Henry III and Richard of Cornwall from their mother Isabelle of Angoulême's second marriage to the French count of La Marche. There were nine Lusignan siblings, and on the dowager queen Isabelle's death in 1246, five of them made their way to England and were warmly welcomed by their half-brother the king.

There were also the Savoyard uncles of Eleanor of Provence, some of the many brothers of the queen's mother Beatrice of Savoy, dowager countess of Provence, who made their career in England. Finally, another important man whom Leonor met was Lord Edward's uncle-in-law Simon de Montfort, earl of Leicester. Simon was a French nobleman born *c.* 1208, who arrived in England in about 1230 and married King Henry's youngest sister Eleanor in 1238; their marriage was the catalyst for Richard of Cornwall's quarrel with the king that year. Henry gave permission for Montfort to wed his sister, though began to regret his decision when it dawned on him that Eleanor's marriage should have been used to benefit his own foreign policy, as the marriages of his other two sisters Joan (1210–38) and Isabella (1214–41) had been; Joan wed the king of Scotland and Isabella wed Frederick II, Holy Roman Emperor and king of Sicily.[14] Leonor of Castile had a family connection to Simon de Montfort: his niece Laure de Montfort married her elder brother Don Fernando.

Queen Eleanor was, like her new daughter-in-law, a lady of the south, having spent the first dozen years of her life in Provence in the south-east of France, close to the Italian border. Eleanor had had to grow accustomed to the cool green dampness of England, as Leonor – raised in the intense dry heat of central Spain and the Andalusian plains – would now also have to do. Unfortunately, some of the winters during the first few years of Leonor's residence in England seem to have been particularly bad. In January 1257 and again throughout January and into early February 1259, there are many references to the 'excessive wind and changeable weather', and the wind was strong enough to destroy buildings across the south of England, especially on the latter occasion. Even the walls of the great stronghold of Dover Castle on the Kent coast were badly damaged, while buildings in the royal manors of Kennington near London and Woodstock near Oxford, and towers, battlements and other buildings in the castles of Oxford, Winchester, Gloucester and Salisbury, were unroofed by the fierce wind.[15] A London chronicler states that on 28 December 1256, there was 'a great tempest, with thunder and lightning', and that the winter of 1262/63 was a particularly bad one: the River Thames froze solidly, and there was a 'great frost and thick ice' for many weeks. A few years later, 'London Bridge was broken by the great frost', and England saw 'such an abundance of frost, cold and snow' that even the oldest English people had never experienced before. On this occasion, five arches of London Bridge were destroyed 'by the violence of the ice'.[16] The English harvest of 1257 failed catastrophically owing to the awful weather and widespread floods, and Leonor's uncle-in-law Richard of Cornwall, elected king of Germany that year, sent fifty ships full of grain from his new kingdom to his homeland in a compassionate attempt to stave off his countrymen's hunger and suffering during the harsh winter of 1257/58.[17]

Leonor had the company of a close relative while she found her feet in England, and the Liberate Rolls are full of references to her father-in-law paying all the expenses of Don Enrique and his household. In November 1256, Henry III even paid for Enrique to travel to France – perhaps he visited his stepmother, Leonor's mother Queen Jeanne – and also paid all the expenses of his retinue in England until he returned. In January and again in June 1257, Enrique was meant to go home to Castile, but failed to do so, and was still in England in July 1259. Eventually, his presence began to embarrass King Henry and to threaten a diplomatic row with Alfonso X as Enrique had led a rebellion against his brother, in the company of their second eldest brother Don Fadrique, before his departure from his homeland. Finally forced to depart from England, Enrique headed for North Africa and became a mercenary.[18]

Chapter 3

Two Battles

Henry III and Louis IX of France had married two sisters, and relations between the English and French royal families were (despite Louis's suspicion over his nephew-in-law Edward marrying into Castile and his transparent attempts at one-upmanship) as warm in the mid-thirteenth century as at any time in the Middle Ages. Leonor's 17-year-old sister-in-law Beatrice ('Bella B'), married John (b. 1239), heir to his father Duke John I of Brittany, in France in January 1260. The kings and queens of England and France, and their children, all attended the wedding, which took place shortly after the funeral of King Louis and Queen Marguerite's eldest son Louis, fiancé of the young Doña Berenguela of Castile. Beatrice, however, never became duchess of Brittany as she died eleven years before her father-in-law. In fact, John I lived long enough to see the birth of his great-grandson, Beatrice's grandson Duke John III, in 1286.

Leonor's other sister-in-law Margaret, queen of Scotland, and her husband Alexander III visited England later in 1260. Queen Margaret remained in her homeland after her husband's return to his kingdom and gave birth to her first child, a daughter she named after herself who later married King Eirik of Norway, at Windsor Castle on 28 February 1261. News must have reached Leonor in England of the death of her half-brother Don Sancho, archbishop of Toledo and chancellor of Castile, on 27 October 1261 at the age of only 28, and shortly afterwards, Lord Edward's aunt Sancha of Provence, queen of Germany and countess of Cornwall, died as well. Sancha was the third sister of Marguerite, queen of France and Eleanor, queen of England, and was married to Richard of Cornwall. The fourth Provence sister was Beatrice, who married Louis IX's brother Charles of Anjou and later became queen of Sicily. The four sisters married two sets of brothers, and all became queens.

Not much is known of the early years of Edward and Leonor's marriage. As far as the extant record shows, Leonor did not become pregnant again until the early 1260s, so it seems that she and Edward were very careful after (apparently) losing their first, unnamed little daughter in 1255. The couple were lucky that Leonor had not been damaged by this too-early experience of pregnancy and birth or miscarriage. Given how fertile Leonor proved to be, giving birth regularly throughout the 1260s, 1270s and into the 1280s when she was past 40 years old, and given that she and Edward seem to have consummated their marriage immediately in November 1254, it is surprising that there was such a long wait after 1255 until she gave birth to another child, unless there were more miscarriages and stillbirths that did not find their way onto record. Not only would the royal family and their subjects have desired the security that came from knowing that the succession to the throne was safe, becoming the mother of a future king of England would have greatly increased the young Spanish woman's status in her new land.

Leonor and Edward's daughter Katherine, their eldest daughter with the exception of the infant assumed to have been born prematurely in Bordeaux in May 1255, was born at an uncertain date in the early 1260s, and died on 5 September 1264. She was buried in Westminster Abbey on 3 October 1264. Katherine must be the daughter who was said to be living with Leonor at Windsor Castle on 17 June 1264, though this record does not provide the child's name.[1] Katherine died two and a half months later. She was presumably named in honour of her aunt, Lord Edward's little sister who had died in 1257 at age 3.

Almost certainly born in November 1241, Leonor was in her early twenties when she gave birth to Katherine sometime between *c.* 1261 and 1264. Leonor and Edward's second or third daughter, Joan, was born in December 1264 or January 1265 and was given the English form of the name of Leonor's mother Jeanne, countess of Ponthieu and dowager queen of Castile. Perhaps the couple also chose the name in honour of Edward's late aunt Joan of England, queen of Scotland.[2] Leonor prepared to go into confinement on 7 December 1264 and was purified (or 'churched') following the birth shortly after 3 February 1365; this ceremony took place forty days after birth, or sometimes only thirty days if the infant was female. Little Joan, like her elder sister, did not live long: she died shortly before 7 September 1265 at only a few months old, a year almost exactly to the day after Katherine. Also like her sister Katherine, Joan was interred in Westminster Abbey, and on 7 September 1265 her grandfather Henry III bought a 'good and beautiful gold cloth' to lie over her coffin or tomb there.[3] The two little girls were buried in the same tomb as their 3-year-old aunt Katherine, and several more of their many younger siblings would be interred with them in later years. The children's tomb can still be seen in Westminster Abbey, though it was moved from its original location in the chapel of St Edward the Confessor after the death of Anne of Bohemia (1366–94), first queen of Edward and Leonor's great-great-grandson, Richard II (r. 1377–99).[4]

The years 1264 and 1265, on top of the sad deaths of Edward and Leonor's two young daughters, were among the most dramatic and turbulent in medieval English history. Simon de Montfort, earl of Leicester, and his brother-in-law Henry III had long had a difficult relationship, and in 1258 Simon led a group of barons who imposed the Provisions of Oxford on the king. The Provisions were a remarkable set of propositions which removed the king's executive powers and made him little more than a figurehead. They were overturned some years later, and it would not be until the seventeenth century that such radical notions of constitutional monarchy were seen again. In 1264, the explosive situation came to a head, and war broke out between the royalist party and the baronial party, led by Simon de Montfort. Simon defeated King Henry, Henry's brother Richard, earl of Cornwall and King of the Romans, and Henry's elder son Lord Edward at the battle of Lewes in Sussex in May 1264. Neither Henry nor Richard demonstrated much ability throughout their long lives as battle commanders, and Richard, humiliatingly, was taken prisoner while hiding in a mill during the battle.[5]

Lord Edward, unlike his father and uncle, was an excellent military leader, but withdrew from the battlefield in order to pursue a vendetta against a contingent of soldiers from London. The previous year, his mother Queen Eleanor had been pelted with rubbish and stones and insulted by a mob as her barge passed along the River Thames between the Tower of London and Westminster, and Edward never forgave the inhabitants of the city for this insult. He and his knights, all on horseback, pursued the London soldiers fleeing on foot for miles, and killed all of those whom they found. Edward finally returned to the battlefield much later to find that his father and his uncle Richard of Cornwall had been captured, that his half-uncle Guy de Lusignan had been killed while fighting for the king, and that his uncle-in-law Simon de Montfort, commanding the opposing side, was in control. He perforce had to surrender to Simon, and he, Henry III and Richard of Cornwall were subsequently held in captivity.

For a few months Simon de Montfort, earl of Leicester, and his allies, including the 21-year-old Gilbert de Clare, earl of Gloucester and Hertford, and the Leicestershire baron Hugh Despenser, justiciar of England (whose son and grandson of the same name were destined to play significant and malevolent roles in the reign of Lord Edward and Doña Leonor's son Edward II), ruled the kingdom. Montfort famously invited representatives from the shires and towns to the two parliaments he held during the fifteen months he ruled England, and is still remembered today as one of the progenitors of the English parliament. In other respects, however, his rule proved unpopular and barely an improvement on the royal regime he replaced, and he showed considerable favouritism towards his five sons, Henry, Simon, Amaury, Guy and Richard de Montfort. He gradually lost the support of the young earl of Gloucester, though Hugh Despenser and other men remained staunchly loyal to him until the end.

Leonor of Castile, unlike her mother-in-law Queen Eleanor, remained in England during the crisis of 1264/65 (Eleanor of Provence and her second son, 19-year-old Edmund, withdrew to France).[6] She was given temporary custody of Windsor Castle on 16 June 1264, a month after the battle of Lewes, and lived there with her little daughter Katherine and her household, including her steward John Weston. Leonor was then about two or three months pregnant with her daughter Joan, born in December 1264 or early in the new year. She seems to have been intensely loyal to her husband, to the point where the baronial opposition considered her Edward's deputy while he was held in captivity.[7] Certainly, being put in command of the important royal castle of Windsor suggests Leonor's loyalty to her husband and his father, as well as her own competence, as it was almost unheard of for a woman to be appointed as custodian of a castle, and Windsor was a particularly important stronghold.

On 17 June, however, her father-in-law the king – or more probably, his brother-in-law Simon de Montfort, issuing the instruction in Henry's name – countermanded the order of the day before. He told Leonor to leave Windsor Castle with her daughter, her steward, a household knight called Sir William Charles, her ladies and damsels, and the rest of her retinue. She was to travel to Westminster and stay there, and King Henry, or Simon de Montfort, told her 'not to fail, as the king undertakes to excuse her to E[dward] her lord and will keep her harmless, and receives them [her household] into his safe conduct'. Joan Munchesni, a wealthy heiress and married to King Henry's younger half-brother William de Valence (one of the Lusignans), was inside Windsor Castle with Leonor and was also pregnant. Joan was ordered to go to some nearby religious house 'until God delivers her of the offspring wherewith she is great'.[8] Tragedy struck the royal family when Leonor and Edward's infant daughter Katherine died in the late summer or early autumn that year. Leonor gave birth to her daughter Joan a few months later.

Lord Edward escaped from his uncle Simon de Montfort's custody in late May 1265. With the aid of the young earl of Gloucester and Hertford, Gilbert de Clare – Edward and Leonor's future son-in-law – who had now switched sides after growing disenchanted with Simon de Montfort's rule, and Gilbert's brother Thomas, Edward raised an army. He annihilated Montfort's forces at the battle of Evesham in Worcestershire on 4 August 1265. Simon himself was killed, as were his eldest son, 26-year-old Henry de Montfort, and his closest ally and one of the men he had appointed as his executors, the justiciar Sir Hugh Despenser. Simon's widow Eleanor, King Henry's youngest sister (b. 1215), and their other children fled overseas. Eleanor was to die in France in 1275, two of her sons made their way to Italy, and her only daughter, Eleanor de Montfort, married Llywelyn ap Gruffudd, prince of Wales, in 1278. Although a group of devoted Montfortians held out at the late Simon de Montfort's great Warwickshire stronghold of Kenilworth for a few months, the rebellion was over, and the queen, Eleanor of Provence, and her second son Edmund returned to England from France. The political situation returned to something approaching normal, except that Henry III, who turned 60 years old in October 1267, was to be little more than a cipher for the remaining few years of his long life and long reign, and his son Lord Edward dominated the political scene.[9]

Chapter 4

Crusading

Around mid- or late October 1265, several months after the royalist victory at the battle of Evesham and a few weeks after losing their second (or third) daughter Joan, Edward and Leonor conceived another child. Leonor gave birth to her first son, John, at Windsor Castle during the night of 13/14 July 1266. Her second son, Henry, was born twenty-two months later, on or a little before 6 May 1268, also at Windsor Castle. In London, the inhabitants rejoiced, danced in the streets, and enjoyed a public holiday the day after John of Windsor's birth, in the belief that the succession to the throne was now assured and that the little boy would, in the distant future, rule as their king after his father.[1]

John was presumably named in honour of his father's grandfather, King John, who had died fifty years previously in October 1216. Although a modern theory has it that the English royal family in the Middle Ages deliberately shunned the name John after King John's disastrous reign, Edward and Leonor's eldest son would have succeeded his father in 1307 as King John II of England if he had not died young. Their fourth son, who did succeed his father on the throne as Edward II in 1307, named his own second son John, and this John (b. 1316) was heir to the English throne from January 1327 until June 1330. Edward and Leonor's grandson Edward III (r. 1327–77) survived his three eldest sons, and there was some debate near the end of his life in 1376/77 as to whether he should be succeeded on the throne not by his first son's son, who was a mere child, but by his fourth and eldest surviving son, John of Gaunt, duke of Lancaster.[2] It was only chance that no other English king bore the name John after 1216, not a deliberate decision on the royal family's part. Edward and Leonor's second son Henry of Windsor, meanwhile, was named conventionally after his grandfather, the reigning king.

On 17 or 18 June 1269, just thirteen months after she gave birth to Henry and on her husband's thirtieth birthday or the day after, Leonor bore another child at Windsor Castle. It was a daughter, whom she named after herself and her mother-in-law Eleanor of Provence, and young Eleanor of Windsor, at least the fifth and perhaps the sixth child born to Leonor and Edward, would be their eldest who lived to adulthood. Eleanor's name in her own lifetime was usually spelt Alianore, sometimes Alianor or Alienore, as was her mother's; Leonor, usually known to posterity as Eleanor of Castile, sometimes appears on record during her husband's reign as 'A., Queen of England'. In 1264, the pope called her 'Alienor, wife of Edward, son of King Henry'.[3] A contemporary pet name for women called Alianore was Alisote.

In later years, Eleanor of Windsor was often called her father's *primogenita*. This literally means 'first-born daughter', and therefore it has often been wrongly assumed that Eleanor must have been born in 1264 or earlier as the eldest of Edward and Leonor's many daughters.[4] In practice, however, *primogenita* meant 'eldest surviving daughter', which Eleanor certainly was, as Katherine and Joan, and the unnamed daughter probably born to Leonor in Bordeaux a few months after her wedding, died in infancy. Eleanor's younger brother Alfonso of Bayonne, born in November 1273 as Edward and Leonor's third son, was also often called Edward's *primogenitus* or 'eldest (surviving) son' in the years when he was heir to the throne, even though he had two older brothers, John and Henry, who died young. Henry III promised Leonor's valet John Beaumes an annual income of either £10 or 10 marks (£6.66) annually in land on 18 June 1269 for bringing him news of his granddaughter's birth. This grant gives the newborn infant's name as Eleanor, and her date of birth is therefore not in question. A medieval work called *Le Livere de Reis de Brittaniae* also states that Eleanor, 'daughter of Sir Edward, the king's son', was born in 1269.[5]

Eleanor of Windsor joined the household of her brother Henry of Windsor, who was very close to her in age, and a third child who came to live with them was their cousin John of Brittany. John was nicknamed Briton, was probably born in 1266, and was a younger son of Henry III's second daughter Beatrice ('Bella B'). Briton's elder brother Arthur (b. 1262) was the heir, after their father, to their grandfather John I's duchy of Brittany, and was brought up in the duchy, but young Briton spent most of his long life in England and later became earl of Richmond. Each of the three children had their own nurse looking after them, and Eleanor's was called Cecile or Cecilia Cleware. The three shared a *rokstere* or 'rocker', i.e. a girl or young woman who rocked their cradle, who was called Alice de la Grave. Almost certainly, this woman is to be identified with the Alice de Leygrave who appears on record in later years as the wet-nurse of Henry and Eleanor's youngest brother Edward of Caernarfon, born in April 1284 and their father's successor on the throne as King Edward II. Edward II called Alice de Leygrave 'the king's mother' in and after 1307, and she was still alive on 1 December 1318 when she must have been a ripe old age.[6]

The extant accounts of the three children's household, written in Latin, refer to Eleanor as *domina* [Lady] *Alianore* and to her brother Henry as *dominus* [Lord] *Henricus*. The children of kings, though no-one else, had the right to be addressed as 'Lord' and 'Lady' from birth, but were not called 'Prince' or 'Princess', titles for royal children which did not yet exist. It is inaccurate and anachronistic to refer to Edward I and Leonor of Castile's daughters as 'princesses'. One exception to this rule is that Eleanor's youngest brother Edward of Caernarfon was made prince of Wales in February 1301 and thereafter was called 'Lord Edward, Prince of Wales' (*Dominus Edwardus, Princeps Walliae* in Latin) or sometimes simply 'the Prince' for short, but he was never called 'Prince Edward'.[7] Henry and Eleanor's cousin John of Brittany, who was a grandson of Henry III but was the son of a duke and not of a king, was not entitled to be addressed as 'Lord' or 'Sir' until he was knighted, and appears in the document simply as 'Britonis' (his nickname in its Latin form) without a title.

The three children were bathed regularly; the women in charge of their bath were each paid 3*d* a day, a rather generous amount by the standards of the day, especially considering that the women's duties were hardly onerous. A gallon of wine was added to Henry's bath on the eve of Pentecost one year, presumably because he suffered from some kind of illness (he was to die at the age of 6), as wine was believed to be strengthening. The three all wore smocks and hose, with little or no difference between Eleanor's clothing and the clothes her brother and male cousin wore, and caps with peacock feathers, slippers, gilded buttons, and furred gloves in cold weather. One Christmas, nine dozen buttons were purchased for Henry and Eleanor, and another dozen were used to decorate their and Briton's saddles. On another special occasion the royal siblings dined on partridge, an expensive delicacy. The children's need to play and to have fun was recognised: a toy cart was bought for Henry, although it was soon broken, and he also received toy arrows, a coronet and a toy trumpet (and a white palfrey horse from his mother shortly before he died, which he never had the chance to ride). In later years, Edward I purchased wooden castles for his and Leonor's two youngest sons Alfonso of Bayonne and Edward of Caernarfon, and wooden siege-engines for Alfonso and for Jan of Brabant, one of the king's sons-in-law. The boys also received wooden swords for mock fighting and skirmishing.[8] Probably little Eleanor had dolls and other toys which were considered by the adults looking after her to be more appropriate for girls.

Crusading fever was in the air in Europe at the beginning of the 1270s. The sultan of Egypt, al-Zahir Baibars, captured Antioch in 1268, and was busily besieging other crusader fortresses and towns. Louis IX of France, who had led a crusade twenty years previously, decided to lead another one. His nephews-in-law Edward of England and Edward's brother Edmund, now earl of Lancaster and Leicester, took a vow to go with him, as did their cousin Henry of Almain (b. 1235, Richard of Cornwall's elder son and heir) and brother-in-law John of Brittany, and numerous other English noblemen including the earls of Surrey and Gloucester. Edward promised on 27 August 1269 that he would accompany Louis IX on crusade, and on 2 August 1270 made arrangements for the custody of his and Leonor's children while they were away.[9] His uncle Richard, earl of Cornwall, was to have the official charge of the children, while Richard's son Henry of Almain accompanied Edward and Edmund overseas. Little Eleanor of Windsor was only 14 months old when her parents left England, and they would not see her again until August 1274 when she was 5.

Edward and Leonor left England on 20 August 1270, rather later than planned. The year before, Edward's only brother Edmund had married the great heiress Aveline de Forz, who, born in Burstwick, Yorkshire in January 1259, was just 10 years old to his 24, and who was set to inherit two earldoms from her parents, William de Forz and Isabella de Redvers. Edmund left his young wife safely behind in England when he travelled to the Holy Land, while Leonor decided to accompany her husband on crusade. The English party missed the planned meeting with their royal uncle Louis IX, and Louis sailed instead to Tunis in aid of his youngest brother Charles of Anjou, king of Sicily. He died there on 25 August 1270, and his 25-year-old eldest surviving son Philip III, a first cousin of Lord Edward and his siblings, succeeded him as king of France.[10]

At an unknown date in late 1270 or sometime in the first few months of 1271, Leonor gave birth to a daughter in the port of Acre in the Holy Land, who died soon after birth; her name is not known.[11] Far away in England, Richard of Cornwall had the official care of Edward and Leonor's first son, John of Windsor. Tragedy struck the English royal family when little John died at the age of 5 on 3 August 1271, at his great-uncle Richard's castle of Wallingford a few miles from Oxford. He was buried at Westminster Abbey five days later. John was never heir to the throne as he died in the lifetime of his grandfather Henry III, but if he had lived until 1307, he would have succeeded his father as John II.

Richard of Cornwall experienced another tragedy in March 1271 when his son Henry of Almain was murdered in Sicily. Henry left his cousins in the Holy Land, and while in the Sicilian town of Viterbo, went to worship at the church of San Silvestro, where he was pursued by his cousins Simon (b. 1240) and Guy (b. *c*. 1244) de Montfort, the second and fourth sons of his late uncle Simon de Montfort, earl of Leicester. They dragged him out of the church and stabbed him to death in revenge for their father's demise and the subsequent mutilation of his body at the battle of Evesham in 1265, even though Henry had not fought in the battle and had nothing to do with the appalling treatment of the earl's remains. Simon de Montfort the younger was excommunicated, and died later in 1271, 'cursed by God, a fugitive and a wanderer on the earth'.[12] Guy de Montfort evaded justice for a few years, married the Italian noblewoman Margherita Aldobrandesca and became count of Nola, but was destined to die in a Sicilian prison in the early 1290s. When the shocking news of his son's murder at the hands of his nephews reached Richard of Cornwall in England, it made him seriously ill; he had a stroke and never recovered, and died on 2 April 1272 at the age of 63.

Chapter 5

The First Marital Alliance

Sometime in the spring of 1272, not long after the death of her uncle-in-law Richard in distant England, Leonor of Castile gave birth to another daughter in the port of Acre in the Holy Land, and called her Joan. The modern names Joan, Joanne and Joanna were spelt Johane, Johanne or Jone in England in the thirteenth and fourteenth centuries, and its pet forms were Jonet(t)e, Johanette or Jony; perhaps little Joan was known by one of these names to her family. Like her sister who was born in late 1264 or early 1265 and died a few months later, Joan was probably named in honour of Leonor's mother Jeanne of Ponthieu, though one historian has suggested that Joan de Valence née Munchesni, countess of Pembroke, was her godmother and gave Joan her name.[1] The name Joan was so extraordinarily common that it is impossible to say for sure, though Joan of Acre did visit Joan de Valence on a number of occasions in 1296/97, a period when the elder Joan's accounts survive. The infant born in 1272 would be the second of the royal daughters who lived into adulthood, and was and is always known as Joan of Acre after her birthplace.

The author of the *Livere de Reis de Brittaniae* noted Joan of Acre's birth in the Holy Land, and called her *Jone la filie sire Eduuard*, 'Joan the daughter of Lord Edward', and *Dame Jone de Acre*. The author of the Middle English *Brut* chronicle called her *Iohne of Acres*, and Piers Langtoft, an English author who wrote a rhyming chronicle in French in the early 1300s, called her *dame Jone*, 'Lady Joan', and *Jone la countesse de Acres surnomez* or 'Joan the countess [of Gloucester], surnamed of Acre'. He says that she was more beautiful than a hundred other women, and called her mother Leonor, meanwhile, whom he named 'Elyanore', a 'beautiful and elegant lady'.[2] Just a few weeks after Joan of Acre's birth, on 17 June 1272, her father's thirty-third birthday and her sister Eleanor of Windsor's third birthday, Edward's adversary Sultan Baibars supposedly sent an assassin to kill him, but he survived and managed to kill his attacker. The 'knife with which King Edward was wounded at Acre in the Holy Land' was kept, and was still held in the English treasury seventy years later.[3] An old and often-repeated story that Leonor sucked the poison out of her husband's wound and saved his life has long been discredited.

Although Edward would not know it until much later, his father died on 16 November 1272 at the age of 65, after a reign of fifty-six years, the fourth longest in English history. In the distant Holy Land with his Castilian wife and their infant daughter, Edward was now king of England. Edmund of Lancaster, earl of Lancaster and Leicester, left his brother and sister-in-law in the Holy Land and returned to England, arriving home near the end of 1272 – apparently by coincidence, not in the knowledge that his father the king had recently died. None of Henry III's four living children (Edward, Margaret, Beatrice and Edmund) were in England at the time of his death, though his widow Eleanor of Provence and most of the English nobility and episcopate attended his funeral in the chapel of St Edward the Confessor in Westminster Abbey, which Henry himself had had built and which had been completed and consecrated three years previously. When Henry's elder son Edward finally received news of the deaths of both his father the king in November 1272 and his 5-year-old son John in August 1271, he is supposed to have made a remark which seems callous even by the standards of the age, to the effect that he grieved far more for his father than for his son as he could always have more sons, but would never have another father. This story may, however, be apocryphal. Possibly this flippant statement, if he ever said it or anything like it, came back to haunt Edward in later years, when he lost another two sons in childhood and had to deal with the possibility of his throne passing to one of his daughters. On the other hand, in the first year of his reign Edward paid a group of men almost £7 to work on 'the tomb of John of Windsor, the king's son' for sixteen weeks, so he showed respect for the memory of his and Leonor's little boy.[4]

Edward and Leonor stopped off for a leisurely visit in his duchy of Aquitaine on their way back to England. On 9 October 1273 in Gascony, Edward came to an agreement with Pere (b. 1240), the Infante of the Spanish kingdom of Aragon, regarding a future marriage between Pere's eldest son and Edward's eldest living daughter, Eleanor of Windsor. Eleanor was now 4 years old and her parents had not seen her since they had departed from England more than three years previously, and though they probably did not yet know it, she had been ill enough in late July and early August 1273 that a wax candle was lit at a nearby saint's shrine in the hope that it would aid her recovery (and she did recover).[5]

Infante Pere of Aragon was married to Constanza, eldest child of the late King Manfredi of Sicily (d. 1266), and was the son and heir of King Jaume I *el Conquistador*, 'the Conqueror', of Aragon. Pere of Aragon and Constanza of Sicily's eldest son was Alfonso, born in November 1265 and thus three and a half years Eleanor of Windsor's senior, and almost 8 years old when his future marriage to her was arranged. He was heir to the throne of Aragon behind his father.

Pere and Constanza had three younger sons as well, Jaume (b. 1267), Frederic (b. 1272) and Pere (b. *c.* 1275), and the admiring Catalan chronicler Ramon Muntaner called the four royal Aragonese sons 'the wisest, the most skilful in the world both at feats of arms and at everything else, the most courteous, and the best brought up'.[6] King Edward's agreement was designed to make his eldest daughter the queen of a large and important territory in southern Europe: Aragon covered much of eastern Spain, and its chief towns were Barcelona, Valencia and Zaragoza (now the second, third, and tenth largest cities in Spain). Until 1276 the Crown of Aragon also contained the island of Majorca, but although King Jaume I left most of his territories to his eldest son Don Pere, Eleanor of Windsor's putative father-in-law, he gave Majorca to his second son Don Jaume (b. 1243), who reigned as king of the island in his own right.

At the same time, King Edward arranged a future marriage for his and Leonor's son Henry of Windsor, then aged 5, and the great heiress Juana of Navarre (b. January 1273), who was set to inherit her father Enrique I's small kingdom of Navarre in northern Spain and his French counties of Champagne and Brie. As it happened, King Enrique of Navarre died a few months later and Juana's planned marriage into the English royal family never went ahead; she married Philip III of France's son and heir the future Philip IV (b. 1268) in August 1284 instead, after her mother, Philip III's cousin Blanche of Artois, fled from Navarre to the safety of the French court after her husband's death.[7]

Queen Leonor was heavily pregnant when these arrangements for her children's future marriages were made, and on 24 November 1273 in the town of Bayonne in the far south of the duchy of Aquitaine, gave birth to her eighth or ninth child and third son, Alfonso. The boy, about eighteen months younger than his sister Joan of Acre, was named after his uncle and godfather Alfonso X of Castile and Leon, who travelled to Bayonne to attend the baptism. It is not the case, as some writers have claimed, that Leonor visited her homeland at this time; as one of her biographers points out, an examination of her itinerary in 1273 makes a trip to Castile impossible unless she travelled at lightning speed.[8] Alfonso of Bayonne was probably born the day after his mother's thirty-second birthday and the day after his uncle and godfather's fifty-second birthday.

English scribes struggled endlessly with young Alfonso's name, to the extent that some later writers, trying to make sense of the strange spelling they saw in documents, mistakenly thought that Edward and Leonor had a daughter called 'Alice'. Had Alfonso been born as heir to the English throne, had Henry of Windsor not been alive in November 1273, Edward would probably have refused to allow his brother-in-law to give the boy a name that was decidedly foreign and exotic to the English, nephew and godson or not.[9] In fairness, King Edward's own name was also very unusual in the thirteenth century, and French scribes struggled with it, spelling it Edduvart or Oudouart or other variants. 'Edward' was an Anglo-Saxon name which had almost entirely disappeared after the Norman Conquest of England in 1066, until Henry III revived it for his first son in 1239, intending to honour Edward the Confessor (d. 1066). Over the centuries, the name spread over the Continent until a variant of it existed in many European languages, but in the thirteenth century 'Edward' was virtually unknown outside England and was not yet at all common there either. When Lord Edward was growing up, his name must have sounded as old-fashioned and downright odd to his contemporaries as Wulfstan or Aethelnoth or Leofwin would have sounded. The given name of Edward's younger brother Edmund of Lancaster is also the name of an Anglo-Saxon saint revered by Henry III, though it had not fallen out of fashion after 1066 to quite the same extent that the name Edward had.

Chapter 6

Many Losses

Edward and Leonor finally returned to Edward's kingdom on 2 August 1274 and were crowned king and queen of England at Westminster Abbey on 19 August. The Middle English *Brut* chronicle says that the streets 'were covered over his [Edward's] head with rich cloths of silk' as he and the queen rode at the head of a great procession through the city from the Tower to Westminster. The great conduit on Cheapside, which usually brought fresh drinking water to the centre of London from the River Tyburn a couple of miles away, ran with red and white wine all day, so that anyone who wished to partake might do so. Edward's sisters Margaret and Beatrice, the queen of Scotland and the duke of Brittany's daughter-in-law, attended with their husbands Alexander III and John, but it seems that their brother Edmund, earl of Lancaster and Leicester, did not. He and Edward had quarrelled over the right to carry the sword Curtana during the procession and over the king's refusal to make his brother hereditary Steward of England, and Edmund is not named among the magnates present during the coronation.[1] The royal brothers soon made up, however, and Edmund of Lancaster was to demonstrate complete loyalty to his elder brother for the remaining two decades of his life. Henry of Windsor and Eleanor of Windsor, meanwhile, now aged 6 and 5, were finally reunited with the parents they could not possibly have remembered, and met their infant brother Alfonso of Bayonne for the first time.

They did not yet meet 2-year-old Joan of Acre, however. When her parents returned to England, she was left in Ponthieu with her maternal grandmother, the dowager queen of Castile and Leon, and did not travel to England for a few years. Queen Jeanne was now married to her second husband Jean de Nesle, lord of Falvy, who in 1270 referred to 'the noble lady Jeanne, queen of Castile and Leon, countess of Ponthieu, our wife' (*la noble dame Jehane … roine de Castele et de Lyon contesse de Pontieu nostre fame*). Sadly, nothing is known of Joan of Acre's life in France, though perhaps her grandmother told her stories about her life in Spain and about the great Spanish warrior king who was her first husband and Joan's grandfather. Edward and Leonor spent time in Ponthieu with Queen Jeanne in June and July 1274 on their way back to Edward's kingdom, which was perhaps the first time the new queen of England had seen her mother for many years. Leonor's elder brother Don Fernando had died a few years previously and their younger brother Don Luis and his children all died sometime before the end of the 1270s, and Leonor was now heir to the county of Ponthieu. Edward and Leonor's decision to leave their daughter with Jeanne seems most likely to have been made entirely on personal, not political, grounds, and because there was a special bond between the dowager queen of Castile and her toddler granddaughter. As Joan of Acre had two brothers and an older sister, it was unlikely that she would ever inherit the county, and unlikely that Edward and Leonor made their decision on the basis that Joan would one day become countess of Ponthieu and therefore should grow up there.[2]

Six-year-old Henry of Windsor, living in Guildford, Surrey with his and his siblings' other grandmother, Eleanor of Provence, fell seriously ill in 1274. His physician, Master Hugh of Evesham, prepared liquorice water and sugar syrups for the little boy to drink, and copious amounts of milk were also purchased, but his condition deteriorated. Thirteen widows were hired to pray all night for Henry's recovery, and candles were sent to be burned at several famous shrines, but the little boy died sometime between 14 and 17 October 1274, two months after his parents' coronation. He was buried in Westminster Abbey with his siblings who had also died young. In the accounts kept for the household of Henry himself, his sister Eleanor of Windsor and their cousin John of Brittany, an absent-minded clerk noted the usual Friday payment of alms made by the young royal children, and had to cross out Henry's name on remembering that he was dead. Henry and Eleanor paid out 16*d* or 17*d* in alms to the poor with their own hands every Friday; the partly struck-out entry was corrected to read that 8*d* was given out only by *domine Alianore*.[3]

King Edward and Queen Leonor did not ride the 30 miles from London to Guildford to visit Henry before his death. One might argue that they had not realised how seriously ill their son was and that their failing to ride the short distance to see Henry does not reveal their lack of interest in their son even when he lay at death's door, though the king's extant accounts do demonstrate that he paid little attention to the anniversaries of the many deaths of his children. There is no record of Edward ordering masses to be sung for the soul of his third son when Alfonso also passed away in 1284, in contrast to the lavish oblations which were made in the duchy of Brittany following the death of Edward's nephew Henry of Brittany, one of his sister Beatrice's sons, after the boy died young.[4] Coupled with the callous remark Edward might have made in the early 1270s that he could always have more sons but would never have another father (assuming he ever did say this, which is far from certain), and with the fact that he and Leonor left their children behind in England for more than three years on two separate occasions even though some of the children were still very young, some historians have found it hard to avoid the conclusion that Edward I and Leonor of Castile were unlikely to win any awards as great parents.

Although other writers have defended the royal couple against the charge of being indifferent parents, their behaviour does seem to stand in stark contrast to Edward's own parents Henry III and Queen Eleanor, who created a loving, affectionate family environment and whose protective concern for all their children, even in adulthood, is not in any doubt. It may be that Edward I, in the last years of his life, showed more interest in his two young sons from his second marriage, Thomas and Edmund, than he had shown in his many children with Leonor; he sent an affectionately scolding letter to the noblewoman Margery Haustede, who looked after Thomas and Edmund, for failing to send him news of them.[5] Edward I and Leonor's youngest son Edward II seems to have been closer to his own children (or his younger children, at least) than his parents were to him and his older sisters, and Edward II's son Edward III and his queen Philippa of Hainault, much like Henry III and Eleanor of Provence, created a happy and loving family environment for their many children.

On the other hand, perhaps we should not assume evidence of absence from absence of evidence, and remember that few personal letters from the thirteenth century survive and that it is exceedingly difficult to establish the nature of people's familial relationships, especially at a remove of more than 700 years and from the perspective of a very different society. There also remains the undoubted fact that Edward and Leonor lost a large number of their sons and daughters very young; the mortality rate of the royal children was brutal even by the standards of the time, and Leonor was only outlived by six of the many children she had borne while Edward was survived by only four of his and Leonor's offspring plus his three young children from his second marriage. As Edward's biographer Marc Morris points out, 'it would be understandable if the king and queen came to regard their children with greater detachment than most parents'. Morris also notes the gifts that Edward showered on his surviving daughters, and indeed there seems little doubt that he loved them dearly and treated them with great indulgence, while Leonor regularly wrote letters inquiring after her children's health, including in April, June, July and October 1273 during her and Edward's long absence from England. A few years later, she sent salmon pies to her youngest son Edward of Caernarfon, and arranged for Dominican friars to join his household to aid with his instruction (Edward was to demonstrate a strong loyalty, which was reciprocated in full measure, to the Dominican order for the rest of his life).[6] There was also the fact that Leonor was about four or five months pregnant when Henry died in October 1274, which was surely a good reason to exercise caution regarding a visit to her ailing, and possibly infectious, son.

Whatever opinion one might form of Edward and Leonor's performance as parents, it is easy to see that the couple formed an extremely close and loving partnership. Leonor's biographer Sara Cockerill has noted that in 1283/84, a year when his accounts survive, Edward gave out extra alms on their wedding anniversary and in the days leading up to Leonor giving birth to their youngest child.[7] As Leonor was then past 40 and giving birth for at least the fourteenth and perhaps sixteenth time, it is both understandable and touching that her husband wished to demonstrate his concern for her well-being. This is just one example of the couple's devotion, and it is apparent that they shared many interests, enjoyed each other's company to the point of being inseparable, and showed consideration and kindness to the other on many occasions. Edward once commissioned a psalter and book of hours for his wife, a thoughtful gift for the book-lover that Leonor was, while for her part, she hired musicians for the king to entertain him on the rare occasions that they were apart. The couple also enjoyed playing chess together.[8]

Young Henry of Windsor's demise in October 1274 left his brother Alfonso of Bayonne, now 11 months old and the only living son of

Edward and Leonor, as heir to their father's throne. Alfonso lived in his own household, which was under the command of Philip Willoughby and William Salinis and, later, Thomas Pampesworth or Pampelworth. By July 1278 and probably much earlier, Alfonso and his household lived at Windsor Castle, as his two older brothers had, and as his father and Edward's own younger siblings had in the 1240s and 1250s as well. Sometime early in Edward I's reign, the king paid Thomas Pampelworth, 'clerk of Geoffrey de Picheford, constable of Windsor Castle' £60 for his sons' expenses at the castle.[9]

The king's 15-year-old sister-in-law Aveline de Forz, heir to the earldoms of Devon and Aumale and married to Edmund of Lancaster since 1269, died on 10 November 1274.[10] She was interred in Westminster Abbey and her tomb can still be seen there, and Edmund was buried next to her decades later, although he had been married to another woman in the meantime and had children with her. Aveline, unsurprisingly given her youth, left no children, though the chronicler Nicholas Trevet or Trivet claims that she gave birth to two infants who died soon after birth, who might have been twins. This is perhaps unlikely, as if Aveline had borne a child to Edmund of Lancaster who lived long enough to take a breath, even if s/he died very soon afterwards, Edmund would have been entitled to hold all of Aveline's large inheritance in his own hands for the rest of his life, thanks to the medieval custom called the 'courtesy of England'. He never did hold any of her lands after her death. On the other hand, Nicholas Trivet wrote his chronicle at the request of Edward I and Leonor's daughter Mary (b. 1279), Edmund of Lancaster's niece, and it seems highly likely, therefore, that he was well-informed about the English royal family.

Soon after Aveline's premature death, on 28 November 1274, Queen Leonor's half-brother Don Felipe, formerly archbishop-elect of Seville, died as well, at the age of 47; Leonor would die on the same day as Felipe, sixteen years later. Yet more deaths struck the English royal family in 1275. Both of King Edward's sisters, Margaret, queen of Scotland, and Beatrice, daughter-in-law of the duke of Brittany, died that year, in February and March, aged 34 and 32 respectively. Beatrice probably died after giving birth, as her youngest daughter Eleanor of Brittany, a future abbess of Fontévrault, was born in 1275. According to the author of the *Lanercost* chronicle, written at Lanercost Priory near the English-Scottish border and a very useful source for events in Scotland and the north of England in the thirteenth and fourteenth centuries, Queen Margaret of Scotland was 'a woman of great beauty, chastity, and humility'. The Westminster chronicle *Flores Historiarum* says that the deaths of Queen Margaret and Beatrice 'left a deep sorrow to the nobles after the great joy of the coronation [of Edward in August 1274]; for they were ladies in the flower of youth, of high character and distinguished beauty'.[11] Margaret left her three children, Margaret, Alexander and David, and her widower Alexander III did not marry again for another ten years. Beatrice also left half a dozen children, and her widower succeeded his long-lived father as duke of Brittany in 1286 and died in 1305 well into his sixties, having never remarried.

Chapter 7

Eleanor at Court

Edward and Leonor conceived another child around mid- or late June 1274 while they were in Ponthieu staying with Queen Jeanne, and perhaps on or about 15 March 1275 at Windsor Castle, Leonor gave birth to her sixth or seventh daughter, Margaret. As Leonor was already in Bury St Edmunds, Suffolk by 17 April 1275, however, and must therefore have set off from Windsor (90 miles from Bury St Edmunds) a few days earlier, this would be a short lying-in period, and Margaret was perhaps born in mid-February rather than mid-March.[1] The royal couple might have named their daughter after her aunt the queen-consort of Scotland, who died on 26 February that year. In September 1275, six or seven months after little Margaret's birth, her future husband Jan of Brabant, son and ultimate heir of the duke of Brabant, was born as well.

Margaret's nurse was Cecile Cleware, who had previously worked as the nurse of her sister Eleanor, now 5 going on 6 years old. Cecile's husband bore the excellent name of Wygeyn Sifrewast, and the couple came from Clewer in Berkshire.[2] The little Margaret was sent to live at Windsor Castle with the brother who was less than sixteen months her senior, Alfonso of Bayonne, and would be the third of the king and queen's many children who lived into adulthood.[3]

Edward and Leonor conceived yet another child probably in August 1275, less than half a year after Margaret was born, while they were travelling north for a possible meeting with Llywelyn ap Gruffudd, prince of Wales.[4] Leonor gave birth to another daughter at Kempton near London probably on 1 May 1276, just thirteen and a half or perhaps fourteen and a half months after Margaret was born. The queen named her latest daughter Berengaria or Berenguela after her grandmother Berenguela (1180–1246), queen of Castile in her own right and queen of Leon by marriage. It was also the name of Edward I's great-aunt by marriage, Berengaria of Navarre (d. 1230), wife of King Richard Lionheart.

The eldest royal daughter Eleanor of Windsor, meanwhile, had already been betrothed to Alfonso of Aragon for two and a half years when her little sister Berengaria was born. Alfonso's grandfather Jaume I, king of Aragon, Majorca and Valencia and count of Barcelona, died on 27 July 1276 in his late sixties, after a reign of sixty-three years. Jaume's eldest son Don Pere, Infante Alfonso's father, succeeded him as king of Aragon and Valencia and count of Barcelona, and his second son Don Jaume as king of Majorca. In contrast to his long-lived father, King Pere of Aragon's reign would be a short one of only nine years. Dramatic news reached England from another Spanish kingdom the following year: not long before 15 September 1277, Queen Leonor's eldest half-brother Alfonso X had his next-eldest brother Don Fadrique executed in Burgos, the city near the monastery of Santa María la Real where Leonor had married Edward twenty-three years before. Fadrique had, like the fourth royal brother Don Enrique, long been a rebellious thorn in King Alfonso's side.

Eleanor of Windsor joined the royal English court around 1276/77, aged about 7 or 8. In contrast to later centuries when the king or queen-regnant spent much of the year in and around London, in the thirteenth and fourteenth centuries the king and his enormous retinue changed location several times a week, moving in a never-ending circuit from town to village to castle around the south and midlands of England, though they only very rarely travelled to the north. Eleanor, even at this young age, had her own large household with a chamberlain, a keeper of her hall, a valet of the bedchamber, and countless others. In 1278, Eleanor and her household met her parents at Devizes in Wiltshire and travelled with them to Glastonbury in Somerset, where they spent Easter, and they travelled onto London that May. Eleanor was particularly close to and spent much time with the dowager queen, Eleanor of Provence, who was as loving and caring a grandmother to her many grandchildren as she had been a mother to her five children. While Queen Leonor could surely have offered extremely useful advice to Eleanor of Windsor to prepare her for her future role as a queen in Spain, it is difficult to get much sense that either Eleanor or her younger sisters were particularly emotionally close to their mother, however, and Eleanor seems to have found much more support and affection in her paternal grandmother.[5]

Chapter 8

A Marriage Proposal (1)

In 1277, King Edward considered the possibility of betrothing Joan of Acre, aged 5 and still resident in Ponthieu with her maternal grandmother, to Hartmann, second son of the German king, Rudolf von Habsburg (r. 1273–91), and Rudolf's late first wife Gertrude von Hohenberg. Hartmann von Habsburg was born in 1263, so was nine years Joan's senior, and his sisters included the queens of Hungary and Bohemia and the duchesses of Bavaria and Saxony. King Rudolf sent two envoys – Heinrich von Isny, doctor of theology, bishop of Basel and future archbishop of Mainz, and Andreas von Rode, provost of Werden – to England on 25 September 1277. Throughout the last quarter of the year, the two men discussed the possibility of Joan of Acre's future marriage to Hartmann with King Edward.

Although Hartmann was only King Rudolf's second son – his brother Albrecht was eight years older than he and was already married to Elisabeth of Carinthia – there was a chance that Hartmann would become King of the Romans, i.e. king of Germany, after his father. Unusually, the German throne did not automatically pass to the eldest son of the previous monarch as most other European thrones did, but was an elected position; Edward's uncle Richard of Cornwall had been elected as German king in 1257, and Rudolf von Habsburg was his successor.[1] Edward, therefore, having already arranged a marriage for his eldest daughter designed to make her a queen in Spain, was attempting to make his second daughter a queen in Germany as well. Ultimately, it would turn out that none of his daughters became queens.

A marriage into Germany for one of Edward and Leonor's daughters would provide a useful counterbalance to the far-reaching influence of his wealthy and powerful uncle-in-law Charles of Anjou, king of Sicily and count of Provence, as far as Edward was concerned, and more generally, Rudolf and his son might become excellent allies against the kingdom of France if this ever proved necessary.[2] Relations between England and

France were still very cordial in the late 1270s, but Edward, being a consummate politician, was well aware how easily that situation might change, as indeed it did when his cousin Philip III died unexpectedly at the age of only 40 in 1285. Philip's teenage son and successor Philip IV proved to have little interest in maintaining his father's and grandfather's amicable relationship with the king on the other side of the Channel, to the extent that England and France spent much of the 1290s at war with each other.

The proposed German-English marriage was the pet project of Edward's aunt, the dowager queen of France, Marguerite of Provence, Louis IX's widow and Philip III's mother. Marguerite had been disgruntled for decades that her father Ramon-Berenger, count of Provence, had left his county in its entirety to his youngest daughter Beatrice on his death in 1245, rather than sharing it out among his four daughters equally or giving it to Marguerite, his eldest daughter. Marguerite had feuded for many years with her brother-in-law Charles of Anjou, Beatrice's husband, over his possession of Provence. She hoped that Rudolf von Habsburg could be persuaded to resurrect and give to his son Hartmann the old kingdom of Arles, a large territory of the Holy Roman Empire dating back to the tenth and eleventh centuries, which comprised much of modern-day Switzerland and south-east France, including Provence. Edward I offered to give Joan of Acre a 10,000-mark dowry in exchange for Rudolf promising to give Hartmann this ancient kingdom.[3]

The negotiations bore promising fruit, and on 2 January 1278, King Rudolf's envoys Heinrich von Isny and Andreas von Rode took oaths regarding the future marriage between Joan of Acre and Hartmann von Habsburg.[4] It was decided that the wedding should take place that same year, preferably on 8 September, the Nativity of the Virgin Mary. King Edward sent Heinrich and Andreas back to Rudolf with his own three envoys, two Dominican friars and Gerhard or Gerard Grandison, bishop of Verdun. He gave the men precise instructions to seek clarification on Joan's dowry, dower lands and the provisions that would be made for her under the unfortunate circumstances that she became a widow. They were also to make careful inquiries as to Hartmann's character and to inform Edward of their findings as soon as possible.

Evidently all went well, as King Rudolf, in Vienna, issued a number of documents at the end of April and early May 1278, specifying which dower and jointure lands would be given to Joan from the Habsburgs' properties in Switzerland. He also promised that the wedding would take place on 8 September 1278, and that he would do everything in his power to ensure that Hartmann was elected King of the Romans if it should happen that he himself was elected Holy Roman Emperor. The kings of Germany were often 'promoted' to emperor by seven powerful men called the *Kurfürsten* or 'Electors': the archbishops of Cologne, Trier and Mainz, and four secular lords, the king of Bohemia, the count palatine of the Rhine, the margrave of Brandenburg, and the duke of Saxony. The fact, therefore, that Hartmann von Habsburg was only a second son was not a mark against him as a future husband for one of the king of England's daughters.

Unfortunately, Rudolf von Habsburg went to war against the kingdom of Bohemia later that year, and the planned wedding day of 8 September 1278 came and went. Hartmann the bridegroom wrote to Edward in about October 1278, stating that he would travel to England as soon as possible but that for various reasons his journey was delayed, and in late February 1279 the German knight Konrad Wernher von Hatstatt travelled to England to offer Rudolf's and Hartmann's apologies for the delay. Edward I prepared to welcome the young bridegroom on 10 June 1279, but Hartmann came down with a serious illness, and again his father had to write to the king of England with apologies.[5] In the end, Joan of Acre's German marriage never took place, and she never even met her fiancé, although she was brought to England from Ponthieu in 1278 to do so; it was the first time she had seen the country which her father ruled and where she would spend the rest of her life, and the first time, as far as is known, that she had met her siblings Eleanor, Alfonso and Margaret. At some point in the late 1270s or early 1280s, she joined her older sister at court and began to take part in the endless royal peregrinations around the kingdom.

Chapter 9

A Marriage Proposal (2)

Queen Leonor was heavily pregnant when the negotiations for her daughter's German marriage were held in late 1277 and early 1278, and on 3 January 1278 she gave birth to a child, most probably a daughter, whose name is not known and who died immediately after she was born.[1] Edward and Leonor lost two daughters in 1278: Berengaria, born around 1 May 1276 and barely 2 years old, died sometime before 27 June that year. Of the eight or perhaps nine daughters Leonor had borne, only Eleanor of Windsor, Joan of Acre, and Margaret of Windsor were still alive by the summer of 1278. The infant mortality rate in the thirteenth century was of course horrific, but to have only three daughters survive from eight or nine births was a low rate even by the standards of the time, and of course Edward and Leonor had already lost two sons as well and would lose their third a few years later.

The early year of 1278 was a hectic time for the English royal family. In addition to the sad death of their newborn child, and the negotiations taking place for Joan of Acre's future marriage, the king of England also received a 'commission from the duke of Brabant to treat of the marriage' between his son and another of Edward and Leonor's daughters on 24 January 1278 ('the Monday before the conversion of St Paul').[2] The duke of Brabant, a large territory in modern-day Belgium and the Netherlands with its capital at Brussels, was Jan I (b. 1252 or 1253), brother of the queen-consort of France, Marie of Brabant, who had married Edward I's widowed cousin Philip III in 1274.[3] Jan sent four envoys to England and wrote a letter, in French, to Edward I. In the letter, the duke talked of the 'covenants of marriage between the very high lord, Lord Edward, by the grace of GOD king of England, on one side, and we on the other; that Jan [*Johan*], our eldest son, shall take to wife my lady Margaret [*madame Margarete*], daughter of the aforesaid king, when they are of an age to marry'.[4] Brabant was an important duchy, part of the patchwork of comparatively tiny but rich and influential counties and duchies which covered what is now Belgium, the

Netherlands, northern France and western Germany. Margaret's marriage into this part of Europe was merely the first of what would become quite a rush of English royal marriages into the Low Countries over the next few decades: her youngest sister Elizabeth married into the county of Holland in 1297, her nephew Edward III into the county of Hainault in 1328, and her niece Eleanor of Woodstock, one of Edward III's sisters, into the county of Guelders in 1332.

It was probably inevitable by the conventions of the time that Duke Jan's son was also named Jan, and the younger Jan of Brabant was a grandson of the very long-lived Guy de Dampierre, count of Flanders (Guy was born in the mid-1220s or thereabouts, became a father in *c.* 1247, and and lived until 1305), via his mother Margaretha of Flanders, duchess of Brabant. Born on 27 September 1275, young Jan was a few months younger than his putative fiancée Margaret of Windsor. The covenant between the kingdom of England and the duchy of Brabant stated that if Margaret could not marry Jan for some reason, the next eldest daughter of the king would do so, and likewise, if Jan could not marry Margaret, then the next eldest son of the duke would do so. The duke and his son would dower Margaret with 3,000 *livres tournois* ('pounds of Tours', a currency often in use on the Continent) of land annually in Brabant, and the lands and rents she would receive after her marriage were minutely and painstakingly laid out in another letter.

Some modern writers have stated that Jan of Brabant was not his father's eldest son, but had an older brother named Godefroy, born in 1273 or 1274, who died as a child or adolescent sometime between September 1283 and May 1294. This cannot, however, be the case; Duke Jan specifically referred to Jan as 'our eldest son' (*nostre eisne filz*) in several of his letters to the king of England in 1278, and it is impossible that Edward I would have arranged the marriage of one of his royal daughters to a mere second son of Brabant. Unlike the throne of Germany, succession to the duchy was based, like the thrones of England and France, on primogeniture, and the duchy passed by right to the eldest son of the previous duke. Edward's daughters were not only the children of a king, they were the granddaughters of two other kings, and Edward would never have dreamed of wasting the marriage of one of them on the younger son of a duke who would not succeed his father. Jan (b. 1275), not his brother Godefroy, was called the duke of Brabant's heir in English records in 1279.[5]

Jan and Godefroy of Brabant had a sister, Margaretha of Brabant, born on 4 October 1276, and Godefroy himself had certainly been born by 1 February 1278, when a letter was written in his name. It stated that he would not do anything to impede the marriage of his brother and Margaret of Windsor, and that he had sworn a sacred oath to this effect in the name of the four Evangelists. The letter called Godfrey 'son of the duke of Brabant', not 'eldest son'. Godefroy was himself betrothed in September 1283 to another Margareta, niece of the count of Berg in Germany, but he died at an unknown date before his father in May 1294, and his sister-in-law Margaret of Windsor almost certainly never met him. Perhaps Godefroy was a younger twin of Jan, hence the modern confusion as to which of them was the elder son and their father's heir.[6] Edward I sent the abbot of Westminster and a knight called Sir Thomas of Sandwich to the duchy of Brabant 'to treat touching all matters which concern the completion of the marriage between John son and heir of J., duke of Lorraine and Brabant, and Margaret the king's daughter' a year later in early 1279.[7]

Chapter 10

Eleanor and Aragon

On 11 or 12 March 1279 at the palace of Woodstock near Oxford, Queen Leonor gave birth to yet another daughter, fourteen months after bearing an infant who died soon after she was born. This latest royal daughter was called Mary, which was an unusual name in the English royal family of the thirteenth century, so little Mary of Woodstock might have been named in honour of the Virgin Mary or after one of her godmothers – or perhaps Leonor had her grandmother Countess Marie of Ponthieu in mind. In the thirteenth and fourteenth centuries, the name Mary was usually spelt 'Marie' in England, the same way as it is spelt in modern French, and two common diminutives or pet forms were Mariote and Marion(e). Mary of Woodstock, the ninth or tenth daughter of the king and queen, would be their fourth who survived childhood, and would become famous as a nun with no vocation.

Mere days after giving birth to her latest daughter, Queen Leonor lost her mother, when Jeanne de Dammartin, dowager queen of Castile and Leon, died on 16 March 1279 at the age of about 60. Her county of Ponthieu in the far north of France, which she had inherited from her mother Marie in 1250, passed to Leonor as her only living child, while her other and much smaller county of Aumale, her inheritance from her father Simon, went to Leonor's French nephew Jean of Aumale, son of her late older brother Don Fernando.[1]

Leonor and Edward knew of her mother's death by 21 March 1279, when they jointly empowered Edward's brother Edmund of Lancaster, earl of Lancaster and Leicester, to take possession of the county of Ponthieu on Leonor's behalf. Edmund was count of Champagne by right of his second marriage in late 1275 or early 1276 to Blanche of Artois, dowager queen of Navarre and countess of Champagne, and he was an important and influential landowner in France as well as in England and Wales. The king and queen both travelled to Leonor's new county a few weeks later: they departed for Ponthieu from Dover on 13 May 1279, and returned to England on 19 June.[2] The county was to pass to the queen's only surviving son, 6-year-old Edward of Caernarfon, after her death in November 1290.

The years 1280 and 1281 are, as far as is certainly known, the only significant period between the early 1260s and 1284 when Queen Leonor did not give birth to any children; as far as the record shows, she gave birth in March 1279 and then again in August 1282. It is possible, however, that she did give birth to a short-lived son sometime in 1280 or 1281. The author of the *Opus Chronicorum*, probably written within twenty years of Leonor's death, stated that the he had overheard King Edward discussing his and Leonor's children, and Edward said that they had five sons. Only four are known for certain: John of Windsor, born in July 1266; Henry of Windsor, born in May 1268; Alfonso of Bayonne, born in November 1273; and Edward of Caernarfon, born in April 1284. If Leonor did indeed bear a fifth son, the years 1280/81 are the only possible years where another birth could be fitted in (unless the boy was a twin to one of her daughters). It is perhaps unlikely, however, that the queen could give birth to a son whose name is not known and whose existence does not appear in any other record; a daughter might plausibly be obscured and fail to appear on record, and indeed the names of two or three of Leonor's daughters are not known, but a son and possible heir born to the reigning king of England was an entirely different proposition. Then again, the royal wardrobe accounts of 1280/81 are missing, so perhaps there was indeed evidence of the existence of another royal son which has not survived today. Sara Cockerill points to the unusually long period of three months which the royal court spent in one area, Gloucestershire and Wiltshire, in the early months of 1281, which could reveal the approximate date of birth of a son who might have been stillborn, or who died not long after his birth.[3]

In June 1281, Edward I contemplated sending Eleanor of Windsor to Spain to marry her fiancé, Alfonso of Aragon. She turned 12 that month, so was rapidly coming to what was, by the standards of thirteenth-century royalty, marriageable age. Two Englishmen, John Vescy and Anthony Bek, were appointed to travel to Spain and to contract the marriage between Eleanor and Alfonso.[4] John, Lord Vescy (1244–89) was an important baron of Northumberland who had been raised with Edward I's younger brother Edmund of Lancaster, and who had lost his Italian wife Agnese di Saluzzo in *c.* 1265. In 1279 or 1280 Queen Leonor arranged Vescy's second marriage to a young partly French, partly Spanish kinswoman of hers, Isabella Beaumont, a granddaughter of Leonor's aunt Berenguela of Leon. Anthony Bek served as bishop of Durham from July 1283, being elected as such at Edward I's request, until his death in early 1311, and in February 1306 became the only Englishman in history to be appointed patriarch of Jerusalem.

King Edward failed, however, to send his daughter to Spain, and claimed that his mother Eleanor and his wife Leonor had persuaded him that Eleanor of Windsor was still too young to travel to another country and to marry: 'The queen her mother and our dearest mother are unwilling to grant that she may pass over earlier on account of her tender age.' John Vescy and Anthony Bek were therefore asked to perform the difficult task of assuring the Aragonese that the English still very much wished the marriage to take place, while delaying it for at least a year and a half and preferably longer.[5]

This might reveal that both Eleanor of Provence, who married Henry III in January 1236 when she was probably only 12, and Leonor of Castile, who married Edward shortly before she turned 13, felt that they had married and moved to another country at too young an age. From a modern and compassionate perspective, this certainly seems a valid and accurate point. On the other hand, Edward I was hardly a man to allow his wife and his mother to talk him out of doing something he truly wished to do, and possibly the two women's intercession was a plausible excuse he had invented for failing to send his daughter to her fiancé. It may be that the king was concerned about an ongoing and very serious quarrel between the kingdoms of Aragon and Sicily on one side and the papacy and the kingdom of France on the other (discussed further below), and decided that sending Eleanor into the middle of it was not in her best interests, or his own. Whatever the reasons, the delay in sending Eleanor to Aragon meant ultimately that she would never travel there and would never marry, or indeed meet, Alfonso or become a queen. Alfonso was only three and a half years her senior and turned 16 in November 1281; it is impossible to know Eleanor of Windsor's feelings on the matter for certain, but perhaps she considered that marrying a young royal man not too much older than herself, a man who would make her a queen, and a man who was deemed courteous, skilful in arms and well brought up, was not such a bad idea, all things considered.

As it turned out, four of the daughters of Edward I and Queen Leonor married, and it is interesting to note that none of their weddings took place when the women were particularly young. Eleanor of Windsor, ultimately, did not marry until she was 24; Joan of Acre married when she was 18 or very soon to turn 18; Margaret married when she was 15, but her husband was six or seven months younger than she and still 14 at the time of their wedding; and Elizabeth married for the first time at 14, but her husband was only 12 or 13. As Elizabeth was widowed from her first husband when she was 17 and he probably only 15, it seems possible that the marriage was never consummated. She married her second husband when she was 20, and gave birth to her first child when she was 21. Joan of Acre was 19, or very close to it, when she had her first child, Eleanor was 25 or 26, and Margaret was 25 when she bore her only child. Only Joan of Acre, therefore, was a teenager when she became a mother, and had already reached the very end of her teens.

Chapter 11

Sicilian Vespers

Joan of Acre's 18-year-old German fiancé Hartmann von Habsburg drowned in the River Rhine between Breisach and Strasbourg on 21 December 1281, when his ship hit a rock in thick fog and capsized. Although Edward I was informed shortly afterwards by the bishop of Verdun, Hartmann's father King Rudolf did not even bother to tell the English king of his son's death until the following August, having evidently lost all interest in an alliance with England.[1] Joan, still only 9 years old, had been deprived of a life in Germany as the wife of its probable future king, and her father would have to arrange another match for her. King Rudolf, who should have been her father-in-law, outlived his second son by a decade. He was succeeded as King of the Romans by Adolf von Nassau in 1292, and in 1298 by his eldest son, Albrecht, who in 1308 would be murdered by his nephew, Johann 'Parracida' of Swabia, son of Albrecht and Hartmann's younger brother Duke Rudolf of Austria. Despite Hartmann's early death and Albrecht's murder, their father had established an extremely long-lived royal dynasty, and King Rudolf's Habsburg descendants ruled large territories in Europe as far apart as Hungary, Croatia, Spain and Portugal until the twentieth century.

Eleanor of Windsor was in Guildford, Surrey with her grandmother Eleanor of Provence on 15 February 1282, when both she and her father sent letters to Aragon regarding her marriage. Eleanor's letter states that she was using her grandmother's seal, as she herself did not yet have one. Letters from Aragon referred to her as *illustris Regis Angliae primogenita*, 'the eldest daughter of the illustrious king of England', meaning, of course, the eldest surviving daughter. In a letter Don Alfonso of Aragon sent to King Edward on 10 February 1282, he called himself *Infans Alfonsus* or 'Infante Alfonso', and in another, sent soon afterwards, he acknowledged receipt of Edward's letters and stated how glad he was to hear of the English king's good health. All the letters between England and Aragon were written in Latin.[2] There was much more correspondence between the two kingdoms in May 1282 owing to a dramatic situation called the Sicilian Vespers, a rebellion against Edward I's uncle-in-law Charles of Anjou, king of Sicily and count of Provence, which resulted in Alfonso's father King Pere of Aragon becoming king of Sicily by right of his wife Constanza, daughter of the late King Manfredi of Sicily. Edward was informed on 26 May 1282 that five cities in Sicily had revolted against Charles of Anjou and had massacred the French, and shortly afterwards Pere told Edward that he would accept the crown of Sicily as requested. His reign officially began on 4 September 1282.[3]

King Edward was very busy in 1282, invading and attempting, successfully, to take over North Wales. Dafydd ap Gruffudd, brother of the prince of Wales, Llywelyn, gave the English king a plausible excuse to invade after he attacked Hawarden Castle in March that year. With his pregnant wife and their eldest daughters Eleanor and Joan in his company, Edward arrived at the new castle of Rhuddlan in North Wales in early July.[4] On *c.* 7 August 1282, Leonor gave birth to her tenth or eleventh, and youngest, daughter at Rhuddlan Castle, and she was named Elizabeth. This was probably an attempt by Edward I to have a son and potential heir born in Wales, which went awry when the infant was a girl. The exact date of Elizabeth's birth is not certain, but the queen was purified or churched on 6 September, and as this usually occurred approximately thirty days after she bore a daughter, this suggests a date of birth of *c.* 7 August.[5]

Elizabeth's name was an unusual one in England in the late thirteenth century, and the name, as was the case with that of Elizabeth's older sister Mary, was not previously found in the English royal family. The royal couple's inspiration for the choice is unknown; the little girl might have been named after a godmother. In Leonor's native language, 'Elizabeth' is 'Isabel', and indeed Elizabeth of Rhuddlan's name occasionally appears on record as Isabel or Isabell, the two names being considered more or less interchangeable. In 1313, for example, in an inventory of some of the items which belonged to Elizabeth's younger brother King Edward II, a gift of a brooch she had given him was stated to have come from *madame Isabell la seor*, 'my lady Isabel the sister'.[6] Mostly, however, her name was written as Elizabeth, and this variant was most probably what Elizabeth of Rhuddlan called herself.

Queen Leonor was apparently closer to her youngest daughter than to any of her other children; unusually, Elizabeth of Rhuddlan remained with the queen, or at the very least visited her often, for the first two years of her life, and was with Leonor in the North Wales town of Caernarfon in April 1284 when Leonor gave birth again. Elizabeth also spent much time with Edward of Caernarfon, the brother who was only twenty months her junior, in childhood and adolescence.[7] There is much evidence of the two youngest royal siblings' closeness.

Eleanor of Windsor, according to one modern writer, married Infante Alfonso of Aragon by proxy on 15 August 1282, a few days after the birth of her youngest sister.[8] Other modern writers, however, state that Eleanor married Alfonso by proxy in Westminster Abbey on 15 August 1290, a year when two of her younger sisters, Joan of Acre and Margaret of Windsor, certainly did get married.[9] It is beyond all doubt that Eleanor and Alfonso never did marry in person, because he died before she could travel to Spain, but as Alfonso's wife and queen, even if only by proxy, Eleanor would have been entitled to receive dower from the kingdom of Aragon for the rest of her life as all widows did. She did not. At the very least, we would expect to find her father corresponding with Alfonso's successor regarding her rightful dower, but he did not. Whether it is correct to state that Eleanor ever married Alfonso III is unclear, but she certainly did not marry him in 1282, as they required a papal dispensation for consanguinity and none had been issued. Pope Martin wrote to King Edward on this issue in July 1283; see below.

On 11 December 1282, Llywelyn ap Gruffudd, prince of Wales, was killed at Cilmeri after falling into a trap led by the sons of his cousin Roger Mortimer, Lord of Wigmore, who had died earlier in the year. Edward I sent Llywelyn's 6-month-old daughter Gwenllian, his own close relative – she was the daughter of Edward's cousin Eleanor de Montfort, who died after she gave birth to Gwenllian – to Sempringham Priory in Lincolnshire, where she spent her entire life, dying in 1337. North Wales fell to the king of England, and Edward had Llywelyn's brother Dafydd, whom he considered a turncoat, grotesquely executed in Shrewsbury a few months later.

Chapter 12

Leonor's Last Child

News of the ongoing arrangements for Eleanor of Windsor's marriage to Infante Alfonso of Aragon, whether it ever took place by proxy or not, reached the ears of Pope Martin IV in Orvieto on 7 July 1283. The pope, who was French by birth and whose previous name was Simon Brion, took the side of the Frenchman Charles of Anjou in France's struggle with the kingdom of Aragon over Sicily, and was at pains to remind Edward I that he had officially deposed Eleanor's future father-in-law Pere as both king of Sicily and king of Aragon. Pope Martin wrote to Edward 'expressing surprise at his offering his daughter Eleanor in marriage to Alfonso, eldest son of Pere, late king of Aragon, whom the pope deprived of his kingdom'. He urged Edward to revoke the alliance, and went on to tell him that 'Alfonso and Eleanor are related in the fourth degree of kindred, as the king must know that the countess of Provence, his mother's mother, was sister of Amadeus, count of Savoy, whose [grand]daughter, King Pere's wife, was the mother of Alfonso.'[1]

Other than mixing up Constanza of Sicily, queen of Aragon, with her mother Beatrice of Savoy (d. 1258/59), queen of Sicily, the pope's impressive knowledge of the intricate familial relations at the highest levels of European society was very nearly correct. Eleanor of Windsor and Alfonso of Aragon were indeed third cousins, i.e. were related in the fourth degree of kindred, both being great-great-grandchildren of Tommaso I, count of Savoy and Marguerite of Geneva, and thus they required a papal dispensation for consanguinity before they were able to wed. It was clear from this letter of Martin IV that the required dispensation would not be forthcoming.

On 27 August 1283, Queen Leonor was a few weeks pregnant for at least the fourteenth, and perhaps even the sixteenth time, when she and King Edward escaped from a fire in Caergwrle Castle (also sometimes called Hope Castle) in North Wales. The fire was not a small one: it reduced the castle to rubble. Nor was this the only time that the king and queen had a dramatic escape: some years later in Gascony, as the couple sat and talked on a couch, a bolt of lightning came through the window behind them, passed between them, and killed two of their servants standing nearby. Edward and Leonor themselves were entirely unhurt, and others who were present exclaimed that it was a miracle.[2] As the child Leonor was carrying in August 1283 was the future king of England, the ancestor of all the later monarchs of England, an ancestor of many or perhaps even most people of English origin alive in the twenty-first century, and the father of the king who began the Hundred Years War against France in the 1330s, European history would be remarkably different if Leonor had succumbed to the flames and smoke. On 3 October 1283, a few weeks after the king and queen escaped from the fire, the unfortunate Dafydd ap Gruffudd, brother of the late Prince Llywelyn, was given the traitor's death by hanging, drawing and quartering in Shrewsbury; Edward had not forgiven what he deemed to be betrayal on Dafydd's part (Dafydd had allied with the English king against his brother, though ultimately was reconciled to Llywelyn).

The king and queen's daughter Eleanor of Windsor was with them in the autumn of 1283, as was her sister Joan of Acre, now 11 years old, though one assumes the two royal girls did not have to watch Dafydd's grotesque execution. Edward I expected his children to make daily offerings when they attended Mass, and also when they visited shrines and altars. Between 1 November 1283 and 6 January 1284, the king gave Eleanor 5*s* 6*d* to make up for offerings which Eleanor had not made and he felt she should have. Extant records of 1284/85 show that he gave her another 5*s* 8*d* because she did not make offerings at masses on sixty-eight feast days in an unstated calendar year in the early 1280s.[3]

On 4 April 1284, the heavily pregnant Queen Leonor's half-brother King Alfonso X of Castile and Leon died at the age of 62, after a reign of thirty-two years, and was succeeded by his second son, Sancho IV (b. 1258). His eldest son, Fernando de la Cerda, had died in July 1275 three months before his twentieth birthday, leaving two infant sons, Alfonso and Fernando. Alfonso X had wished to be succeeded by the elder of these two grandsons, but Sancho IV set his nephews aside and took the Castilian throne for himself, an act for which King Alfonso cursed his son on his deathbed. King Sancho was succeeded in later years by his son, grandson and other descendants, though the de la Cerda branch of the Castilian royal family also continued. Don Carlos de la Cerda, a great-grandson of Fernando de la Cerda (d. 1275), was a notorious pirate who preyed in the English Channel and who had a distressing habit of throwing sailors overboard after plundering their ships. In 1350, Edward I and Leonor of Castile's grandson Edward III defeated him and his fleet at the naval battle of Winchelsea (often colourfully known as 'the Spaniards on the Sea'), and although Carlos survived the battle, some years later he was murdered in France.

On 25 April, exactly three weeks after losing her eldest half-brother, Queen Leonor gave birth to her youngest child, Edward, in the town of Caernarfon in North Wales. She gave birth either on the site of the castle which her husband was having built, on the location of a previous small fortification, or in the town itself, which Edward was also rebuilding. If she did give birth on the site of the castle, her son was almost certainly born in a temporary wooden building, and it is highly unlikely that his birthplace was a higher floor of the Eagle Tower, as is claimed today. Her youngest daughter Elizabeth of Rhuddlan, not yet 21 months old, was with her in Caernarfon, as was her second daughter Joan of Acre, either recently 12 or almost 12.

Leonor was now 42 years old and there seems little doubt that Edward of Caernarfon was the youngest of her many children. Two other children claimed by some writers to have been daughters of Leonor and Edward I, Beatrice born in 1286 and Blanche born in 1290, are almost certain to be much later inventions, and there is no real evidence that they ever existed. They first appear on record in a document dating to, or even after, the reign of Edward I and Leonor of Castile's great-great-great-great-grandson Henry VI (r. 1422–61).[4] Given Leonor's fertility, it is certainly not impossible that she did become pregnant again in 1286 when she was 44 years old (she turned 45 in *c.* late November 1286), but in the absence of any evidence from the thirteenth or fourteenth centuries which proves the existence of children born to her in or after 1286, it is safest to assume that Edward of Caernarfon was her youngest child, and he was certainly her youngest child who survived infancy.

Little Edward was not born as the heir to his father's throne as his 10-year-old brother Alfonso of Bayonne was then still alive, but on 19 August 1284 when his baby brother was 4 months old, Alfonso died. He was the third son of his parents to die in childhood, and it was the tenth anniversary of Edward I and Leonor's coronation as king and queen of England. The cause of his death is impossible to ascertain. For a decade the people of England had grown accustomed to the notion that one day a king named Alfonso of Bayonne would rule over them, and had young Alfonso lived into adulthood and ruled England, his name, or at least a variant of it, would have become a common one in Britain and subsequently in other English-speaking countries; but it was not to be. Although she had lost many of her other children as well, Queen Leonor was particularly devastated at the death of her third son, and would be buried with Alfonso's heart a few years later. Separate heart burial was routine and usual in the English royal family of the thirteenth and fourteenth centuries, though the custom might seem macabre and bizarre to a modern audience.

Edward of Caernarfon thus became heir to his father's throne, and unlike his three older brothers was a sturdy, healthy child who grew up to become – in stark contrast to the ridiculous caricature of him as a weak and feeble fop in the Hollywood film *Braveheart* – a man of enormous physical strength. Numerous chroniclers commented on this, one stating that Edward was 'one of the strongest men in his realm', and others that he was 'handsome in body and great of strength' and 'elegant, of outstanding strength'.[5]

Chapter 13

Amesbury and Holland

King Edward and Queen Leonor's future son-in-law Jan of Brabant, who turned 9 years old in September 1284, visited England and the English court that year, and the following year came to live in the kingdom permanently. An ordinance drawn up by royal officials for the boy's household in England still exists, and shows that Jan, called 'Jehan de [of] Brabant', had his own chamberlain, marshal, cook, tailor, priest, clerk, two falconers, officials in charge of his pantry (for bread, spices and other dry goods) and buttery (for drinks and other wet goods), and eight personal attendants, called *garzons por son cors*, literally 'boys for his body'. He was entitled to have three palfreys, i.e. riding horses, two coursers, i.e. hunting horses, two pack-horses, and an unspecified number of dogs, presumably also for hunting. Jan had one knight with him whose name was Sir Daniel, a companion from Brabant called Hukelin or Hughenins de Reigny, and another servant called Hennekin, evidently also from the boy's homeland. Jan's cook was named Gerars, and other servants were named Watrelos Ligne, Stenes, and Addinet.[1]

In or before late 1284, Jan's fiancée Margaret of Windsor, also now 9, joined her sisters Eleanor of Windsor and Joan of Acre at court, and an extant account of 1285 shows that golden bowls and plates of gold were bought for her that year, as well as two dozen gloves, pearls and basins. Her tailor, Roger, made her new robes for Christmas and for the feast of the Nativity of St John the Baptist (24 June), a very popular feast day in the English royal family.[2] The 1st of November 1284 marked the royal couple's thirtieth wedding anniversary, and it is remarkable that King Edward and Queen Leonor were still producing children in 1284, so many years after their wedding at Las Huelgas near Burgos. The period of Leonor's childbearing, assuming she did give birth in 1255, was an unusually long one, and even if she did not, she bore her first child in the early 1260s, almost a quarter of a century before the last. King Edward fathered three children in his second marriage when he was in his sixties;

his youngest child was born in May 1306, the month before his sixty-seventh birthday, more than forty years after his eldest child was born and possibly as long as half a century.

Eleanor of Provence, widowed from Henry III in November 1272 and now in her early sixties, decided in 1285 to retreat to Amesbury Priory, a Benedictine house founded by her late husband's grandfather Henry II in 1177. It stood in the Wiltshire countryside 8 miles north of Salisbury and close to the palace of Clarendon, where the royal family often stayed in the thirteenth and fourteenth centuries. According to the Lanercost chronicler, the dowager queen now 'despised the withering flower of this world wherein she had formerly delighted'.[3] She requested the company of two of her granddaughters: Eleanor of Brittany, born in 1275 and the youngest child of the late Beatrice ('Bella B'); and Edward and Leonor's fourth surviving daughter Mary of Woodstock. Eleanor of Brittany entered the priory first and was veiled on 25 March 1285, the feast of the Annunciation, not long after her tenth birthday. On 15 August 1285, Mary duly entered Amesbury Priory as well to provide more company for her grandmother the dowager queen, who herself did not join the Amesbury community until 7 July 1286. Mary was just 6 and a half years old in August 1285, and her parents, especially Queen Leonor, seem to have been opposed to her taking the veil, but were overruled by Edward's mother. All of Mary's family were present at Amesbury on 15 August to witness her entry into the priory, even her 16-month-old brother Edward of Caernarfon.[4] The king respited the sum of £80 which Amesbury Priory owed to the Exchequer, 'for love of his daughter Mary, whom he lately caused to be veiled in their house'.[5] On 23 August 1285, Edward I gave Mary, 'whom the king has caused to take the veil', a generous allowance of £100 a year for her chamber.[6]

Time would tell that Mary had absolutely no vocation as a nun, though her cousin from Brittany did, and ultimately Eleanor of Brittany became prioress of Fontévrault in France, Amesbury's mother house. Eleanor of Provence's biographer Margaret Howell has stated that in part, the dowager queen's insistence that two young girls be veiled as nuns to keep her company whether they wished it or not should be seen as 'blatant selfishness', but that in fairness, Queen Eleanor's decision was not without precedent. Ela, countess of Salisbury (d. 1261), founded Lacock Abbey in Wiltshire in the late 1220s and became its abbess, and took two of her own granddaughters into the convent with her.[7]

Over the course of her life, Mary of Woodstock left the priory whenever she felt like it to visit her family. Her much younger kinswoman Isabella of Lancaster (b. *c.* 1305/08), a great-granddaughter of Henry III and Eleanor of Provence, joined Amesbury Priory in 1327, and her extant accounts of the early 1330s reveal that she also often left Amesbury to visit her father Henry, earl of Lancaster, her siblings, and her aunt. Isabella's father was the richest nobleman in the country and a generous benefactor of the priory, which enabled her to have more freedom than other nuns enjoyed. One year, Isabella left the priory for a total of ninety-six days, and often exchanged gifts, letters and visits with other members of the nobility.[8] Despite her frequent absences from Amesbury, Isabella of Lancaster became its prioress only a few years after she entered the convent as a nun. Mary, as daughter and sister of kings of England, was also given considerably more latitude than other nuns would ever have been allowed. She visited her family in March and May 1286, the second visit lasting about a month, and was at court again for about a month in early 1290.[9] Many years later in the early 1300s, she often stayed with her little half-brothers, Edward I's young sons from his second marriage, and in the 1310s she spent several festive seasons with her brother Edward II and spent months with him and his queen in 1312 when their son was born. Her father and brother paid off her gambling debts and paid for a generous wine allowance.

On 10 April and 11 June 1285, Edward I sent letters to Floris V, count of Holland, about the potential future marriage of Floris's son and Edward's daughter.[10] The young couple were specifically named on 2 October 1285, for the first time: Edward's youngest daughter Elizabeth of Rhuddlan, born in August 1282 and then 3 years old, and Floris's only surviving son Jan, born sometime in 1283 or 1284 and only a few months old when his future marriage was arranged. Edward's third son Alfonso of Bayonne had been betrothed to Floris of Holland's daughter Margaretha on 9 September 1281, and the king wished to maintain his alliance with the county of Holland, so a few months after Alfonso's premature death in August 1284, he arranged the betrothal of his youngest daughter and Floris's son and heir. Edward and Floris agreed that the little boy would grow up in England, and he might have travelled to England with his carers in 1285 in the company of Jan of Brabant, who was also a future son-in-law of the king of England and was Jan of Holland's cousin.

Young Jan of Holland had as many as six older brothers, who had all died young, and four sisters, who also all died young; even Margaretha, betrothed to Alfonso of Bayonne between September 1281 and August 1284 and a girl who would have become queen of England if she and her fiancé had lived into adulthood, vanished from the record after Alfonso's death. Jan himself outlived his father and became count of Holland, but died at 15 or 16 and had no issue from his marriage to Elizabeth of Rhuddlan, and although Floris fathered eleven known legitimate children, he had not a single grandchild from them. His illegitimate children fared rather better, and several lived into adulthood and produced children of their own.[11] To have eleven children yet to have none of them live past the age of 16 or so was a brutal mortality rate even by the standards of the time, and even more brutal than Edward I and Queen Leonor's, six of whose many children lived into adulthood.

Floris V of Holland was born in Leiden on or shortly after 24 June 1254 as the son of Count Willem II and his German wife Elisabeth, daughter of the duke of Brunswick-Lüneburg. On 28 January 1256, Willem was leading an expedition against the rebellious Frisians near Hoogwoud, when he and his horse fell through some ice. The Frisians caught him, dragged him out of the icy water, and smashed his skull. When Floris came of age many years later, he decided to avenge his father's murder on the Frisians, but his campaign proved an abject failure and gave the peasants of Kennemerland another opportunity to rebel against his rule. Floris could only quell the rebellion by granting Kennemerland a number of privileges, and was thereafter sneered at as *der keerlen god*, 'god of the peasants'.[12] In the early 1270s, Floris married Beatrijs van Vlaanderen (d. 1291), or Beatrice of Flanders in English. She was one of the many children of the long-lived Guy de Dampierre, count of Flanders. Margareta of Flanders, another of Guy de Dampierre's many daughters, married Duke Jan I of Brabant and was the mother of Margaret of Windsor's fiancé.

Edward I sent further letters to Floris V of Holland on 22 September 1285, and they came to an agreement that the king would pay the count '50,000 pounds of black *Tournois*' for his son's marriage. Edward wished young Jan of Holland to be raised in England and promised to pay Floris £10,000 if the boy arrived before he completed his seventh year, with another £10,000 to be paid when he did complete his seventh year. The remainder was due when Jan and Elizabeth 'shall have arrived at the lawful age for contracting matrimony'. In return, Floris agreed to give Elizabeth 6,000 pounds of 'black Tournois' annually in land as dower. In case Jan died without a child from his marriage to Elizabeth – as did in fact happen – a portion of the £50,000 was to be restored to the king of England or his heirs. The agreement went on and on, detailing all the arrangements that would be made in case either Jan or Elizabeth died before they married, or in case they did marry and had children, or did not have children. Edward paid Floris some of the money he owed him in May and September 1291.[13]

Chapter 14

A Battle in Germany

Eleanor of Windsor's fiancé succeeded his father Pere as King Alfonso III of Aragon on 11 November 1285. Alfonso had just turned 20, and was crowned king of Aragon on 2 February 1286 in Valencia and on 9 April in Zaragoza. Soon afterwards the young king declared war on his uncle King Jaume of Majorca and took over the islands of Majorca and Ibiza in 1286, while his younger brother, also called Jaume, reigned as king of Sicily, their inheritance from their mother Constanza, from 1285 to 1295. King Edward's first cousin Philip III of France had died a month earlier on 5 October 1285 at the age of only 40, and was succeeded by his 17-year-old son Philip IV. Philip's wife Juana of Navarre, who might have married into England if Henry of Windsor had not died at the age of 6, became queen-consort of France as well as queen-regnant of Navarre, though she was still only 12.

King Alfonso of Aragon was embroiled in a long-standing dispute with the papacy which was not of his own making. His maternal grandfather King Manfredi of Sicily and Manfredi's father, the Holy Roman Emperor Frederick II (d. 1250), had quarrelled with and warred against a succession of popes. This resulted in Pope Clement IV (d. 1268) inviting Louis IX's brother Charles of Anjou to invade Sicily with an army, which he did, successfully, and killed Manfredi. Manfredi's daughter Constanza and her husband Pere of Aragon invaded Sicily in 1282, defeated Charles of Anjou, who died in 1285 expelled from his kingdom, and captured Anjou's eldest son Charles of Salerno (also sometimes called Charles of Naples). King Edward of England was asked in 1286 to negotiate between Aragon and Sicily on one side, and France and the papacy on the other, over the whole affair. Now in his late forties, Edward was a highly experienced and respected statesman, and he had a personal interest in the matter as well; Charles of Salerno, as the son of Queen Eleanor's sister Beatrice of Provence, was his first cousin, and Alfonso III of Aragon was his daughter's fiancé.

In May 1286, therefore, Edward I and Queen Leonor left England again, and would not return until August 1289. During the king's long absence, his cousin Edmund, earl of Cornwall, was keeper of the realm. Before their departure, Edward and Leonor spent some pleasant times with their children: they all went on a boating trip at Brentford, and travelled to Gravesend in Kent, the royal couple by barge and their children by ship. The king and queen sailed from Dover on 13 May 1286, and the dowager queen Eleanor of Provence and the royal children were all present to wave them off. Queen Eleanor and Mary of Woodstock returned to Amesbury Priory, and the dowager queen was veiled as a nun on 7 July. Around 1286 or 1287, during their parents' absence, Eleanor of Windsor and Joan of Acre sent a letter regarding an ongoing feud between the wealthy and well-connected young nobleman Sir Hugh Despenser 'the Elder' (b. 1261), his adherent Sir Ralph Gorges, Sir John Lovel, and someone called 'John Lovel the bastard'.[1] Nothing else is known about this feud or what the outcome of the royal sisters' intervention was, but despite their youth Eleanor and Joan clearly took an interest in maintaining the peace and stability of their father's realm while he was overseas.

In Germany, the battle of Worringen took place near Cologne on 5 June 1288. Margaret of Windsor's future father-in-law, Jan I, duke of Brabant, defeated Siegfried von Westerburg, archbishop of Cologne, in their struggle over possession of the duchy of Limburg. Archbishop Siegfried's brother Heinrich was one of the many men killed during the battle, and Siegfried himself was taken prisoner. Jan I of Brabant thereafter added 'duke of Limburg' to his titles, and news of the battle must have reached his 12-year-old son and 13-year-old future daughter-in-law in England. A rhyming chronicle written in the Dutch language about the battle of Worringen soon afterwards, called the *Rymkronyk van Woeringen*, stated:

> As Lady Margaret of England [*Vrouwe Margriete van Inghelant*], who is betrothed to the duke of Brabant's son Jan, does not understand Dutch speech, I wish to send her a present of Dutch poetry, so that she may learn Dutch; and besides I send her an account – as I can give her nothing more beautiful – of her father-in-law the duke's fine deeds of knighthood.[2]

Although Margaret would have had to learn Dutch (or Flemish) to communicate with the bulk of the population in Brabant, she would almost certainly have been able to speak French with her husband and his family, as the Dutch-speaking courts of Brabant and Holland were well accustomed to using that language. Count Floris V of Holland, future father-in-law of Margaret's sister, was taught both Dutch and French as a child. Despite her husband's knowledge of French, Margaret was to spend well over thirty years living in a partly Dutch-speaking duchy, and presumably came to speak and understand the language well. Her father-in-law was the first ruler of Brabant who issued his charters in Dutch, and his son and successor followed in his footsteps. Margaret had other concerns in 1288/89 besides a battle in Germany and learning the Dutch language, however: silk and gold thread was purchased for her spindle and for 'the making of garlands'. Evidently she was a keen embroiderer who loved working with rich fabrics, and another account mentions her 'embroidery work' and the purchase of gold thread and silk for her.[3] Doubtless all the daughters of the king and queen were taught how to spin and embroider, though it seems from extant evidence that Margaret took up the activity with far greater enthusiasm than did her sisters.

Edward I and Queen Leonor finally returned to England in August 1289, a couple of months after the king's fiftieth birthday, and landed at Dover. Their children Eleanor, Joan, Margaret, Elizabeth and Edward, who had been staying at Langley in Hertfordshire (Leonor's, and subsequently her son's, favourite residence), went to meet them there. The children's journey of a little more than 100 miles from the Hertfordshire countryside to the Kent coast took a painfully slow two weeks. On his return to England, King Edward heard that Joan of Acre had quarrelled with a wardrobe clerk and refused to accept money from him to pay her expenses, and so he had to pay off the debts she had accumulated.[4] Alfonso III of Aragon kept in close touch with his future father-in-law after Edward's return to his kingdom. On 24 November 1289 and again on 10 January 1290, Alfonso wrote to the English king, complaining about the insincerity and bad faith of Edward's cousin Charles of Salerno, and also that he had suffered by the actions of his uncle, Jaume, formerly king of Majorca.[5]

Now that he was home again, King Edward turned his attention to the vital issue of his children's marriages, and, as the future king of England, the most important was 5-year-old Edward of Caernarfon's. Edward betrothed his son and heir to the boy's first cousin once removed, the king's great-niece, Margaret 'the Maid' of Norway. Aged 6 in 1289, she was the only child of King Eirik Magnusson of Norway and Margaret of Scotland (1261–83), herself the eldest child and only daughter of Alexander III of Scotland and Edward I's sister Margaret of England (1240–75). Little Margaret of Norway, great-granddaughter of the dowager queen of England, Eleanor of Provence, was the only heir of her late grandfather Alexander III. Alexander, who had succeeded his father on the Scottish throne as a child in 1249 and is often considered to have been one of Scotland's greatest kings, died in March 1286 when he rode his horse off an escarpment during a storm and was found the next morning with a broken neck.

All three of Alexander III and Margaret of England's children died before he did, and only his daughter left a child, Margaret of Norway, born in or a little before April 1283.[6] Marriage to the partly Norwegian, partly Scottish and partly English Margaret was intended to give Edward of Caernarfon control of Scotland as well as of England one day, and ultimately Margaret 'the Maid' and Edward would have had a strong claim to the throne of Norway as well, as her father King Eirik had no sons and was succeeded on the throne by his younger brother Haakon. Eirik, born sometime in 1268, was only 14 or 15 when his daughter was born and was a good seven years younger than his half-Scottish, half-English wife (b. February 1261 in Windsor), who died not long after giving birth to her daughter. After King Alexander's death in March 1286, and having ascertained that his second wife Yolande de Dreux was not carrying his posthumous child, the Guardians of Scotland proclaimed Margaret of Norway as their queen – surely reluctantly, given that she was barely even 3 years old, the wrong sex, and far away in another country. They realised, pragmatically, that if a young girl were to rule successfully in Scotland she and they would need the support of the powerful leader of their southern neighbour, and if King Eirik wanted an alliance with King Edward of England, as indeed he did, there was little they could do but accept it; his daughter and her future marriage were in Eirik's control, not theirs. The Treaty of Salisbury was signed on 6 November 1289 and the Treaty of Brigham on 18 March 1290, arranging Edward of Caernarfon and Margaret's future marriage; Pope Nicholas IV issued a dispensation for consanguinity on 16 November 1289; and on 17 March 1290, the clergy and nobles of Scotland asked Eirik to send his daughter to her kingdom. Edward I added his voice to the chorus a month later.[7]

Chapter 15

Books and Education

The three eldest royal daughters, 20-year-old Eleanor of Windsor, 17-year-old Joan of Acre, and 14-year-old Margaret of Windsor, travelled with their parents and with thc royal court for a few months in 1289/90, after the king and queen's return to England. Elizabeth, who turned 8 in early August 1290, and her brother Edward of Caernarfon, who turned 6 on 25 April 1290, occasionally visited court, though were apparently considered too young to cope with the incessant travelling on a regular basis. In the summer of 1290, the two youngest royal children set off on a limited tour of the countryside with their own households rather than joining the royal court on a permanent basis.[1] Joan of Acre seems to have visited a manor belonging to Richard Swinfield, bishop of Hereford, in late 1289, as he gave her a gift of wine, bread and fish worth 20*s* 3*d*.[2] On 16 November 1289, Pope Nicholas IV issued a dispensation for Joan's impending marriage to Gilbert de Clare, earl of Gloucester and Hertford.[3]

Little is known about the education of the royal children of the late thirteenth century, even of the boys. The Wardrobe Book of Edward I for 1285/86 records the purchase of 'writing tablets for Eleanor the king's daughter', so evidently Eleanor of Windsor could read and write, and in 1291 more *tabliaus a liure* were bought for Eleanor.[4] There is not a great deal of evidence for literacy among the English nobility and royalty in the late thirteenth and early fourteenth centuries, but the evidence we do have suggests a general ability to read, and perhaps also to write. Margaret Wake, born into a fairly minor baronial family of the north of England in the mid or late 1290s, who married the five royal sisters' much younger half-brother the earl of Kent in late 1325, was able to write well enough to compose a long letter in her own hand in *c.* 1329.[5] The copious surviving correspondence of Hugh Despenser the Younger, born in the late 1280s as a grandson of the earl of Warwick, Joan of Acre's son-in-law, and later lord of Glamorgan and the powerful chamberlain and 'favourite' of Edward II, makes clear that Despenser was a fluent reader. Although, like everyone else of his class and era, Despenser hired scribes to write his letters and thus we do not know for certain if he could write or not, he told his correspondents on several occasions that he had read their previous letters out loud to the king and the royal council.[6] Edward II's teenage son Edward III wrote the words *Pater Sancte* ('Holy Father') in his own hand in a letter to Pope John XXII in 1329 or early 1330, and as he was certainly taught to read and write, it seems very possible that his father and his five aunts were as well.[7] Mary of Woodstock cared enough about the writing of literature and history to act as the patron of the historian and chronicler Nicholas Trivet or Trevet (*c.* 1258/68–*c.* 1334); see Chapter 38 below.

French was the primary written language of the English elite in this era, and probably their primary spoken language as well. As the sisters, however (with the exception of Joan of Acre until she was 6), grew up in England and would have been surrounded by English-speaking servants, they must have at least understood the language and most probably also spoke it fluently. Their father could speak English, and their brother Edward II became famous, or infamous, for his friendships with commoners such as sailors, fishermen and carpenters – people whose social status makes it apparent that they would never have learned French.[8] This surely means that Edward must have been fluent in English. The royal siblings' first cousin Margaret of Scotland, queen of Norway, is said by one chronicler to have taught French and English to her husband King Eirik's subjects, which of course implies that she and presumably her father Alexander III of Scotland and other members of her family were fluent in both languages. The royal English siblings were perhaps not entirely conversant with Latin, though they did learn it in childhood. Pope John XXII (1316–34) once thanked the archbishop of Canterbury for translating one of his letters from Latin into French for Edward II, and one modern author has suggested that Nicholas Trivet wrote the work which he dedicated to Mary of Woodstock in French because she would not have understood it in Latin.[9]

The dowager queen Eleanor of Provence, despite her retreat into Amesbury Priory in 1285/86, took as strong an interest in the well-being of her grandchildren as she always had. Probably in 1289, she sent a letter to her son the king, expressing her unease that Edward planned to take his little son Edward of Caernarfon with him when he travelled to the north. 'We feel uneasy about his going. When we were there, we could not avoid being ill, on account of the bad climate. We pray you therefore, deign to provide some place in the south, where he can have a good and temperate climate, and dwell there while you visit the north.'[10] Apparently, after more than half a century in England, the woman who had spent her early life in Provence had never grown accustomed to the chilly dampness of the north. Eleanor's granddaughters surely also benefited from her care and concern for them, and she presumably also kept herself informed of the welfare of her great-granddaughter Margaret of Norway, now the fiancé of Eleanor's grandson Edward of Caernarfon and the only living descendant of Eleanor's eldest daughter Margaret, the late queen-consort of Scotland.

Chapter 16

Eleanor, Possible Queen-Regnant of England

Joan of Acre and Gilbert 'the Red' de Clare, earl of Gloucester and Hertford, were due to marry on 30 April 1290. On 17 April, a number of important men travelled to Amesbury Priory in Wiltshire, and witnessed Earl Gilbert seal a fascinating and important document. Eleanor of Provence is not specifically mentioned as being present, but presumably she was there given that she lived at Amesbury Priory, and she might well have played a more important role in conceiving and dictating the document than appears from the extant record.

The important men present who witnessed this document, which was written in French – the dowager queen of England, being female, did not 'count' as a witness – were the archbishop of Canterbury and the bishops of Bath and Wells, Winchester, Durham, Exeter and Worcester; Henry III's half-brother William de Valence, earl of Pembroke; Edward I's brother Edmund of Lancaster, earl of Lancaster and Leicester; Henry de Lacy, earl of Lincoln; and Sir Otto Grandisson, Sir William Brecuse, Sir John St John, Master William Lue and John de Berwick. Referring to his future wife as *dame Johane*, 'Lady Joan', Gilbert de Clare began 'As our lord the king, by his grace, has consented to give me Lady Joan, his daughter, to wife, I, to prevent all doubts and suspicions, have sworn on the saints' that if Edward I died and he himself were still alive, he would swear fealty to Edward's son Edward, who on 17 April 1290 was not quite 6 years old, as his rightful liege lord, and would guard the rights of the realm. If Edward of Caernarfon died without male heirs but Edward I had other sons of his body, or if Edward of Caernarfon died but left male heirs of his body, Gilbert would swear allegiance to whomever of the king's male heirs was his rightful liege lord.

The most fascinating part came next: if Edward I and all his sons were dead and none of them had male heirs born of their bodies, the earl of

Gloucester promised that he would swear fealty to 'Lady Eleanor', *dame Alianor*, Edward I's eldest daughter, as his liege lady, and subsequently to the heirs born of her body. The document stated:

> And if by misfortune it should happen that GOD makes his commandment to our lord the king, and to his sons, and they have no heirs of their bodies, if the Lady Eleanor, eldest daughter of my lord the king above-mentioned, is alive, I will bear good faith to this same Eleanor, and to the begotten heirs of her body, and in no manner, not by force, nor by deceit, disturb her rights, nor her, nor the heirs of her body, should she have them, nor the kingdom of England nor the land of Ireland, according to the ordinance of our lord the king above-mentioned; which ordinance is:
>
> That our lord the king wishes and ordains that should Lord Edward [of Caernarfon], his son, or another son, should he have one, remain without heirs of his body; that therefore, after the death of our lord the king above-mentioned, the kingdom of England, and the land of Ireland, remain to Lady Eleanor, his eldest daughter, and the begotten heirs of her body.

Edward I thus acknowledged the possibility that, one day, his daughter might inherit his kingdom in her own right. It is very interesting to note that the king preferred the idea of his throne passing to his daughters rather than to his younger brother Edmund, earl of Lancaster and Leicester, and subsequently to Edmund's sons Thomas and Henry of Lancaster, who in April 1290 were about 12 and 9 years old respectively.[1] If Eleanor died without heirs, then the kingdom of England would belong to her sister Joan of Acre and her heirs, then to the next sister, i.e. Margaret, though she was not named, 'and so from daughter to daughter, and heir to heir'.[2]

This was a startling decision by Edward I, given that the only precedent for a queen-regnant in England was the disastrous example of the Empress Maud (or Matilda) a century and a half previously. Maud was the only surviving legitimate child of Henry I (r. 1100–35), William the Conqueror's youngest son, and her father forced his barons to swear fealty to her as their next ruler. On Henry's death in 1135, however, Maud's cousin Stephen of Blois, son of William the Conqueror's daughter Adele, took advantage of Maud's absence in France and had himself crowned king instead. Maud and Stephen battled over the throne for the next few years during a period of English history now known as the Anarchy, and Maud came close to being crowned queen at one point, but managed to alienate the Londoners to the extent that they chased her out of the city before her coronation. Edward I, Empress Maud's great-great-grandson, must have been familiar with the history, yet did not let this rather unfortunate precedent dissuade him from the decision to make his daughters heirs to his throne, failing his and Edward of Caernarfon's male issue.

In England in the late thirteenth century, the system of primogeniture, whereby the eldest son inherited everything, did not apply to female heirs, who – in the absence of male heirs, who took precedence over their sisters wherever they came in the birth order – were entitled to equal portions of any inheritance. It is very interesting to note that Edward I did not intend this system to apply to his kingdom, but wished his eldest daughter, or failing her, his second eldest daughter and so on, to inherit England in its entirety. He did not wish his kingdom to be divided into four equal parts for his four secular daughters (Eleanor, Joan, Margaret and Elizabeth), as would have happened had Edward been merely a landowner in England and not its king. In April 1290, Eleanor was still betrothed to the king of Aragon, and Edward must also have realised that his daughter's Spanish children, assuming she had any, would have a strong claim to the kingdom of England; yet this did not dissuade him either.

Edward I's decision suggests that he found much to admire in his daughters' personalities and abilities, and thought that Eleanor and her younger sisters would be able to cope with the challenges of ruling his kingdom. Ultimately, however, this situation never came about as Edward of Caernarfon was a healthy, strong child who survived his father (though Eleanor of Windsor herself did not). In 1300 and 1301, Edward I fathered two more sons with his second wife Marguerite of France, who entered the line of succession behind their much older half-brother; the elder of these two boys was heir to the English throne between 1307 and 1312. Edward of Caernarfon himself, as King Edward II, fathered two legitimate sons in 1312 and 1316 from his marriage to Isabella of France, and his elder son succeeded him as Edward III in 1327 and fathered seven legitimate sons, of whom five survived infancy.

The question of the rightful succession to the English throne arose again in 1376 when Edward III's eldest son Edward of Woodstock, prince of Wales, died in his father's lifetime. The prince left a 9-year-old son, Richard of Bordeaux, as his only surviving legitimate child, and the boy duly succeeded his grandfather as King Richard II in 1377. Edward III's second eldest surviving son Lionel of Antwerp had died in 1368 also leaving only one child, a daughter called Philippa of Clarence (1355–*c*. 1379), countess of March and Ulster. Philippa's Mortimer children, born in the 1370s, came to have an excellent claim to the throne in the 1390s, because Richard II had no offspring. In 1399, however, Henry IV, son of Edward III's third eldest surviving son John of Gaunt, became king of England after the forced abdication of Richard II, and Henry thus set aside his cousin Philippa of Clarence's descendants. This had perhaps been in line with Edward III's own wishes. The king dictated a document after the death of the prince of Wales in 1376, stating that he wished his eldest son's son Richard to succeed him, and subsequently, failing any issue of Richard, his third son John of Gaunt and his male issue, his fourth son Edmund of Langley and his male issue, and his fifth and youngest son Thomas of Woodstock and his male issue. Edward did not mention his granddaughter Philippa, the only child of his dead second son Lionel, or her children, as possible successors.[3] Given that Edward III himself began to claim the throne of France via his mother Isabella in 1337 and thus obviously believed that the succession to a kingdom could be inherited from a woman, his decision to exclude his granddaughter and her children from the succession to his own English throne is rather startling, and stands in contrast to his grandfather Edward I's decision in 1290 to leave his kingdom to one of his daughters, failing his and his only living son's male issue.

Chapter 17

Two Royal Weddings

Gilbert 'the Red' de Clare, earl of Gloucester and Hertford, had been married in the early 1250s to Alice de Lusignan, whose French father Hugues, count of La Marche, was a younger half-brother of Henry III and an older full brother of William de Valence, earl of Pembroke. The couple were both children when they wed, and the *Flores Historiarum* calls Alice 'a damsel of a very tender age, indeed I may say an infant'. Gilbert was scarcely older. After they were finally of an age to consummate their marriage, he and Alice produced two daughters, Isabella, Lady Berkeley, in 1262 and Joan, countess of Fife, in *c.* 1264/65, but their marriage was an unhappy one, and the couple lived apart from about 1267 onwards. Edward I sanctioned Gilbert's future marriage to Joan of Acre as early as May 1283, even though the earl's marriage to Alice de Lusignan, called 'Alice de la Marche' or 'Lady Alice de Marchia' in English records, was not annulled until May 1285. That month, Gilbert granted his former wife half a dozen of his manors to hold for the rest of her life, 'in consideration of the nobility of her kin and being unwilling that for lack of suitable maintenance she should have cause for sadness'.[1] The papal dispensation for Gilbert and Joan to marry was granted in November 1289, after King Edward and Queen Leonor returned from their long sojourn in Aquitaine. Alice de Lusignan died in 1290, the year Gilbert married Joan of Acre.

Gilbert de Clare was born in Christchurch, Dorset on 2 September 1243, so was almost three decades older than his royal second wife and 46 going on 47 years old when they married on 30 April 1290.[2] He was the second child and first son of Richard de Clare, earl of Gloucester and Hertford (1222–62) and Maud de Lacy (1223–89), daughter of Margaret de Quincy, countess of Lincoln in her own right, and one of his two younger brothers was Bogo, a wealthy pluralist who forged a successful career in the Church. Maud de Clare née de Lacy played favourites among her children and went out of her way to promote the career of her son Bogo, and showed a stark preference for him over her other two sons and three daughters.[3] She and her eldest son Gilbert feuded endlessly and went so far as to sue each other on occasion, and although Gilbert de Clare fathered five daughters, he named none of them after his mother. This was so unusual and so unconventional by the standards of the English nobility of the thirteenth and fourteenth centuries that it reveals much about his and Maud's mutually hostile, unamicable relationship. The earl was perhaps not too distraught when Maud died in early 1289 and he could finally, in his mid-forties, take possession of his large inheritance, including the third his mother had held as dower.[4]

Gilbert and Alice de Lusignan's younger daughter Joan de Clare, born *c.* 1264/65, married Duncan or Donnchadh MacDuff, earl of Fife in Scotland, and gave birth to her son Duncan MacDuff the younger in late 1289, several months after her husband was murdered. Gilbert de Clare was, therefore, already a grandfather when he married the teenaged Joan of Acre, and Joan was a few years younger than her two stepdaughters. Isabella de Clare, the elder of Gilbert and Alice de Lusignan's two daughters, seems to have been briefly married to the much younger Guy Beauchamp, earl of Warwick (b. *c.* 1271/75), in 1297, but their marriage must have been annulled for some reason.[5] She married secondly the widowed Maurice, Lord Berkeley (b. 1271 and also much her junior) in *c.* 1316/17, when she was about 55 years old.

Joan of Acre's new husband was known as 'the Red' as much for his choleric disposition and touchiness as for his flaming hair, and he and his new father-in-law, only four years his senior, had long had an uneasy relationship. During the baronial wars of the 1260s, Gilbert had at first supported Henry III's brother-in-law Simon de Montfort, earl of Leicester, against the king and his son Edward, though he switched sides and played an important role in the royalist victory of 1265. He commanded one of the divisions which defeated the earl of Leicester at the battle of Evesham in August that year; Simon de Montfort supposedly exclaimed 'This red dog will eat us today' before the battle.[6]

Gilbert surrendered his many lands to Edward I before his wedding to Edward's daughter, and on 27 May 1290 they were granted back to him and Joan jointly with the condition that any children Gilbert had with Joan would inherit them. This grant gave precedence to any children Gilbert might have with his second wife over his two daughters with his first, who had probably been disinherited anyway by the 1285 annulment of their parents' marriage, and the question of who exactly the correct de Clare heirs were became a pressing matter in and after 1314 when Gilbert and Joan's son was killed in battle and left no children. Well into the 1400s, 150 years after Gilbert de Clare and Joan of Acre's wedding, royal officials often examined and confirmed Edward I's May 1290 grant of Gilbert's lands back to him, the birth order of Gilbert's three daughters with Joan, and the subsequent ownership of his lands by his daughters, their husbands and their descendants.[7] The de Clares were one of the great noble families of thirteenth-century England, and owned lands in every county of the south of England, in Wales, and in Ireland. One of their great strongholds was Caerphilly Castle in Glamorgan, South Wales, which Gilbert had built himself as a young man twenty years before he married Joan of Acre.

For her wedding, Joan purchased a girdle of gold studded with rubies and emeralds in Paris, which cost the large sum of £37 12*s*, and a matching head-dress also made of gold and worked with rubies and emeralds, which cost over £12.[8] A famous Scottish minstrel called 'King Capenny' or 'King Caupenny', a king of heralds, performed at the wedding and received 50 shillings. Other minstrels called Oysillet, Ernulph, who was a vielle-player in the household of Guy, count of St Pol, and 'Poverett of the marshal of Champagne' also played for Joan and her wedding guests. Oysillet was named in the records of Joan's wedding as the 'minstrel of the king of Scotland', but the problem is that there was no king of Scotland in 1290; perhaps this meant Alexander III, Edward I's brother-in-law and Joan of Acre's uncle, who had died four years earlier. Robert Berneville, a minstrel of Philip IV of France, travelled to England to perform for Joan and Gilbert and received 50*s* for his routine, and was still in England on 1 June 1290 when he was given another 50*s* in exchange for performing again for Edward I. The earl of Gloucester himself employed a harper called Ricard, who is likely to have been present at the wedding as well.[9]

Soon after the wedding, Joan and Gilbert left court without royal permission and took themselves off to Gilbert's castle of Tonbridge in Kent, to the annoyance of her parents: an example of Joan's determination to do what she wanted to do rather than what she was told to do, which she would demonstrate again and again. The king and queen retaliated by confiscating seven gowns laid aside for her and giving them instead to her 15-year-old sister Margaret, whose wedding took place also at

Westminster a few weeks later.[10] The couple eventually returned: Gilbert 'the Red' held a banquet at his mansion in Clerkenwell to celebrate his marriage on 3 July 1290, and a few days later rode with his household knights and with six ladies in the wedding procession of his sister-in-law Margaret and Jan of Brabant.[11] Edward I, who loved his daughters dearly and was often very indulgent towards them, had obviously forgiven Joan by then for leaving court without permission. He gave her a large amount of plate and other equipment for her household at Clerkenwell, including four beds, forty-six golden cups, sixty silver spoons, many bowls of silver and one of pure gold. The king told the 'keeper of the exchange of London', Gregory Rokesle, on 2 July to send 'white refined silver of Ghent of the weight of 300 marks' to Master William of Louth, bishop-elect of Ely near Cambridge, to have utensils made for Joan. The Westminster chronicler refers to Joan of Acre and Margaret of Windsor at the time of their weddings in 1290, somewhat creepily, as 'illustrious virgins ... daughters of the illustrious Edward'.[12]

Another important wedding which took place in 1290 was that of Roger Bigod, earl of Norfolk, and his second wife Alicia of Hainault, on 24 June. It was held at the royal manor of Havering-atte-Bower in Essex, apparently with Edward I and Queen Leonor present, as the king arrived at Havering from Westminster on that day.[13] Norfolk was about 45, and had been widowed in 1281 when his first wife Aline Despenser, née Basset, passed away. Alicia was probably in her teens, and her parents Jan of Hainault and Philippa of Luxembourg, count and countess of Hainault, were both some years younger than her new husband. The marriage, like Norfolk's first, produced no children, and the next earl of Norfolk would be the elder of Edward I's sons from his second marriage. Joan of Acre perhaps attended Norfolk's wedding: she was at Havering-atte-Bower on 26 June with her parents, and gave 66*s* 8*d* to a minstrel of Flanders called Adinet de Pyrewe who performed for them.[14]

Margaret of Windsor, now aged 15 years, married her long-term fiancé Jan of Brabant, aged 14 years, at Westminster Abbey on 3 July 1290. It was a splendid occasion, far more of a public event than Joan of Acre's wedding had been, and King Edward paid the huge sum of £100 to no fewer than 426 minstrels who performed at Margaret and Jan's wedding. The king's harper Walter Storton was the chief minstrel who gave all the other performers their fees, and who arranged the journeys of nineteen of them from various parts of England to Westminster.

Many of the performers came from overseas: Robert, count of Artois in northern France, whose sister Blanche of Artois was married to Edward I's younger brother Edmund of Lancaster, sent his (unnamed) court fool to the wedding, and who received 40*s* from Edward I. Bastin Noblet of Liège and Janyn le Coc of 'Dowayto' received 10*s* each; Bastin was an acrobat, and perhaps Janyn was too. Floris V, count of Holland, sent a minstrel called Jan Celling to the wedding, and Duke John II of Brittany – widower of Edward I's sister Beatrice, and Margaret of Windsor's uncle – sent Robin the Fool. Margaret's new brother-in-law Gilbert de Clare, earl of Gloucester, rode in the procession with 103 knights, and her 6-year-old brother Edward of Caernarfon also rode with his own retinue and eighty knights. Her aged grandmother Eleanor of Provence remained at Amesbury Priory and did not travel to London for the wedding, though the teenaged bridegroom Jan went to visit the dowager queen before he wed Margaret, and spent most of the summer of 1290 hunting in various parks and chases across England.[15]

The impressed author of the *Livere de Reis de Brittaniae* or 'Book of the Kings of Britain' stated that '[n]othing so magnificent was ever seen or heard of in our time' as Margaret of Windsor and Jan of Brabant's wedding (though, as is annoyingly often the case with medieval chroniclers, he provided few details of this hitherto unseen magnificence). Margaret wore a chaplet and a belt of gold studded with pearls and rubies and decorated with sapphires in the form of the royal English leopards, and her eldest sister Eleanor wore an outfit with no fewer than fifty-three dozen silver buttons. The splendid occasion was, however, somewhat marred by an irate King Edward hitting a servant on the head with a stick and wounding him quite badly, and he later had to pay the servant the large sum of 20 marks, over £13, in compensation. The reason for the assault was not recorded; perhaps the king was simply in a bad temper.[16]

On 28 March 1290, Duke Jan I of Brabant had settled lands in his territories to the annual value of 6,000 pounds of Tours on 'Lady Margarete, daughter of the very noble king of England, consort of Johan, our eldest son'. The duke subsequently travelled to England with his brother Godefroy, lord of Aarschot and Vierzon, and their cousins 'Ernout, lord of Walehain and Florens' and Bertrand, lord of Berlare, to attend his son's royal wedding. Edward I sent a letter to Jan I on 8 September 1290 a couple of months after the wedding, when the duke had returned to his own territories, referring to 'Jan, your son and ours, and Margaret his wife, our daughter and yours' (*Johan vostre fiz e le nostre, e Margarete sa femme, nostre fille e la vostre*). The king appointed two attorneys, a clerk named William Carlton and a knight named Sir Roger Tilmanston, to take possession of the assigned lands in Brabant on the young couple's behalf.

Margaret and Jan dictated a joint letter on the same day, agreeing to the appointment of the two attorneys. They sealed the letter with Jan's seal, and, because Margaret's own seal was 'not known', with the seal of 'the noble lady Alianore, queen of England, consort of our lord the king aforesaid', i.e. Leonor of Castile.[17] In 1282, Eleanor of Windsor had had to use her grandmother Eleanor of Provence's seal as she did not yet have one, and although her younger sister did have one a few years later, Margaret knew that it would not be widely recognised, so sensibly borrowed her mother's. Her 19-year-old first cousin Margaret of Scotland still had no seal of her own in 1280, the year before she married Eirik Magnusson and became queen-consort of Norway: when Margaret wrote to her uncle Edward I sometime that year, she sealed the letter with the seal of one of her attendants, Dame Luce de Hassewel, though she did not explain why her attendant had a seal while she herself, daughter and niece of kings, did not.[18]

Depending on their physical and emotional maturity, Margaret and Jan might have consummated their marriage immediately, but they did not live together as a married couple until a long time afterwards. Their marriage appears to have been an unsatisfactory one; they lived apart for more than three years from 1294 to 1297, and only had one child together, though Jan fathered at least four or five illegitimate children from relationships with several mistresses. Mary Anne Everett Green wrote in the nineteenth century that Margaret of Windsor was particularly kind and generous to one of these children, but that he had been born when Jan was very young, before his marriage. Given that Jan was still only 14 when he wed Margaret, it does not seem terribly likely that any of his children with other women were born beforehand. Whether the existence of Jan's out of wedlock children truly was the 'painful humiliation' to Margaret that Green claims, cannot be known; this is only an assumption. Perhaps this was indeed the case, or perhaps, raised in a world where women were firmly enjoined to be faithful but men were not, she did not care all that much.

A couple of weeks later on 18 July 1290, Edward I began in earnest to plan the wedding of his son Edward of Caernarfon and young Edward's 7-year-old first cousin once removed, Margaret, the Maid of Norway. On 28 August, young Edward appointed John de Warenne, earl of Surrey (b. 1231), as his procurator to contract his marriage.[19] Sadly, Margaret died in the Orkneys a few weeks later, on her way to Scotland and to her impending wedding to the English king's heir. As the Orkneys belonged to her father King Eirik, the young queen never set foot in her own kingdom, and her body was returned to the Norwegian mainland and buried next to her mother's in Bergen. King Edward heard the bad news from William, bishop of St Andrews.[20] In 1291, he arranged another future marriage for his son and heir with Blanche (b. *c.* early 1280s), youngest child of Philip III of France from his second marriage to Marie of Brabant, though this was destined never to take place either.

Clearly in a mood to sort out his young family's future marriages, Edward I also arranged one in July 1290 for his 12-year-old nephew Thomas of Lancaster (b. *c.* late 1277 or early 1278), eldest of the three sons of Edmund of Lancaster and Blanche of Artois, and the heir to Edmund's numerous manors, castles and lands and several earldoms. Thomas's potential future bride was Beatrice, daughter of Hugh, viscount of Avallon, himself one of the sons of Duke Hugh IV of Burgundy.[21] Hugh of Avallon's much older half-sister Adelaide of Burgundy was the mother of Duke Jan I of Brabant, who perhaps suggested the match to Edward while he was in England for his son and Margaret of Windsor's wedding, though ultimately the planned marriage did not go ahead as Beatrice died in childhood. Some years later, Edward arranged a brilliant match for Thomas with Alice de Lacy (b. 1281), daughter and heir of the earl of Lincoln, which, although it proved unhappy on a personal level for the unfortunate and childless couple and ended with Alice walking out on Thomas, increased the Lancasters' already considerable wealth and influence.

Chapter 18

The First Royal Grandchild

Joan of Acre became pregnant with her first child around late July or early August 1290, a month or so after she and Gilbert 'the Red' de Clare attended her sister Margaret's wedding. Margaret herself, with her sisters Eleanor and Elizabeth and her new husband, remained at court with the king and queen, and they all travelled to St Albans and made offerings at the abbey church. King Edward fed 300 poor people at Silverstone in early August because Margaret and Jan of Brabant failed to attend Mass.[1] On 16 November, Elizabeth of Rhuddlan and Edward of Caernarfon attended a special Mass for the soul of their grandfather Henry III; it was the eighteenth anniversary of his death.[2]

Their mother Queen Leonor fell seriously ill in the summer and autumn of 1290, and Joan of Acre rushed to Nottinghamshire to see her, despite her pregnancy. Elizabeth of Rhuddlan and Edward of Caernarfon were summoned as well. Young Edward, or rather his servants, had sent his mother 'medicinal waters' in July 1290 not long after Margaret and Jan's wedding, so evidently she was already ailing.[3] The queen died on 28 November 1290 in Harby, Nottinghamshire, and was buried at Westminster Abbey on Sunday, 17 December, presumably with her six surviving children all present, though her heart was given to the church of the Blackfriars (Dominicans) in London with that of her third son Alfonso of Bayonne, and her viscera were given to Lincoln Cathedral. Her tombs in Westminster Abbey and Lincoln Cathedral still exist.

As the queen's only living son, 6-year-old Edward inherited the county of Ponthieu which Leonor had inherited from her mother Queen Jeanne in 1279, and Edward was to give the county to his French wife Isabella shortly after their wedding in 1308; it later passed to their son Edward III. If Edward of Caernarfon had not been born or if he had died before his mother as his three older brothers did, Ponthieu would have passed to Eleanor of Windsor as Leonor's eldest daughter. Although in England the law of primogeniture did not apply to female heirs, in

France it was the custom that in such cases, the eldest daughter inherited everything. Jeanne de Dammartin herself had three younger sisters, Mathilde, Philippa and Marie, yet inherited the counties of Ponthieu and Aumale in their entirety on the deaths of her parents in 1239 and 1250, and, as the sole heir to them, made a far more impressive marriage than her landless younger sisters did. Had it not been for the existence of her little brother, fifteen years her junior, Eleanor of Windsor stood a chance of becoming queen-regnant of England after her father died, and would certainly have inherited Ponthieu in 1290 on her mother's death. Whether she resented Edward of Caernarfon taking precedence over her despite his youth, simply by virtue of being born male, or whether she accepted it as an unavoidable and unquestionable fact of the world she lived in, is impossible to know.

Leonor's grieving widower built the magnificent series of 'Eleanor Crosses' at every place where the queen's funeral cortège rested on its way to London, and some of them still exist. King Edward sent a sad and moving letter to the abbot of Cluny in France, describing Leonor as 'whom in life we dearly cherished, and whom we cannot cease to love, now she is dead'.[4] The Westminster chronicler remarked on the queen's death, calling her the 'daughter of Ferrand [Fernando], formerly the most mighty king of Spain', and Henry Burg of the London Dominicans wrote a poem in Latin on the occasion of Leonor's heart being buried at the convent, part of which ran:

> Mourn not too long; than canst not by much weeping,
> Bring back her soul who in this tomb lies sleeping;
> But pray that she abide with Christ in glory;
> While here below her virtues live in story.
> Long live the king, and prosper in achievement!
> Wouldst thou record the year of his bereavement?
> Write once a thousand and a hundred thrice,
> Add them, and from the total take five twice,
> Also the month and day thou must remember,
> Queen Alianora died on fifth [*sic*] November.[5]

Leonor's date of birth is not known for certain, but as her biographers John Carmi Parsons and Sara Cockerill have pointed out, forty-nine candles were carried by paupers during a procession at her memorial service in 1291.[6] The odd number strongly implies that she was 49 years old or in her forty-ninth year when she died. If she was born on 23 November 1241, as Cockerill suggests, she died five days past her forty-ninth birthday. There is little doubt that the marriage of Doña Leonor and Lord Edward, arranged in 1253/54 to avert a war between England and Castile over the duchy of Aquitaine, had proved to be one of the great royal love stories of the Middle Ages. Edward remained a widower for nine years after losing Leonor, only re-marrying Philip IV's half-sister Marguerite in September 1299 because he had gone to war against France and the marriage was part of the price he paid for peace. The king's decision to remain a widower for nine years is all the more remarkable given that the undisputed succession to the English throne hung on the young life of Edward of Caernarfon, and is yet more proof, if more proof were needed, of Edward I's devotion to his Spanish wife.[7] The king was evidently not in any pressing hurry to father more sons with a second queen, which is, one assumes, also proof that he was happy enough for his kingdom to pass to his daughter Eleanor of Windsor should any unhappy fate befall Edward of Caernarfon.

Leonor's will, assuming she ever made one (as a married woman, she would have needed her husband's permission to dispose of her goods and property), does not survive. To her fifth and youngest daughter Elizabeth of Rhuddlan, at an unknown date, Leonor gave or bequeathed a 'great crown' (*grande coroune*) with rubies, emeralds, pearls and sapphires, and she surely left similar items to her other daughters as well.[8] She may have left an enamelled gold cup studded with precious stones to her only surviving son; in 1312, Edward of Caernarfon owned one given to him 'with her blessing' by 'Queen Alianore', which means either Leonor or her mother-in-law Eleanor of Provence, who outlived her. Leonor perhaps also left her son a brooch, as he had one in 1312 said to have been 'a gift from my lady the queen, the mother', though it is not impossible that this meant Edward of Caernarfon's stepmother, Edward I's second wife Marguerite of France, rather than Queen Leonor. Contemporary idiom, most confusingly, did not differentiate between a mother, a stepmother and a mother-in-law.[9]

Leonor's youngest daughters Mary of Woodstock and Elizabeth of Rhuddlan paid for a special Mass in honour of their mother in 1297, and her son made a special point of marking the twenty-fifth anniversary of the queen's demise in November 1315 by paying thirty-five Dominican friars to 'perform divine service at the anniversary of the lady the queen, mother of the present lord the king'. In May 1302, Elizabeth successfully asked her father to grant a favour to Alice Breton, one of Leonor's former attendants, because of Alice's good service to her mother.[10] Edward of Caernarfon was just 6 years old when he lost his mother, and as she had spent over three years of his life outside England, he cannot have spent all that much time with her. He was well aware, however, both of his relatives on his mother's side, and of some of the actions Leonor had taken. In 1304, he knew that Leonor had arranged the marriage of Sir Hugh Mortimer of Richard's Castle in Herefordshire to a woman named Maud, a kinswoman of Leonor, and he called the late queen 'our dearest lady and mother' (*nostre treschere dame e mere*), though this is a conventional expression and does not say anything in particular about Edward's feelings for his late mother.[11] His paying Dominican friars to perform divine service for his mother's soul was, however, a respectful gesture, and honoured the queen's memory; Leonor was a staunch supporter of the Dominican order, as was Edward himself. As prince of Wales and king of England, Edward of Caernarfon was to show much favour to his mother's Beaumont relatives as well as to her kinswoman Maud Mortimer: Henry, Lord Beaumont, Louis Beaumont, bishop of Durham, and their sister Isabella, Lady Vescy.

Leonor, a bookworm who had grown up in a dazzlingly intellectual court, probably left her daughters a collection of books as well, though which ones, and what became of them, is unknown.[12] Although the five royal sisters themselves are not known to have commissioned any books and perhaps never even purchased any, Leonor's granddaughter Elizabeth de Burgh, née de Clare (1295–1360), Joan of Acre's fourth child and third daughter, was famously a lover of books, and gave nine to her foundation at the University of Cambridge in 1338, known as Clare Hall in her lifetime and now as Clare College. Elizabeth borrowed seven books from the royal collection in 1327, and three years earlier had paid a scribe to make a copy of the *Vitae Patrum*, 'Lives of the Fathers'. In 1350/51, she had to hire no fewer than seven horses to carry the books she had purchased in London to her own lands. Elizabeth de Burgh's cousin Margaret Courtenay, née de Bohun, countess of Devon (1311–91), one of the two daughters of Elizabeth of Rhuddlan who survived childhood, left a book of medicines, a book of the prophecies of Merlin, and a book about the story of Tristan in her will.[13]

Edward II, although not usually famed as an intellectual king, perhaps inherited his mother's love of books more than his older sisters did. He once borrowed two books from the library of Canterbury Cathedral – the lives of St Thomas Becket and St Anselm – but failed to return them. Among other manuscripts in his possession, Edward owned an illuminated biography of Saint/King Edward the Confessor, a history of the kings of England in Latin, a Latin prayer book, a romance (any kind of fiction, not just a love story) in French, which he had inherited from his paternal grandmother Queen Eleanor, and a book called *De Regimine Regum* or *On the Ruling of Kings*. In 1326, Edward gave a large and lavish copy of the story of Tristan and Isolde to the nobleman Hugh Despenser the Younger, his chamberlain and co-ruler, who might have been his lover. A search of the English Exchequer in 1323 discovered a booklet 'written in a language very strange to the English', which was in fact Welsh, and a book bound in green leather containing the chronicle of Rodrigo Jiménez de Rada, one of the predecessors of Queen Leonor's brother Don Sancho as archbishop of Toledo. As king of England in 1317 and 1326, Edward of Caernarfon founded colleges at both Oxford and Cambridge, the first of only two people in history to do so (the second was his descendant Henry VI, born in 1421). In 1312, Edward supported the creation of a new university in Dublin, which opened in 1320 and operated for a few years, and in 1317/18 he successfully persuaded Pope John XXII to recognise Cambridge University officially as a *studium generale*. Edward II stated in February 1317 that 'the realm is enriched by two universities [Oxford and Cambridge] as by two special jewels'.[14] Although none of Leonor of Castile's children could possibly be described as a bookworm to anything like the same extent that she was, her son and several of her granddaughters placed a high value on education, and, as will be discussed later, Mary of Woodstock became the patron of a historian and chronicler in *c.* 1320.

Sometime between 23 April and 13 May 1291, Joan of Acre gave birth to her first child, a year after her wedding and just before her birthplace of Acre fell to the Mamluks (a dynasty of Muslim warriors) after a six-week siege and the Holy Land was lost to the Christians, on 18 May 1291.[15] It was a boy, whom she named Gilbert after his father, though it would have been more usual by the standards of the era to have named him Richard after his paternal grandfather Richard de Clare, earl of Gloucester and Hertford, who died in 1262. Edward I, delighted at the birth of his eldest grandchild, gave £100 on 21 May to Joan's messenger, William, son of Glay, for bringing him news of little Gilbert's birth.[16] The infant became sole heir to his father's two earldoms and vast landholdings in England, Wales and Ireland from the moment of his birth. Joan would have been purified or 'churched' forty days after giving birth, sometime between the beginning and middle of June 1291. After this, she and Gilbert 'the Red' would have been allowed to resume marital relations. Just after she gave birth, on 12 May 1291, Joan and Gilbert presented the bishop of Worcester, Godfrey Giffard, with two bucks and does as a gift to settle a dispute over a foss in the Malvern Hills.[17]

Chapter 19

The Death of Alfonso III

On 24 June 1291, a few weeks after the birth of her great-grandson Gilbert de Clare and nine months after the death of her great-granddaughter the young Norwegian queen of Scotland, the dowager queen of England, Eleanor of Provence, died at Amesbury Priory. She was in her late sixties when she passed away, and is usually assumed to have been born in *c.* 1223. According to the Lanercost chronicler, her birthday was the feast day of St Andrew, i.e. 30 November, on which date in 1291, the chronicler says, her heart was buried in London. If this is true, Eleanor was perhaps born on 30 November 1222 or on 30 November 1223, and was either 12 or 13 when she married the much older Henry III (b. October 1207) in January 1236 and 15 or 16 when she bore her eldest child, Edward I, in June 1239.[1]

Eleanor's body minus her heart was buried at Amesbury Priory on 8 September 1291 rather than with her husband Henry III in Westminster Abbey, her place in the chapel of St Edward the Confessor having already been given to her daughter-in-law Leonor. She was survived by her sister Marguerite, the dowager queen of France, who died in her seventies in December 1295 ten years into the reign of her grandson Philip IV and when she was, like her sister, a great-grandmother a good few times over. Louis IX, whom Marguerite outlived by a quarter of a century, was canonised in August 1297, and it was a great triumph for the French royals to have a saint in the family. Louis's first cousin Fernando III of Castile and Leon, grandfather of Edward I's daughters, would also be made a saint of the Catholic Church, though he would have to wait until 1671, more than four centuries after his death.

News must have reached England soon after Eleanor of Provence's death that Eleanor of Windsor's long-term fiancé Alfonso III of Aragon had died on 18 June 1291 at the age of only 25, while he was in Barcelona making preparations for his and Eleanor's impending wedding. The chronicler Ramon Muntaner says that the king had a rash on his upper thigh which became infected, and that the consequent fever plagued Alfonso so violently for ten days that any other man would have died long before.[2] He was buried in the house of the Franciscan friars in Barcelona, and was succeeded on the throne of Aragon by his brother Jaume II (b. 1267, r. 1291–1327), second of the late King Pere's four sons. Alfonso's mother Queen Constanza outlived her eldest son and, as it turned out, her putative English daughter-in-law Eleanor, and died in 1302.

In stark contrast to his father Pere, who fathered seven known illegitimate children, and his younger brother Jaume, who married four times and fathered ten legitimate children and several illegitimate ones, Alfonso III supposedly, according to Ramon Muntaner, died a virgin and never even touched a woman. Muntaner states further than Alfonso only wished to sleep with his wife and therefore never concerned himself with any other woman; assuming this is true, and assuming Eleanor came to hear of it, she must have deeply regretted the loss of such an unusual man who desired only her. Although royal and noble women were strictly enjoined to preserve their virginity until marriage, men were not held to anything like the same standards, and nobody, including Eleanor herself, would have considered it to be anything out of the ordinary if Alfonso had taken mistresses before his wedding to her (and indeed even afterwards). Alfonso was also said to be wise, courteous, well-bred, and skilful in feats of arms, and if this is true, it makes him sound like the perfect medieval royal husband.[3]

Eleanor, who had been betrothed to Alfonso of Aragon since she was a toddler, never met him and never set foot in Spain. Her mother and grandmother had done their best to safeguard her interests in 1282 by requesting that she remain in England until she was older and more mature, but ultimately their actions meant that Eleanor did not become a queen in Spain as she had expected to for almost all her life, and did not have a chance to meet the man who had forsaken all other women for her. She was now 22 years old and still unmarried even though two of her younger sisters were already wed, and her father would have to negotiate another match for her. As it happened, no royal marriage between the kingdoms of England and Aragon would take place until Henry VII's elder son Arthur, prince of Wales, married Katherine of Aragon in 1501, though this was certainly not for want of trying. Eleanor of Windsor's brother Edward II attempted to arrange the marriage of his half-brother

Thomas of Brotherton (b. 1300) to Jaume II's widowed daughter María (b. 1299) in 1320/21, and the marriage of his youngest child Joan of the Tower (b. 1321) to Jaume's grandson, the future King Pere IV (b. 1319, r. 1336–87), in 1324/25. Eleanor's nephew Edward III also pursued the possibility of a marriage between the future Pere IV and his sister Eleanor of Woodstock (b. 1318) in 1330.[4]

Eleanor of Windsor's 12-year-old sister Mary, meanwhile, was settling into her new life as a nun of Amesbury Priory, whether willingly or not, and took her binding, final vows in 1291. Three months after the death of her grandmother the dowager queen, her father the king allowed her a generous income of 300 marks (£200) a year from the Exchequer. Half was payable at Easter and the other half at the feast of St Michael, 29 September.[5] On 2 January 1292, Edward I granted 'Mary, the king's daughter, nun of Fontevraud [Amesbury's mother house]', forty oaks annually from royal forests in Wiltshire and Hampshire for her chamber at Amesbury, i.e. for firewood, and 'for her health'. He also gave her an allowance of twenty tuns (about 5,040 gallons or 22,912 litres) of wine a year.[6]

In early 1292, Gilbert 'the Red' de Clare, earl of Gloucester, became embroiled in a violent feud with Humphrey de Bohun, earl of Hereford (b. 1248). Edward I imprisoned both men, and made Gilbert acknowledge a huge debt of £10,000 as surety for his future good behaviour. His lordship of Glamorgan was temporarily confiscated, though was given back to him on 7 May 1292.[7] The king could not long imprison his own son-in-law, the fine was never paid, and apparently Gilbert was allowed conjugal visits, as Joan of Acre became pregnant around late January 1292. She was at court with her father on or shortly before 28 February, when she successfully requested a pardon for a John Breetun, who had killed another man in self-defence.[8]

Joan was purified after childbirth at Caerphilly Castle, an enormous and highly defensible fortification in Glamorgan, on the feast day of St Clement, or 23 November, in 1292.[9] If the purification took place the standard forty days after childbirth, Joan bore her child on *c.* 14 October; if, because it was a daughter, she followed her mother's procedure and was purified only thirty days later, the girl was born on *c.* 24 October. Joan named her eldest daughter Eleanor, or rather Alianore, after her mother Queen Leonor and her grandmother Eleanor of Provence. On 24 November 1291, eleven months before Joan of Acre gave birth to her eldest daughter in her husband's castle, Joan Mortimer, elder daughter and ultimately the co-heir of Sir Hugh Mortimer (b. 1274) of Richard's Castle in Herefordshire, had also been born at Caerphilly Castle, and was baptised in the chapel there.[10] The parentage of Hugh Mortimer's wife Maud is uncertain, but she is known to have been a relative of the late Queen Leonor, which perhaps was a reason why Maud bore her daughter at a castle belonging to Joan of Acre's husband. Leonor had arranged the marriage of Hugh and Maud Mortimer, perhaps another reason for Maud's closeness to Leonor's daughter and son-in-law.[11]

Gilbert de Clare might have been present at Caerphilly Castle when his daughter (his third, after Isabella and Joan de Clare from his first marriage) was born there in *c.* mid or late October 1292, but by 7 November 1292 he was far to the north, in the port of Berwick-on-Tweed on the north-east coast of England with his father-in-law the king. He therefore missed Joan's purification two weeks later. Not long after Eleanor de Clare's birth, Gilbert sent a letter to Robert Burnell, bishop of Bath and Wells, chancellor of England and a close ally of the king, apologising for being unable to attend Edward as he should. He explained that he had been forced to remain in Glamorgan for longer than he had anticipated, as when he travelled there, he had found one of his children ill.[12] Whether he meant his and Joan's toddler son Gilbert or their newborn daughter Eleanor is not clear, but this letter lends a pleasantly human touch to Gilbert 'the Red', a famously irascible man prone to sulking, and reveals that he cared for his and Joan's children.

Chapter 20

Margaret and Jan's Marriage

By late 1292, Joan of Acre's sister Margaret of Windsor and her husband Jan of Brabant were both 17. By the standards of the time, they were certainly old enough to live together as husband and wife, and indeed were past the usual royal age of cohabitation; yet for some reason they did not. Jan's household account fortuitously survives for a few months between 8 November 1292 and late May 1293, and reveals that he spent much of that period with Margaret's cousins Thomas and Henry of Lancaster, called 'the sons of Lord Edmund', i.e. Edward I's younger brother the earl of Lancaster and Leicester. Thomas of Lancaster probably turned 15 in *c.* late 1292 or early 1293 and Henry was born in 1280 or 1281, so they were both some years younger than Jan. Jan also spent much time with Humphrey de Bohun (his name appears in the account as 'Anfridus de Boum' or 'Anfroy(e) de Boum'), heir to the earldom of Hereford, born *c.* 1276 and thus very close to Jan's own age. Humphrey, son of the man with whom Gilbert 'the Red' de Clare had feuded earlier in 1292, would later marry Margaret's youngest sister Elizabeth of Rhuddlan after Elizabeth was widowed by her first husband. Humphrey had three attendants in 1292/93 whose names appear in Jan of Brabant's account as Pieres Maubu, Willelmes Loys and Varles.

Jan's brother-in-law Edward of Caernarfon, who was almost nine years his junior, appears a few times in the account: Jan dined alone with 9-year-old Edward on 7 May 1293, for example, stayed with him for several days after 17 May, and went hunting with him. Edward of Caernarfon also dined with his sister Joan of Acre at the beginning of 1293, about two and a half months after she gave birth to her daughter Eleanor de Clare; Joan visited Edward with 'her knights, ladies, clerks and certain squires' at Langley, Hertfordshire and stayed for two nights. A month later, Joan visited her much younger brother again, this time in the company of her husband the earl of Gloucester and no fewer than 200 attendants, and once more stayed for two nights.[1]

Curiously, Margaret of Windsor is not mentioned even once in her husband's account, except that on 3 May 1293 Jan dined with Edward of Caernarfon and his sisters, 'the king's daughters', at the archbishop of Canterbury's manor of Mortlake next to the River Thames west of London. Margaret, who turned 18 in February or March 1293 and who was still not living with her husband, must have been among 'the king's daughters', yet was not singled out in any way. This all tends to suggest that Margaret and Jan were not a particularly compatible nor happy couple, as does Margaret's refusal to leave England with Jan in 1294 when he went home to Brabant after his father's death. The couple subsequently lived apart for more than three years, and it may be significant that they had only one child together in the twenty-two years of their marriage. It seems highly unlikely that at 17, the couple were not yet physically mature enough to sleep together, or were not yet deemed emotionally mature enough to live together as husband and wife, so there must have been some other reason why they still lived apart.

With a pleasing familiarity, Jan of Brabant's clerks referred to him simply by his first name in his extant account of 1292/93, rather than calling him 'the lord' or similar. Something of his private life is revealed by his leaving his nightshirt (*tunicam nocturnam*) and other items behind when he departed from the port of Berwick-on-Tweed, and he paid 9*d* to hire a hackney horse for a servant to ride back there and fetch his prized possession. It seems to have been common in the Middle Ages for people to sleep naked, and therefore Jan's attachment to his nightshirt seems rather remarkable.[2] Conventionally, Jan loved hawking and dicing, and also played bowls on two occasions: he lost 12*d* and 6*d* doing so. He played chess at Christmas 1292, lost a falcon near Cambridge on one occasion while he was out hawking (though did recover the bird later), and had the same enjoyment of music and the performing arts as most royal and noble people of the era.[3] A minstrel from Jan's native Brabant who lived in his household in England for three years was called Baldewyn the Skirmisher (meaning 'Fencer'), though Baldewyn had returned to Brabant in 1290 and hence does not appear in Jan's account of 1292/93.[4]

By May 1293, although she was still only 14 years old, Mary the nun had become embroiled in a quarrel between the prioress of Amesbury and the abbess of Fontévrault, their French mother house. The enrolment of this dispute on the Close Roll states that 'Lady Mary, the king's daughter, a nun of the house of Aumbresbury [Amesbury]' took the side of the (unnamed) abbess of Fontévrault, against the (also unnamed) prioress of Amesbury. Brother Peter, the prior of Fontévrault, like Mary of Woodstock, took the side of the abbess. In the usual vague manner of medieval documents, the dispute was described as having something to do with 'the promotion of the prioress in the monastery of Aumbresbury and concerning certain other things pertaining to the jurisdiction of the monastery of Fontévrault'. The bishop of Durham, Anthony Bek, had taken the abbess's side, and the bishop of Lincoln, Oliver Sutton, the prioress's side.[5] Mary, another five nuns of Amesbury, and a woman confusingly called 'the abbess of Amesbury' in Edward of Caernarfon's accounts (by which his clerk probably meant the abbess of Fontévrault), visited young Edward in early June 1293, and stayed with him for four nights. They were accompanied by a 'great retinue' as well as by Mary's cousins Thomas and Henry of Lancaster, who by now were no longer travelling with Jan of Brabant.[6]

Sometime soon after 1 June 1293, a few months after giving birth to her daughter Eleanor, Joan of Acre set off with Gilbert 'the Red' de Clare for Ireland, where Gilbert owned a considerable amount of land. Among the large retinue they took with them were Joan's attendant Alice Middleton and Gilbert's harper, Ricard or Richard, and another was a man called Gaudinus or Gandinus de Clare. Joan's inquisition post mortem of 1307 mentions a brother of Earl Gilbert called Gandin de Clare, and as his parents had no legitimate son of this name, Gandin (or Gaudin) was presumably a son of Gilbert's father Richard born out of wedlock.[7] Joan and Gilbert intended to be away for two or even three years, though in the end returned to England much sooner than they had anticipated. Margaret de Clare, future countess of Cornwall and Gloucester, Joan and Gilbert's third child and second daughter, was perhaps born in Ireland while they were there in 1293/94, though, unlike those of her three full siblings, Margaret's date of birth is not known. Assuming a regular spacing between the four children of Joan of Acre and Gilbert de Clare, Margaret was probably born sometime between *c.* March and *c.* June 1294, around fifteen to eighteen months after Joan of Acre gave birth to Eleanor and fifteen to eighteen months before she bore her youngest de Clare child, Elizabeth.

Chapter 21

Eleanor's Wedding and Children

The 24-year-old Eleanor of Windsor finally married on 20 September 1293, over two years after the death of her long-term fiancé Alfonso III of Aragon. Her husband was Henri III, count of Bar in eastern France, a county which was, despite its location, part of the Holy Roman Empire rather than the kingdom of France. It bordered the duchy of Lorraine, and its capital was Bar-le-Duc, 150 miles east of Paris and now in the Meuse department of modern France. Henri, like his wife, came from a huge family, being the eldest son and probably the second child in a list of fifteen siblings. His father Thibaut, count of Bar, had died in October 1291, and his mother was Jeanne de Toucy, who lived until 1317. Two of Henri's younger brothers, Thibaut and Renaud, served as bishops of Metz; Thibaut was transferred to the bishopric of Liège in 1302, and was succeeded in Metz by his brother Renaud. Even though he was a bishop, Thibaut of Bar was killed fighting near Rome on behalf of the Holy Roman Emperor in 1312. Another of Henri's younger brothers, and the one closest to him in age, John or Jean of Bar, fought in England and Scotland in 1300 with King Edward, and yet another brother, Érard, visited England on several occasions in the late 1200s and early 1300s.[1]

It is impossible to ascertain Henri of Bar's date of birth, even approximately. He first appears on record as *Henris ainsneis filz le comte de Bar* or 'Henri, eldest son of the count of Bar' in 1277 when he put his seal to a charter agreeing to help the duke of Lorraine in a dispute against the bishop of Metz (who was John of Flanders, not Henri's younger brother Thibaut), and might already have been an adult then, or perhaps he was merely a teenager. His sister Philippa of Bar, probably their parents' eldest child and certainly their eldest daughter, first appears on record in 1258/59 when a future marriage to Othon of Burgundy was arranged for her.[2] At any rate, Henri was definitely a few years older than his royal English wife, born perhaps *c.* 1260, or even as early as *c.* 1255. Two of his many younger siblings, Pierre and Marie, lived into the late 1340s, suggesting they might have been born around 1280 or later.

The royal wedding took place in Bristol, and Edward I ordered Sir John Botetourt, keeper of the Forest of Dean in Gloucestershire, to hunt 'four harts and thirty bucks' in the forest to provide meat for the guests at Eleanor's wedding banquet. *Le Livere de Reis de Brittaniae* says that 'Lady Eleanor [*dame Elyanore*] was married at Bristol. .. with high magnificence and great feasting.'[3] Otherwise, not much else can be said about the occasion, as few details have survived of the wedding of the king's eldest daughter.

Joan of Acre must have missed the grand occasion as she was in Ireland with her husband, and might have been pregnant with her third child.[4] The sisters' 9-year-old brother Edward of Caernarfon was, however, there, and spent the period from 19 to 26 September in Bristol.[5] On 1 October 1293 a few days after the wedding, Edward I promised his new son-in-law Henri a hugely generous gift of 10,000 marks (£6,666) in cash. The count, however, had not yet received his money by 25 April 1299, when Edward gave him permission to request the sum from his (Edward's) cousin Charles, king of Naples and Jerusalem. Edward had lent Charles the same amount when he was prince of Salerno.[6]

Eleanor of Windsor and Henri of Bar stayed in England for a few months after their wedding, and began preparing to depart around 12 April 1294, though they were still in Eleanor's homeland on the 21st. The retinue who would accompany the countess of Bar to her new home included Sir Guy Ferre, a knight of Queen Leonor's household who later joined Edward of Caernarfon's retinue, and Sir William Leyburne (*c.* 1245/50–1310), a baron of Kent who was the son and heir of a late close friend of Edward I, Sir Roger Leyburne (d. 1271). Four men, including Guy Ferre, were appointed to examine the dower lands that would be given to Eleanor in the county of Bar, and to ensure that their value reached the amount agreed between Henri and Edward I: 15,000 pounds of Tours annually.[7]

Possibly Eleanor was already pregnant when she left England for the last time in April 1294: she bore two children to Henri of Bar, a son named Edward or Édouard after her father and a daughter named Jeanne, and her first child was born sometime in 1294 or 1295 (it is not totally clear whether Édouard or Jeanne was the elder of Eleanor's children). From his birth in *c.* 1294 or 1296 until Eleanor's death in

August 1298, Édouard of Bar was heir to the English throne behind his uncle Edward of Caernarfon and his mother. Between 29 August 1298, when his mother died, and 1 June 1300, when his uncle Thomas of Brotherton, Edward I's first son from his second marriage, was born, the French-born Édouard of Bar was next in line to the English throne behind Edward of Caernarfon.

Margaret of Windsor's father-in-law Duke Jan I of Brabant died on 3 May 1294; he was killed while jousting during the wedding celebrations at Bar-le-Duc, capital of the county of Bar. Margaret's eldest sister Eleanor must have been present during the festivities held to mark her recent arrival in her husband's capital. Jan of Brabant, now aged 18 going on 19, succeeded his father as Duke Jan II. He departed for Brabant from Harwich at the end of June 1294, but left Margaret, now a duchess, behind in her homeland. She would remain in England without her husband for more than three years, which surely emphasises that their marriage was an unhappy one, or at the very least, not a close one. Duke Jan II had other consolations and fathered at least four illegitimate sons with four different women. All of his known and certain illegitimate sons, recognised by him as such – and there might have been other children as well – were called Jan.

It may be that Margaret did intend to depart from England not long after her husband: in 1305, two sailors from the Sussex port of Winchelsea, John Ive and Thomas Alard, presented a petition to the king. They claimed that they had fitted out their ship, the *Nicholette*, ready to take the duchess of Brabant across the sea at the beginning of Edward I's twenty-third regnal year, i.e. in November 1294, and had sailed it to the port of the River Orwell in Suffolk, but Margaret failed to make the crossing. Ive and Alard had spent 100 shillings fitting out the *Nicholette* to make it suitable for the king's daughter, and requested twenty years later that the money be finally reimbursed.[8] Jan II, duke of Brabant, visited England again several times after his return to his homeland in 1294. On 28 April 1295, Edward I granted that 'on his [Jan's] present return home' he might take 200 sacks of wool with him, though he had to pay the usual customs duties on it. Duke Jan was with Edward I again at Berwick-on-Tweed on 12 April 1296.[9]

The five royal sisters' first cousin Sancho IV of Castile and Leon died on 25 April 1295, still only in his thirties, and was succeeded by his eldest son, Fernando IV, who was not yet 10 years old. At the accession of a child to the Castilian throne, its neighbours licked their lips at the prospect of invading and conquering part of mighty Castile's territory, but Sancho's widow María de Molina defiantly held the kingdom for her son and kept it intact. She was to do the same for her infant grandson Alfonso XI in and after 1312 after Fernando IV died in his twenties. A Castilian cardinal who visited England in 1306/07 supposedly stated that the 'counts and barons of the land of Spain' (i.e. the kingdom of Castile) wished Edward of Caernarfon to succeed his cousin Fernando IV, who still had no children from his marriage to Constança of Portugal.[10] Fernando and Constança's son Alfonso XI was, however, born in 1311.

Joan of Acre gave birth to her fourth child in Tewkesbury, Gloucestershire, one of the many towns owned by Gilbert de Clare, on 16 September 1295.[11] It was another daughter, her third and Gilbert's fifth and youngest, and they named her Elizabeth, presumably in honour of Joan's youngest sister, then 13 years old. Elizabeth of Rhuddlan may have been her niece's godmother. Just a few weeks later, on 7 December 1295, Joan was widowed when Gilbert 'the Red' died at Monmouth Castle at the age of 52; she was only 23.[12] What kind of personal relationship the two had had is unclear, but they produced four children in the five and a half years of their marriage, and therefore must have spent quite a lot of time together. Gilbert was buried in the Clare mausoleum of Tewkesbury Abbey with his father Richard (d. 1262) and grandfather Gilbert (d. 1230). His and Joan's son Gilbert and daughter Eleanor, and many of Eleanor's descendants, would also be buried there over the decades. In March 1310, young Gilbert ('Gilleberd de Clare') complained that his father had bequeathed a valuable silver vessel and unspecified other items to him, and had left them with the abbot of Tewkesbury for safe-keeping until Gilbert was older, but the abbot had allowed the items to be taken from his custody. Gilbert petitioned his uncle Edward II about it, and in the ensuing investigation it transpired that ten men had removed the young man's 'jewels of gold and silver, gems, goods, charters, writings and muniments' from Tewkesbury Abbey. One of the ten men was, rather astonishingly, Anthony Bek, bishop of Durham and patriarch of Jerusalem, who in 1282 had been sent to Aragon to negotiate Eleanor of Windsor's marriage to Don Alfonso.[13]

A royal child was a valuable piece on the chessboard of diplomatic relations, and at an uncertain date in or before early 1297, Edward I began negotiations for Joan of Acre to marry a second husband: Amadeus V, count of Savoy. As Gilbert 'the Red' had also been, Amadeus was much Joan's senior: he was born at the end of the 1240s or in the early 1250s, and his first wife Sybille of Baugé, with whom he had eight children, died in 1294. Amadeus and Sybille named their first son, born *c.* 1284, Eduard, almost certainly in honour of the king of England. Amadeus's father Thomas was one of the Savoyard uncles of the late Eleanor of Provence, so he was closely related to the English royal family, and a papal dispensation would be required for consanguinity if he were to marry Joan of Acre.

In eastern France, Eleanor of Windsor, countess of Bar, gave birth to her second child sometime in 1295 or 1296. Possibly this was her son Édouard, or possibly it was her daughter Jeanne. Little Jeanne de Bar, though French by birth, was destined to spend almost all of her life in her mother's homeland. Eleanor of Windsor did not, as sometimes claimed, give birth to a second daughter who married into a princely Welsh family; this was a later myth invented by the Tudor dynasty to bolster their alleged royal descent.[14] Although she was married to the English earl of Surrey for forty-one years, Eleanor of Windsor's only daughter Jeanne de Bar had no children, and therefore all of Eleanor's descendants were and are via her son Édouard I, count of Bar. One of them was Elizabeth Woodville (d. 1492), who married Edward IV of England in 1464 and was the grandmother of Henry VIII.[15]

Edward I spent most of the second half of the 1290s at war with his first cousin once removed, Philip IV of France, a young man who was not remotely interested in maintaining his father's and grandfather's cordial relations with England and who bitterly resented the English kings' long-term possession of a large territory in south-west France. Philip used a quarrel between English and French fishermen in 1294 to provoke Edward into a war over Aquitaine and subsequently confiscated the duchy, and even the intercession of Edward's brother Edmund of Lancaster, the stepfather of Philip's wife Queen Juana of Navarre, only made matters worse. Edmund died in Bayonne in June 1296 while on campaign against the French, a few weeks after King Edward requested his sons-in-law Duke Jan II of Brabant and Count Henri III of Bar to be present during tense negotiations to attempt to make a truce with the powerful kingdom of France.[16] As it turned out, the war would not be settled until 1299.

Chapter 22

The Count's Murder and Elizabeth's Wedding

Floris V, count of Holland, whose only surviving legitimate son had been betrothed to Elizabeth of Rhuddlan since 1285, was murdered in Muiderslot (Muiden Castle) near Amsterdam on 27 June 1296. Jan, now 12 or perhaps 13, succeeded him as Jan I, count of Holland and Zeeland and lord of Friesland. Jan's mother Beatrijs van Vlaanderen had died some years before, and the boy now found himself an orphan. Although it has sometimes been stated that Count Floris was murdered after his decision to switch allegiance from England to France, the chroniclers Jan van Naaldwijk and Willelmus Cappellanus, and other Dutch sources, tell a very different tale. They claim that Floris suggested to his friend and courtier Gheraert (or Gerrit) van Velzen that Velzen might consider marrying Floris's former mistress, Isabella. The indignant Velzen stated that he would never marry that prostitute (*loddeghinne* was the medieval Dutch word he used), whereupon Floris countered that he would make any future wife of Velzen his whore. Supposedly, he did in fact send Velzen out of Holland on some pretext so that he could go to his castle and rape or otherwise abuse and dishonour the woman Gheraert had recently married. On his return to Holland, a furious Velzen and some friends kidnapped Floris near Utrecht, took him to Muiden Castle, and stabbed him twenty times. Gheraert van Velzen was himself executed, or rather lynched, shortly afterwards, either by being broken on the wheel or by being rolled around in a barrel with sharp nails driven into it.[1]

Floris's son Jan named a Dutch knight called Sir Jehan de Renesse as one of his 'enemies' and another of his father's murderers in a letter to Edward I of 18 October 1297, yet earlier that year Jehan accompanied the count of Holland to his wedding in England, and the young count had, rather curiously, not taken any exception to his presence on that occasion; perhaps he only discovered Renesse's involvement later. For his part, Edward I showed conspicuous favour to Jehan de Renesse, giving him a horse worth the large sum of £40. If Count Jan was correct that Renesse had helped to kill his father, this tends to suggest a certain degree of English involvement in Count Floris's murder, or at the very least that the king of England was not displeased about it.[2] Perhaps not coincidentally, King Edward sent a letter to the King of the Romans grumbling about the 'ingratitude' of Floris V on 26 June 1296, the day before the count's murder.[3] Several modern Dutch writers have speculated that as well as the king of England, other noblemen of the Low Countries such as the young Duke Jan II of Brabant and Guy de Dampierre, count of Flanders, might have been involved in a conspiracy to murder the count.[4] Guy de Dampierre was Floris V's father-in-law; Jan II of Brabant was Floris's nephew-in-law.

Whatever the truth behind Floris's death, Elizabeth of Rhuddlan's fiancé was now count of Holland and Zeeland, and was in England in 1296 at the time of his father's murder. The 'men of Holland' wrote to Edward I on 1 July four days after Floris's death, informing the king that Floris was dead and asking him to send Jan back to his homeland now that he had succeeded as count.[5] King Edward, busy in Scotland, did not reply until 14 September 1296, when he sent letters to the barons, knights, burgesses and other 'good men' of Holland, Zealand and Friesland from Berwick-on-Tweed, talking of Floris's 'horrible death'. The king decided to press ahead with Jan and Elizabeth's wedding, and asked the barons, knights, burgesses and other people of Jan's new territories to 'arrange for two or more men of every good town' and three, four or more noblemen from every part of the territories to come to him in England to discuss the marriage. Four men, two knights and two clerks, were given a safe-conduct to return to Holland on 12 November 1296 after coming to see Jan and his father-in-law in England.[6]

Elizabeth and Jan's wedding duly went ahead, and on 30 December 1296 at Ipswich, Edward I sent invitations to various men and women to attend; it was due to take place on Monday, 7 January 1297. The wedding invitees included the bishop of London, the abbot of Colchester, the earls of Norfolk, Hereford and Oxford, the countesses of Norfolk, Oxford and Cornwall, and five other noblewomen whom the king probably intended to serve as Elizabeth's attendants on the day. A number of Jan of Holland's subjects travelled to England to attend the wedding, including contingents of knights, squires, priests and burgesses from

Kennemerland and North Holland and from Jan's towns of Dordrecht, Haarlem, Leiden, Delft and Middelburg.[7] As one Dutch writer stated in the 1990s, the marriage of a Dutch count to an English king's daughter counted as a great success for young Jan's family and for his subjects.[8]

The bridegroom and his retinue arrived in London on 5 December 1296, and stayed there until Sir Reginald Ferre, accompanied by a group of other knights, travelled to the city to collect Jan. On their way to Ipswich, the Dutch party spent five days in Colchester, where they arrived on Christmas Eve, and Edward I ordered fish, meat, poultry, bread and ginger to be purchased there for the young count and his retinue. Jan had nine personal attendants taking care of him, and his party required six carriages for the last leg of their journey from Colchester to Ipswich, which took two days.[9] These towns lie barely 20 miles apart, so evidently Jan's journey was a painfully slow one, probably owing to wintry conditions and snow and ice or floods; that the weather was seasonably cold is revealed by the king buying fire-wood for Jan while he stayed in Colchester.

Adam, a goldsmith of London, hired five horses and a cart to transport Elizabeth's wedding jewels to Ipswich. Another London goldsmith came by horse to Ipswich with jewels for Margaret of Windsor, duchess of Brabant, but, rather haughtily, she rejected them as inadequate. King Edward, indulgent as so often towards his daughters, purchased other pieces for her. These included items for her chapel such as two silver candelabras, four silver dishes and two silver basins, a silver spoon, a silver vessel for holy water, a silver pot and a large silver alms-dish. He also bought a silver alms-dish and vessel for the Host for his daughter Elizabeth. Thirty-five tailors, meanwhile, worked for four days and four nights on the wedding robes, which were embroidered with silk and decorated with numerous silver-gilt buttons. Some of the jewellery which Elizabeth had intended to wear on her wedding day was not ready in time, so King Edward gave her 12 marks in cash and a gold brooch to make up for the disappointment.[10]

The royal family arrived in Ipswich on or about 23 December 1296, and Edward I fed large numbers of poor people in the town throughout the festive season: 200 on Christmas Day, 700 on the feast of St Stephen (26 December), 700 on the feast of St John the Evangelist (27 December), 700 on the feast of the Holy Innocents (28 December), and 100 on the feast of St Thomas Becket (29 December). On Christmas Day, the royal family heard Mass several times in the king's private chapel and in the church of St Peter and St Paul's Priory, and Margaret of Windsor and Elizabeth of Rhuddlan gave 21*s* and 8*d* in oblations during one Mass.[11] On 27 December 1296, the famous acrobat or 'tumbler' (*saltatrix*) Matilda or Maud Makejoye performed for 12-year-old Edward of Caernarfon in the King's Hall in Ipswich, and received two shillings for 'making her vaults' for his entertainment.[12]

Elizabeth of Rhuddlan had some kind of argument with her father at the beginning of January, a few days before her wedding: King Edward had to pay 40*s* for a large ruby and a large emerald to be set into Elizabeth's coronet, which, exasperated with his wilful daughter, he had snatched from her head and thrown into a nearby fire.[13] This implies that the coronet was hastily plucked from the fire either by the king himself, Elizabeth or (more likely) a servant, and that most of it was saved, though two large precious stones in it had been destroyed. During her wedding, Elizabeth wore another coronet, made of gold and worth £90, which had previously belonged to the countess of Luxembourg.[14]

The wedding of 14-year-old Elizabeth and 12- or 13-year-old Jan of Holland took place probably on 7 January 1297, or possibly on the 8th, and Edward I spent a fortune on the minstrels who entertained the guests. They included nine harpers, including one from the household of the Scottish nobleman John 'the Red Comyn', lord of Badenoch (who almost certainly attended the wedding); two trumpeters; two taborers or drummers called Baudet and Martinet; three who performed together called Griscote, Visage and Magote (their professional names; Magot or Magote was a nickname for women called Margaret); Lambin Clay; lute, estive and vielle players; the acrobat Matilda Makejoye; Thomas the Fool; and three Kings of Heralds, John Monhaut, Nicholas Morel and Jakettus de Scocia or 'Jamie of Scotland'. Jakettus or Jakett appears to be the same man as the 'King Capenny' who had performed at Joan of Acre's wedding in 1290, and he was hired again by the royal family for another important event in 1306. His real name was apparently James Cowpen.[15] The earl of Norfolk, Roger Bigod (born *c.* 1245) and his much younger second wife Alix or Alicia of Hainault, a kinswoman of the young bridegroom, attended Elizabeth and Jan's wedding, and two of Norfolk's minstrels were among the performers.

The Anglo-Irish earl of Ulster's daughter Eleanor de Burgh had married Thomas, Lord Multon of Cumberland a few days previously on 3 January, and Edward I gave her a gold chaplet to wear during her wedding.[16] Isabella Beaumont, Lady Vescy, the partly French and partly Spanish noblewoman who was a second cousin of Edward I's daughters, was also with the royal family at this time.[17] Sixty shillings or three pounds was 'thrown among the men standing round at the door ... when the count of Holland married Elizabeth the king's daughter with a ring of gold.' Throwing coins was a popular contemporary custom intended to bring the bridal couple luck, and the money was afterwards distributed to the poor as alms. Another twelve shillings were given out as alms during the wedding Mass celebrated at the great altar. Edward I also gave his daughter Elizabeth and new son-in-law Jan a considerable amount of costly plate as wedding gifts.[18]

While in Ipswich, Edward I dealt with another possible future marriage for his heir Edward of Caernarfon, this time into the county of Flanders. Having lost his first fiancée Margaret of Norway in 1290, and having had his second betrothal to Blanche of France broken off in 1294 as a result of the war between his father and Blanche's half-brother Philip IV, the 12-year-old was now betrothed to one of Count Guy de Dampierre's daughters, either Philippa, the first choice, or Isabella, the second. The count of Flanders was an important ally of the English king against King Philip of France. The planned Flanders match would, however, not work out either, and the agreement was annulled in July 1298, whereupon Edward was betrothed to his fourth fiancée, Philip IV's daughter Isabella, instead.[19]

As had been the case with her older sister Margaret of Windsor in and after 1294, Elizabeth of Rhuddlan failed to leave England with her husband, and remained in her homeland for much of the rest of 1297. Count Jan himself departed for Holland from Harwich within a week or two of the wedding, taking with him a gold cup as a gift from his brother-in-law Edward of Caernarfon and a saddle studded with pearls and embroidered with the royal arms of England from his father-in-law.[20]

Chapter 23

A Secret Wedding

Another royal daughter married in January 1297, but, unlike her younger sister Elizabeth, did so secretly. Joan of Acre, widowed from Gilbert 'the Red' de Clare for just over a year, wed a squire named Ralph de Monthermer without her father's knowledge or permission. Supposedly, Joan declared 'It is not ignominious or shameful for a great and powerful earl to marry a poor woman of low rank. So, it is neither reprehensible nor problematic if a countess promotes a young strong man.'[1] According to the chronicler John Trokelowe, the English magnates were not happy about the marriage but kept quiet out of fear and reverence; fear because Joan was the king's daughter, and reverence because she was the mightiest noblewoman in the kingdom. Another reason might have been Joan's own personality: she was not scared to stand up for herself and defied her father on other occasions as well as in 1297, and could be argumentative and, perhaps, somewhat intimidating.[2]

Edward I heard news, or least rumours, of Joan's secret marriage on 22 January 1297, when he ordered Malcolm Harlegh, a royal official, to take all of Joan's lands, goods and chattels into his own hands immediately. Harlegh was 'warned not to omit to do this as he loves himself and his own things and wishes to escape the king's wrath, certifying the king without delay as to how he has executed this order'.[3] The wording of the royal command to Malcolm Harlegh reveals Edward I's fury with his daughter, and almost two months later on 16 March, he decided to press ahead with the 'marriage of A[madeus] count of Savoy, and Joan, countess of Gloucester and Hertford, the king's daughter'.[4] Perhaps he believed that her Monthermer marriage could be annulled, or was still not sure whether her marriage had taken place or not and whether Joan had truly dared to defy him. According to a chronicler, Ralph de Monthermer was imprisoned in Bristol Castle after daring to marry the king's daughter without permission, though there is no confirmation in the chancery rolls of Edward I giving the order to do so.[5]

Joan sent her three little de Clare daughters, Eleanor, Margaret and Elizabeth, to her father to soften him up before she approached him in person; Eleanor was 4, Margaret 3 or almost, and Elizabeth about 18 months. An undated letter still exists in the National Archives, wherein Joan wrote to her father asking him to accept the envoys she was sending to him.[6] Given the excellent relations between the king and his second daughter and given that they did not usually require envoys in order to communicate, it seems possible that this letter dates to 1297 and represents Joan's efforts to reconcile with her father.

A London annalist calls Ralph 'the bastard of Monthermer', so apparently he was illegitimate or at least was believed to be, and almost nothing is known about his background. The *Complete Peerage* suggests he may have been a grandson of William de Meisnelhermer, lord of Tunstal in Northumberland in 1242. As well as apparently being illegitimate, Ralph also seems to have fathered an illegitimate son, who was also named Ralph, perhaps either before he married Joan or in the eleven years between her death and his second marriage.[7] He appears to have been born *c.* 1262, so was about a decade Joan's senior and in his mid-thirties in 1297, and had served as a squire in the household of Gilbert 'the Red' de Clare.[8] His heir after his death in 1325 was his elder son with Joan of Acre, and as this was the case, he cannot have had any surviving children from any previous marriage he might have had. Possibly Joan and Ralph had known each other for a long time, and after Gilbert's death, her feelings for him blossomed.

Joan of Acre visited Goodrich Castle in Herefordshire on 9 and 10 April 1297, and went hunting for deer with her pack of hounds. Members of her household caught partridges and rabbits as well. Goodrich belonged to Joan Munchesni, widow of William de Valence, earl of Pembroke, a half-brother of Joan's grandfather Henry III. Joan Munchesni had been with Joan of Acre's mother Queen Leonor in Windsor Castle in June 1264, when both women were pregnant, and as noted above, one historian has suggested that the older Joan was Joan of Acre's godmother. Joan of Acre evidently was fond of her kinswoman: earlier in the year, in February 1297, she and her son Gilbert, 5 going on 6 years old, had visited Joan Munchesni, and spent three days and nights with her.[9] This visit took place soon after her secret wedding, and perhaps Joan's motive, at least in part, was to stay well away from her father. If Ralph de Monthermer accompanied her during this visit, or during the hunting trip a couple of months later, he was not mentioned.

On 15 May 1297, Joan was to be given 'reasonable maintenance' for herself and her four Clare children, as her lands had been taken into the king's hands after Edward found out about her marriage.[10] She and Ralph de Monthermer were officially pardoned at the palace of Eltham on 2 August 1297, and Monthermer did homage to the king and to his 13-year-old son Edward of Caernarfon for the lands he held with Joan on this occasion.[11] Eltham still belonged to Anthony Bek, bishop of Durham, in 1297; he was to give the palace to Edward of Caernarfon in 1305, and it remained in royal hands for centuries.

On 28 August, Ralph and Joan appeared on the Patent Roll when they appointed attorneys in Ireland; Joan was called 'Countess of Gloucester', but Ralph was not yet acknowledged as earl. By May 1298, he was addressed as Earl of Gloucester, and would hold the title for the rest of Joan's life.[12] Joan's lands and goods were restored to her, though she had to acknowledge liability for a debt of 8,000 marks 'to have again her goods which for certain reasons he [the king] had taken into his hands'. Joan's eldest child and heir Gilbert de Clare made a reference in *c.* 1307, in a petition to his uncle Edward II, to the fact that 'the countess his mother took Sir Ralph de Monthermer to husband without his [Edward I's] permission, after which all the lands of his [Gilbert's] inheritance were taken into the king's hands'.[13]

Edward I had apparently forgiven his daughter privately as well as publicly by 16 September 1297, when he ordered the constable of Windsor Castle to deliver the 'houses of the outer bailey of the castle' to Joan and Ralph as 'the king has lent the houses to them for the residence of themselves and their households'.[14] It is highly likely that Joan was heavily pregnant at the time with Mary de Monthermer, her fifth child and her first with Ralph, and Mary may have been born in one of these houses in Windsor Castle. Mary's date of birth is not known, but is often estimated as *c.* October 1297, so she was only about two years younger than Elizabeth de Clare, youngest of Joan's four children from her first marriage. A gift of ten does sent by the king to Joan on 10 November 1297 was perhaps Edward's reaction to hearing the news of the birth of his latest granddaughter, and if so, perhaps also represents something of an olive branch on the king's part.[15] Joan and Ralph de Monthermer's second child was another girl, the fifth in a row Joan had borne, probably in 1299. She was also named Joan and, like her aunt Mary of Woodstock, became a nun at Amesbury Priory. Almost nothing is known of Joan de Monthermer's life, not even the year – or even the decade – of her death. After her two daughters, Joan of Acre gave birth in 1301 and 1304 to two Monthermer sons, Thomas and Edward, as well. Her would-be fiancé Amadeus, count of Savoy, deprived of his royal bride, married his second wife Marie of Brabant sometime before 1304 and perhaps in the late 1290s. Probably born in or after 1280, Marie was a good thirty years Amadeus's junior.

Chapter 24

Travelling to the Continent

Margaret of Windsor planned to leave for Brabant on 11 January 1297, just days after Elizabeth's wedding, when the king granted protection to John Weylond, 'going to Brabant in the company of the said duchess'. Five days later Weylond appointed two attorneys to act on his behalf while he was absent from England, and on 20 January the king also gave protection to John Ferrers to travel to Brabant with his daughter. Two important noblemen named on 14 January 1297 as those who would accompany Margaret to Brabant were John, Lord Hastings (b. 1262) and Humphrey de Bohun, earl of Hereford (b. *c.* 1248). A man called Geoffrey de la Mare was also appointed to travel with her, in Hereford's company.[1] The earl of Hereford, who would die at the end of 1298, was the father of the man of the same name who would later marry Elizabeth of Rhuddlan as her second husband.

Yet again, however, Margaret failed to depart from England until later in the year, when she and Elizabeth finally went to join their husbands. Isabella Beaumont, Lady Vescy, was ordered to accompany her kinswoman Elizabeth abroad in August 1297, having attended the wedding in Ipswich a few months previously.[2] Lady Vescy (d. 1334) was the widow of John Vescy, sent to Aragon in 1282 to negotiate Eleanor's marriage to Don Alfonso. She and her siblings Henry, Lord Beaumont (d. 1340) and Louis (d. 1333), elected bishop of Durham in 1317, who used the name of their mother Agnès Beaumont in preference to that of their father Louis Brienne, were French by birth and had a Spanish grandmother, but spent their adult lives in England.[3]

It is possible that the eldest royal daughter, Eleanor of Windsor, was in England in 1297 and visited the city of Bristol, where she had married Henri III of Bar some years before. The author of the chronicle *Flores Historiarum*, written at Westminster Abbey, wrote that 'Lady Alianora, countess of Barz, eldest daughter of King Edward' died in Bristol on 12 October ('the fourth day before the Ides of October') in 1297, and was buried in Westminster Abbey. In fact, Eleanor was certainly alive at Christmas 1297 and New Year 1298 when she spent time with her natal family, and a death date of 29 August, not 12 October, was entered into her youngest sister Elizabeth's psalter. Elizabeth would seem to be a highly reliable, and surely definitive, source for the date of her own sister's death.[4] On the other hand, a chronicle written at Westminster Abbey would seem to be a reliable source for a burial at Westminster Abbey. It may be that the author garbled his account somewhat, and it is possible that Eleanor gave birth to a child while visiting England in 1297, perhaps in Bristol, and that the child died young and was buried in the abbey. Or perhaps the author was correct that it was indeed Eleanor herself who was interred at Westminster, but he erred on the place and date of her death. Eleanor had only two children who lived into adulthood, Édouard, count of Bar and Jeanne, countess of Surrey, but it is certainly possible that she gave birth to another infant who was stillborn or who died in infancy.

Edward I, with his daughters Elizabeth and Margaret in tow, left England and arrived at the port of Sluys in the county of Flanders on 27 August 1297; he remained overseas until mid-March 1298.[5] Margaret's possessions were taken from London to Harwich on a cart pulled by five horses, and it took a total of eighteen days for all her goods to be carried from London before her departure. She was issued with robes for her household servants, mostly made of red and green cloth, shortly before she said a final farewell to her family.[6] Edward I's 13-year-old son Edward of Caernarfon was left behind in England as nominal 'keeper of the realm', or regent, with a council of barons and bishops to advise him. King Edward sent a letter to the deputy treasurer and barons of the exchequer from Orpington in Kent on 2 August 1297 a few weeks before departure, regarding the wine allowance of 'Mary, our dear daughter' (*Marie nostre chier[e] fille*). He stated that the tuns of wine which Mary was supposed to receive twice yearly at Amesbury from the county of Hampshire were four terms in arrears, and that Mary had been forced to 'purchase wines for the sustenance of her household' and was rather considerably in debt as a result. The treasurer and barons were ordered to pay the wine debts as soon as possible.[7]

After her arrival in Ghent, Elizabeth of Rhuddlan purchased red and green silk, a colour combination the royal family obviously loved, for the curtains in her bedchamber. Like Margaret, she was, however, in no great rush to join her husband, and she and her father might have suffered from a malady of the stomach around this time: pomegranates, long considered a cure for stomach and digestive disorders, were purchased for them both in Ghent.[8] On 9 October 1297, Count Jan I of Holland sent a pleading letter, in French, to Edward I. Spelling his name as 'Jehans', using all his titles, count of Holland and Zealand and lord of Friesland, and addressing the king respectfully as the 'wise, noble, honourable and mighty prince, his very dear lord and father', Jan wrote:

> Very dear father, on other occasions we have requested of you that it might please you to send our dear consort to her land; dear lord, once again we humbly beseech you, for the great well-being of herself and of us and of our land and our people, who very strongly desire to see their lady, our dear consort, that it might please you that you might arrange a certain day and a certain place where we can come to meet you, and that it might please you to bring our consort to her own country, as honourably as befits her.[9]

To what extent Elizabeth's failure to leave England in the first place, and her failure to travel to Holland even after she arrived on the Continent, was her decision or her father's is not entirely clear. Perhaps she was in no hurry to travel to her new home, suggesting that she did not much like Jan, or did not wish to leave her family and her homeland, or both. Michael Prestwich, one of Edward I's biographers, however, considers that the king took a 'rather high-handed attitude' towards the young Jan of Holland, and, unwilling to allow Elizabeth to join her husband in Holland, treated his daughter 'virtually as a hostage'. Elizabeth and Jan were, of course, both still very young, and not yet physically or emotionally mature enough for their marriage to be consummated. Communication is not, likely, however, to have been an issue; Jan was evidently fluent in French and always wrote to his English father-in-law in that language. In his own lands, of course, the young count dictated his letters and charters in Dutch, and in his native language called himself Jan, Janne or Johan, not Jehans as he did in French.[10]

Count Jan sent Edward another letter on 18 October 1297, from the island of Walcheren in the Scheldt estuary, bitterly complaining about Edward showing favour to Sir Jehan de Renesse and other men whom

Jan deemed his enemies, 'against our profit, and against our honour'. He sent a letter on the same day to the inhabitants of his town of 's-Hertogenbosch warning them against receiving his father's murderers, but it was intercepted by his cousin Duke Jan II of Brabant, who sent it to their mutual father-in-law (the two Dutch cousins feuded badly in 1296/97, at least partly as a result of Jan of Brabant welcoming some of Count Floris V's killers in his territories, and on the count of Holland's wedding day in Ipswich in January 1297, they mutually appointed Edward of England to arbitrate between them). Jan of Holland's remark that 'although we are still young, we are neither so immature nor so misguided' that he was willing to allow his father's murderers to return to his own lands, reveals that he found Edward I's attitude towards him, at least in this respect, patronising and dismissive.[11]

Whether Eleanor, Countess of Bar, visited England in 1297 or not, she certainly travelled to Ghent to visit her father and her sisters Margaret and Elizabeth at Christmas that year. Margaret and Jan II travelled to Ghent from Jan's capital of Brussels, and the count of Flanders and the sisters' cousin Marie of Brittany, countess of St Pol, were also there. The count of Flanders was the elderly Guy de Dampierre, now at least 70 years old, who was the grandfather-in-law of both Margaret, duchess of Brabant and Elizabeth, countess of Holland; Marie of Brittany was one of the daughters of Edward I's late sister Beatrice.

Three of the six royal English siblings were together for the first time in several years. While in Ghent, Eleanor gave her father a comb, a silver enamelled mirror, and a pricket (a spike for holding a candle), probably on the Feast of the Circumcision, 1 January, when the royal family usually exchanged gifts. The items eventually passed to Eleanor's brother Edward of Caernarfon after the king's death. Isabelle of Luxembourg, countess of Flanders, Guy de Dampierre's much younger second wife, gave Edward I a purse with an ornament of pearls, which eventually also passed to Edward's son and heir Edward of Caernarfon.[12] Edward I returned to England in March 1298, while his third and fifth daughters settled into their new lives in Brabant and Holland respectively.

Chapter 25

A Royal Death

Countess Eleanor did not have much longer to live after seeing her father and two of her sisters at Christmas 1297. She died on 29 August 1298 at the age of only 29, either in Ghent in the county of Flanders, according to the nineteenth-century work *Lives of the Princesses of England*, or in Bristol, according to the fourteenth-century Westminster chronicle *Flores Historiarum*.[1] A medieval chronicle would seem to be a more reliable source, though it would be unusual for the body of an English royal or noble lady to be returned to her homeland rather than being buried in her husband's lands. Given her age and given that she had borne two children between 1294 and 1296 (and had perhaps borne another in 1297, though this is uncertain), it seems entirely possible that Eleanor died as a result of pregnancy or childbirth, though if this is the case, any child she bore this year does not appear on known record. It is also possible that she died of a sudden infection or illness.

Eleanor's husband Count Henri III of Bar was imprisoned in 1297, and was still in captivity at the time Eleanor died; Juana I, queen-regnant of Navarre, queen-consort of France and countess of Champagne and Brie, whose betrothal to Henry of Windsor had been under consideration when they were both infants, supposedly led an army into the county of Bar personally in 1297, after Henri III took his forces into Juana's county of Champagne in support of his father-in-law Edward I. Henri was captured and imprisoned in a dungeon in Paris, then moved to a less harsh incarceration in Bourges.[2]

The four surviving royal sisters acquired a stepmother on 8 September 1299, when Edward I married Marguerite of France in Canterbury. Edward was 60, and Marguerite, born in 1278 or 1279, was 20. She was, therefore, several years younger than some of her stepdaughters, the late countess of Bar, the countess of Gloucester and the duchess of Brabant, was about the same age as Mary the nun of Amesbury, and was three or four years older than the countess of Holland. Her marriage to

Edward I was arranged as a means of ending the war between France and England which had begun in 1294: Marguerite was a half-sister of Philip IV, being the second of the three children of Philip III (d. 1285) and his second wife Marie of Brabant.[3] Adam, the London goldsmith who had provided the jewels for Elizabeth of Rhuddlan's wedding to Jan of Holland, travelled to Paris to purchase plate and jewels to be given by Edward I to Marguerite and her attendants, and to the wedding guests. The guests included the dukes of Brittany (Edward I's brother-in-law John II, d. 1305) and Burgundy (Hugues V, a grandson of Louis IX of France), Eleanor of Windsor's brother-in-law Sir Érard of Bar, and the countesses of Eu, Luxembourg and Dammartin. Philip IV of France did not travel to Canterbury to attend the wedding in person, but sent a couple of dozen servants to England with his half-sister, who doubtless reported back to him on their return to France.[4]

The royal sisters' younger brother Edward of Caernarfon was betrothed to Philip IV and Juana of Navarre's only surviving daughter Isabella (born *c.* late 1295), Marguerite's niece, at the same time, though he did not marry her until after Edward I died and he became king. For some reason, perhaps because she was a second wife and would not be the mother of a king, Marguerite of France was never crowned as queen of England. She did, however, secure the male succession to the English throne by becoming pregnant immediately, and gave birth to her first son a week short of nine months after her wedding.

Two months after her father and stepmother's wedding, on 10 November 1299, Elizabeth of Rhuddlan, countess of Holland, was widowed when Count Jan I died of dysentery. He was only 15 or perhaps 16 and she was 17, and they had no children; it may be that their marriage was never consummated, depending on Jan's physical maturity and state of health. The count had outlived all ten of his full brothers and sisters, though was survived by his illegitimate half-siblings, Witte van Haemstede, Catheryne, Gheraerd, Alide, Pieter, and Dirk. Witte van Haemstede called himself 'brother of the count of Holland' in a charter he issued a month before Jan's death, and Jan addressed him as 'our dear brother' (*onsen lieven broeder*).[5] In the Dutch town of The Hague on the eve of the feast day of Saints Simon and Jude in 1299, i.e. on 27 October, two weeks before the count died, Jan's father's first cousin Jan II, count of Hainault, who was his heir, confirmed Elizabeth's rightful dower in the county of Holland as negotiated some years previously between Edward I and

Count Floris V. As it happened, her dower included the town of The Hague itself.[6] Rumours that young Jan I, count of Holland had been killed by Jan II, count of Hainault were probably inevitable given his youth when he died and given that the older man benefited from his death by increasing his territories, and hardly deserve to be taken seriously.

Elizabeth eventually returned to England, once more her father's responsibility, and it is impossible to say anything very much about her life in Holland or about her feelings for Count Jan and their short marriage. Had she been the mother of a future count of Holland, no doubt she would have stayed there, and her subsequent life would have been remarkably different. She and Jan had spent the festive season of 1298 in Dordrecht, and Jan's charters show that he travelled around his small county rather often, so Elizabeth probably came to know Holland well despite the comparatively short time she lived there. The couple were in Dordrecht again on 13 October 1299 just a few weeks before Jan's death, and on 27 October sent a long joint letter, in Dutch, to Count Jan II of Hainault. Mary Anne Everett Green claimed in the 1850s that Elizabeth spent most of her marriage to Jan 'neglected and often alone at her palace of the Hague', which may well be true, but as no primary source is cited, it is hard to know for sure.[7] Jan of Holland was still lucid enough on 7 November to issue a very long charter in The Hague, which is probably where he died three days later. Elizabeth herself dictated a letter in The Hague on 24 November 1299, two weeks into her widowhood, regarding the purchase of lands in an area called the Ambacht van Kralingen near Rotterdam; the letter was written in Dutch though was surely translated from Elizabeth's dictated French. She called herself 'We, Elizabeth, daughter of the king of England, and countess of Holland' (*Gravinne van Hollant*). The dowager countess of Holland had Masses sung for her husband's soul on 10 November 1300, the first anniversary of his death, while she was in Carlisle in the far north of her father's kingdom.[8]

Elizabeth was still in Holland in March 1300 when her father sent William Burnton and Henry Spigurnel there to help her gain her rightful dower. Edward I instructed her to receive them courteously and to 'advise and inform them as to her said affairs, as the honour of her estate shall require'.[9] Despite Jan II of Hainault and Holland's confirmation of her dower in Holland shortly before the death of Elizabeth's husband, she would have huge problems accessing her rightful lands and income for the rest of her life, both from Jan II and his son and successor Willem.

Chapter 26

Two Royal Half-Brothers

On 1 June 1300, the royal sisters' half-brother Thomas was born in the Yorkshire village of Brotherton, a manor belonging to the archbishop of York. Edward I was almost 61 years old, and must have been delighted to have another son and to have secured the succession to his throne: being male, Thomas immediately displaced his much older half-sisters and entered the succession directly behind Edward of Caernarfon. Until Thomas of Brotherton's birth, the heir to England after Edward of Caernarfon was the late Eleanor of Windsor's son Édouard of Bar. The birth of another son, Edmund of Woodstock, to Queen Marguerite and King Edward on 5 August 1301 pushed Édouard farther down the line of succession. Edmund's birth also meant that the chances of any of Edward I's daughters inheriting their father's throne had become very slight.

Edward I besieged the Scottish castle of Caerlaverock for a few days in July 1300, and one of the hundreds of noblemen and knights present with him was Sir Jean of Bar, the late Eleanor of Windsor's brother-in-law. The English heralds who wrote a long text (in French) in praise of the knights and noblemen at Caerlaverock called him 'Johans de Bar'. The sisters' first cousin 'Briton', i.e. John of Brittany, was there and was called 'handsome and gentle' by the heralds, and their 16-year-old brother Edward of Caernarfon, 'a well proportioned and handsome person ... of a courteous disposition' and said to be an excellent horseman, also took part in the siege. Humphrey de Bohun the younger, who had now succeeded his father as earl of Hereford and Essex, the future second husband of the widowed Elizabeth of Rhuddlan, countess of Holland, was called 'a young man, rich and elegant' in the *Roll of Arms of Caerlaverock*.[1]

Edward I's cousin Edmund, earl of Cornwall, died in late September or early October 1300, and the king himself was heir to Edmund's vast lands across the south of England, being his nearest male relative.[2]

Earl Edmund left a brooch to the king's youngest daughter Elizabeth, which she later gave to her brother Edward of Caernarfon. The two youngest royal siblings were always on close and affectionate terms, and during the festive season of 1300/01, Edward presented his sister with a sorrel horse.[3] After the death of his cousin, Edward I took the opportunity to give Edmund of Cornwall's manor of Corsham, Wiltshire (30 miles from Amesbury) to Mary of Woodstock. In November 1302, Edward granted Mary, 'during her life and residence within the realm', the right to hold a market in the town every Thursday. She would benefit financially by receiving the rents which traders paid for stalls in the market. In April 1305, Edward gave his daughter seven more manors in Wiltshire, Dorset, Somerset and the Isle of Wight.[4]

Sometime not long before 8 November 1300, the king's third daughter Margaret of Windsor gave birth to her only child, a son. Inevitably, he was named Jan after his father and his late grandfather. Margaret sent a messenger, Cornelius Gysingham, to her family in England to inform them of the happy news, and on 8 November, Edward I gave Cornelius 100 marks (£66), Queen Marguerite gave him 50 marks, and Edward of Caernarfon gave 40 marks.[5] Although both Margaret and Jan were still only 25, they were to have no more children; perhaps Margaret had some fertility issues (as Jan fathered a few illegitimate offspring as well, he apparently did not), or perhaps the couple, having produced a male heir for the duchy of Brabant and having decided that they had done their duty, rarely spent any more time together.

On 26 November 1300, Edward I wrote to Duke Jan II and to Margaret, and told them that he was sending Richard Havering to them as an envoy 'for the expedition of certain of the king's arduous affairs' in the duchy.[6] A few months later in April 1301, the king sent two men to Holland on the affairs of his daughter Elizabeth as well.[7] This was connected to Elizabeth's rightful dower as Jan I's widow, which she had huge problems accessing from her late husband's kinsmen and successors for the remaining decade and a half of her life, and Edward also sent letters to Count Jan II of Holland and Hainault commenting on the way 'the affairs of the said countess [Elizabeth] progress badly nowadays owing to the hindrances of certain men'. Elizabeth herself sent her valet Hugh Soyrn or Soyru to Holland 'on her affairs' in September 1302, and sent Gerard de Fraxineto in March 1304 and again in April 1305. Sometime around 1300, she sent John Otheleth to the King of the Romans (now Albrecht von Habsburg, older brother of the late Hartmann), on her business as well.[8]

There is much evidence that Elizabeth became very close to her stepmother Queen Marguerite after her return to England. Elizabeth had lost her mother when she was only 8 years old, though it seems doubtful that Marguerite, only three or four years Elizabeth's senior, proved much of a maternal substitute; perhaps the two women's relationship was more like that of sisters. Mary, the sister closest in age to Elizabeth, was a nun, albeit a nun who often left her priory, her eldest sister Eleanor was dead, and her other sister Margaret lived in Brabant and rarely, if ever, visited England. Joan of Acre was Elizabeth's only sister who still lived in England and whom she might have seen on a regular basis.

On 13 May 1301, the king granted the marriage rights of Joan of Acre's 10-year-old son and heir, Gilbert de Clare, to her stepmother Queen Marguerite, and on 27 September 1301 ordered Joan to deliver the custody of her son to the queen. Joan, however, failed to do so: Edward repeated the order after Marguerite informed him that she had sent John de Vastome and John de Godley to find Gilbert and to deliver the letter to his mother.[9] Evidently Joan was reluctant to hand over her son to Marguerite's custody, so it would seem that the countess's relations with the stepmother who was about seven years her junior might not, in contrast to Joan's youngest sister Elizabeth, have been particularly harmonious.

Earlier in 1301, Joan and Elizabeth's brother Edward of Caernarfon had been created prince of Wales and earl of Chester by their father in a magnificent ceremony in the chapter-house of Lincoln Cathedral which was perhaps attended by his three sisters who lived in England. Edward, who turned 17 on 25 April 1301, was the first heir to the English throne to be made prince of Wales.

Chapter 27

The New Countess of Hereford and Essex

Eleanor of Windsor's widower Count Henri III of Bar died in Naples in September 1302, and left his and Eleanor's son Édouard, aged about 6 or 8, as his successor. Edward I heard the news of his son-in-law's death on or shortly before 13 October 1302, via a messenger called 'le Guellars de Ermoyses' or 'le Guellard des Ermeyses' or 'Guellard de Hermosiis, knight', and declared himself 'much grieved' at Henri's death. He wrote to Henri's brothers Sir Jean and Bishop Thibaut, asking them to look after the interests of Henri's children, his grandchildren.[1] On 15 October 1305, Edward sent four men to the county of Bar to negotiate the arrival of his orphaned granddaughter Jeanne de Bar in England, where she would spend most of the rest of her life, and she had certainly travelled to her mother's homeland by May 1306. The four men were William Langton, bishop of Coventry and Lichfield, Henry de Lacy, earl of Lincoln, Sir Otto Grandisson, and Sir Hugh Despenser. A few months earlier on 15 May 1305, in his chamber at Westminster, Edward I had offered Jeanne's marriage to John de Warenne (b. June 1286), heir to the earldoms of Surrey and Sussex, whose wardship had been in the king's hands since the death of John's grandfather in 1304. John, then in his late teens, 'willingly accepted the marriage', though in later years and decades, he spent much time and effort trying to have the marriage annulled and surely came to regret his acceptance of Jeanne as his future wife.[2]

Elizabeth of Rhuddlan spent at least part of 1302 at court with her father, and he granted several favours to courtiers and servants at her request in May that year.[3] Mary of Woodstock left Amesbury on one of her regular visits to see her family in October 1302, and she and her stepmother the queen jointly made a request of the king that month, when they asked that Roger de Troye, one of Mary's servants, might be given the custody of two parks in the county of Cornwall. Edward I granted the request. The following month, Queen Marguerite and Edward of Caernarfon made another joint request of Edward I, so it would seem that the late Queen Leonor's three youngest children had a rather better relationship with their young stepmother than Joan of Acre had.[4]

Now 20 years old, Elizabeth married her second husband at Westminster Abbey on 14 November 1302. Humphrey de Bohun, earl of Hereford and Essex, was some years older than Elizabeth, probably born in 1276: he was said to be 22 or 23 years old at the inquisition post mortem of his father in January/February 1299. The annalist of St Paul's in London, erroneously calling Elizabeth *domina Margareta* or 'Lady Margaret', claimed that the couple married at Caversham near Reading. Although this is incorrect, the manor of Caversham was held by Joan of Acre as part of her dower from Gilbert de Clare, so it is possible that Elizabeth and Humphrey stayed with her sister for a while after their wedding.[5] Humphrey's mother Maud, daughter of Enguerrand, Lord Fiennes, was French, and his uncle Guillaume de Fiennes had been killed at the battle of Courtrai, also known as the Battle of the Golden Spurs, earlier in 1302.[6] On 10 August 1302, Pope Boniface had given permission for Elizabeth and Humphrey to marry, as they were 'related in the third and fourth degrees of kindred'.[7]

Elizabeth's siblings Joan of Acre, Mary of Woodstock and Edward of Caernarfon presumably attended her wedding, though in contrast to Elizabeth's first wedding to the count of Holland in 1297, very little is known about her second. Mary of Woodstock was certainly at court on 12 October 1302, and surely delayed her return to Amesbury to attend her little sister's wedding. She might still, or again, have been with her family in early January 1303, and if so, her stay away from the priory on this occasion was a particularly long one. Sometime between November 1303 and November 1304, Mary went on pilgrimage at various sites around England, and at one point stayed at Ludgershall Castle in Wiltshire, 10 miles from Amesbury. Her father paid her considerable expenses for her journey from Amesbury to visit him at Windsor on two further occasions.[8]

Presumably because the earl was about to marry his daughter, King Edward ordered an inquisition into the extent of Humphrey de Bohun's lands on or a little before 8 October 1302.[9] He owned castles and manors in eight English counties, Essex, Hertfordshire, Middlesex,

Above and below: The monastery of Santa María la Real de Las Huelgas near Burgos, northern Spain, where Lord Edward of England married Doña Leonor of Castile on 1 November 1254. (Bartwatching on Flickr)

Above: The exterior of the Royal Chapel of Seville Cathedral, southern Spain, where Leonor's father Fernando III was buried in 1252 and her brother Alfonso X in 1284, and the Giralda Tower. (Author's Collection)

Left: Burgos Cathedral, northern Spain. Its foundation stone was laid by Fernando III in 1221. (santiago lopez-pastor on Flickr)

Westminster Abbey, burial place of the royal sisters' parents Edward I and Leonor of Castile, and of their grandfather Henry III. Margaret of Windsor married Jan of Brabant here in 1290, and Elizabeth of Rhuddlan married her second husband Humphrey de Bohun in the abbey in 1302. (Author's Collection)

The medieval Palace of Westminster was destroyed in a fire in 1834 and rebuilt as the Houses of Parliament. In 1239 it was the birthplace of King Edward I. (Author's Collection)

Caerphilly Castle, Glamorgan, built by Joan of Acre's first husband the earl of Gloucester, and where she gave birth to her eldest daughter Eleanor in October 1292. (David on Flickr)

Above: Muiderslot or Muiden Castle near Amsterdam, where Elizabeth of Rhuddlan's father-in-law Floris V, count of Holland, was murdered in June 1296. (Martin Morris on Flickr)

Left: The Cathedral of St Michael and Ste Gudule, Brussels, Belgium, where Margaret of Windsor and her husband Duke Jan II of Brabant were buried. (Thomas Quine on Flickr)

The church of St Mary and St Melor, Amesbury, Wiltshire, possibly the abbey church of Amesbury Priory until the Dissolution, and possibly the burial place of Mary of Woodstock in 1332. (Matthew Black on Flickr)

Clare Priory, Suffolk, Joan of Acre's burial place in 1307, converted into a house 300 years later. (sps1955 on flickr)

Left: Tewkesbury Abbey, Gloucestershire, burial place of Joan of Acre's first husband Gilbert 'the Red' de Clare, her son and heir Gilbert de Clare, and her eldest daughter Eleanor Despenser. (Author's Collection)

Below: Ruins of Pleshey Castle, Essex, where Elizabeth of Rhuddlan gave birth to her eldest surviving son John de Bohn, earl of Hereford and Essex, in 1305, and where she spent much of her married life. (Richard Nevell on Flickr)

Audley End, Essex, which stands on the site of Walden Abbey, where Elizabeth of Rhuddlan and several of her children were buried. (sps1955 on Flickr)

Tonbridge Castle, Kent, where Joan of Acre spent time with her new husband the earl of Gloucester after their 1290 wedding. It later passed to their second daughter Margaret de Clare and her Stafford descendants. (Brian Toward on Flickr)

Rhuddlan Castle, North Wales, birthplace of Elizabeth of Rhuddlan in 1282. (Author's Collection)

Above: Windsor Castle, birthplace of Eleanor, countess of Bar, in 1269, and her sister Margaret, duchess of Brabant, in 1275. (Dave-resting on Flickr)

Left: St Peter's Church, Ipswich, which stands on the site of St Peter and St Paul's Priory, where Elizabeth of Rhuddlan married Count Jan I of Holland in January 1297. (Leutha on Wikimedia Commons)

Caldicot Castle, Monmouthshire, where Elizabeth of Rhuddlan gave birth to her twins Edward and William de Bohun in *c*. 1309 or *c*. 1312/13. (Sian on Flickr)

Buckinghamshire, Huntingdonshire, Wiltshire, Gloucestershire and Herefordshire, and was also an important Marcher lord, i.e. was one of the men who held castles and lands in the turbulent English-Welsh borderlands and in Wales itself. Two royal officials, John Barham and Nicholas Wedergrave, took the fealty of Humphrey's tenants at Caldicot Castle in Monmouthshire, Wales, and its vicinity. Even though the tenants claimed that they 'were not accustomed to seek their lord beyond the water of [the River] Severn to do homage', John Barham subsequently told the king that 'after reasoning with them I made them do fealty in the following form: "I will be faithful and loyal, and bear faith and loyalty to King Edward and his heirs, kings of England."' Another of Humphrey de Bohun's important Welsh castles was Brecon, then known as Brecknock or Breghenoke to the English, and John Barham informed the king that more than 2,000 Welsh people performed fealty there. As 'they did not know how to do fealty in English', however, Barham – whose report to King Edward was written in French – took a bilingual clerk with him to translate and to take the Welsh tenants' fealty in their own language. Humphrey de Bohun would, like all of the English elite of the era, have been fluent in French and presumably also in English; one wonders if he and other Marcher lords learnt the Welsh language as well.

Elizabeth's second marriage would prove to be a fruitful one, and in late September 1303, a little over ten months after her wedding, she gave birth to her eldest child, Margaret de Bohun, in Tynemouth, Northumberland on the north-east coast of England. Elizabeth sent a messenger with the odd name of Huward de Seyru to her father to inform him, and the king rewarded Huward with 50 marks (£33.33).[10] She soon conceived again: the heavily pregnant countess of Hereford left Linlithgow in Scotland (her father spent the first few months of 1304 in Scotland), on 27 July 1304 and set out for Knaresborough Castle in Yorkshire. She arrived there on 12 August. Among the people accompanying Elizabeth were her brother Edward's confessor and two monks of Westminster Abbey, Robert Bures and Guido Asshewell, and the two Westminster monks brought one of the abbey's most sacred relics with them for Elizabeth's use: the girdle of the Virgin Mary, which was believed to offer great assistance to women in labour.[11]

On 10 September 1304, rather less than a year after the birth of her daughter Margaret, Elizabeth bore her first son, whom she named Humphrey after his father, at Knaresborough Castle. Elizabeth was churched or purified at Knaresborough on 11 October, and was entertained by Robert, the king's minstrel, and fifteen of his fellow minstrels.[12] A damaged account of Elizabeth's household exists for the year 1304/05, and reveals that she offered 4*s* 5*d* while attending Mass on the day of her purification, 11 October 1304. She was still in Knaresborough on 13 October, when she made another offering at the shrine of Saint Robert of Knaresborough.[13]

Elizabeth suffered a tragic loss on 28 October 1304, when her 7-week-old son Humphrey de Bohun died at Fulham in Middlesex, and he was buried on 8 November at Westminster Abbey. Humphrey was placed in a lead coffin at Fulham with four candles burning around his body, and on the day of his burial, 120 candle-holders were purchased and a hearse was hired. Offerings for his soul were made at Mass, the sum of five shillings was given to the Friars Preacher of London, and four shillings was paid for ringing bells at the end of the funeral. Another great loss came twenty-five months later, when Elizabeth's eldest child Margaret de Bohun died as well at the age of 2, and she was buried with her brother.[14]

The countess of Hereford kept in frequent touch with her father, and in one year on the Octave of the Assumption (22 August), either 1303, 1304 or 1305, while she was staying at the royal place of Woodstock near Oxford, Elizabeth wrote to the king with family news.[15] Sometime between 20 November 1304 and 19 November 1305, her father's thirty-third regnal year, she stayed at the Tower of London.[16] In 1304/05, Elizabeth had £98 from her father to buy clothes, and £109 in 1305/06. She was also given £50 to buy a new carriage, and Edward I paid off her debts in Holland.[17] Carriages or coaches, pulled by five horses, were a common way for noble ladies of the era to travel, but were very expensive to buy and to maintain, and as they had no suspension were hardly the most comfortable mode of transport on the rutted, dusty or muddy roads and tracks of medieval England.

Chapter 28

The Prince of Wales and his Sisters

The copious correspondence sent by Edward of Caernarfon, prince of Wales, earl of Chester and count of Ponthieu, fortuitously survives for a few months in 1304/05. The young heir to the throne had a terrible quarrel with his father in August 1305, and Edward I banished him from court for a few weeks and temporarily broke up his household. Edward of Caernarfon's letters reveal that his sisters Joan of Acre, Mary of Woodstock and Elizabeth of Rhuddlan came to his aid during this difficult time, as did their young stepmother Queen Marguerite. The prince's main aim was to persuade his father to restore to him two young noblemen who were his close companions, Piers Gaveston and Gilbert de Clare of Thomond (born in 1281 and the namesake nephew of Joan of Acre's late husband Gilbert 'the Red', earl of Gloucester, though often confused by modern writers with Joan's son and heir, yet another Gilbert de Clare). Edward wrote to Elizabeth of Rhuddlan on 4 August to tell her that their father had allowed him the company of two valets, John Haustede and John Weston, and asked his sister to ask Queen Marguerite to intercede with the king and to try to persuade him to allow the prince the company of Gilbert and Piers as well.[1] John Haustede was Edward of Caernarfon's milk-brother, having shared a wet-nurse; Piers Gaveston was a young Gascon placed in the prince's household by the king in or a little before 1300, and Edward fell passionately in love with him.[2]

King Edward was often exasperated with his children, but could and did easily forgive his daughters, whom he loved dearly and to whom he often showed remarkable indulgence. His son and heir was, however, another matter; Edward of Caernarfon would one day become king of England, and was, understandably and necessarily, held to higher standards than his older sisters. Their dreadful quarrel of 1305 was eventually resolved, though not easily, and in early 1307 the two men quarrelled again badly. Joan of Acre once again defied her father, and lent her brother her seal so that he could order goods; Edward, whose own seal had been confiscated by their father, gratefully returned Joan's to her on 21 July 1305.[3] As well as his direct correspondence with Joan, the prince of Wales also sent eleven letters to her husband Ralph de Monthermer, calling him 'the noble man, his dearest brother'. The prince referred to Edward I as 'our dear lord the king, our father and yours' in the letters to Ralph. It certainly appears that the prince of Wales felt considerable affection and respect for the humble squire his sister had married in 1297.[4]

Edward of Caernarfon wrote to Mary seven times in 1304/05. He sent her a greyhound as a gift on one occasion, and on another, ordered an organ (i.e. a musical instrument) for her, though it arrived at Langley, where he was staying, broken and had to be repaired before he sent it on to Mary at Amesbury Priory. Mary also wrote to her brother, and invited him to come and stay with her.[5] Edward called Elizabeth of Rhuddlan his *bele soer*, 'fair sister', as well as *la noble dame sa treschere soer* ('the noble lady, his dearest sister'), and it seems that the two siblings, only twenty months apart in age, were genuinely very close. Edward sent six letters to Elizabeth directly in 1304/05, and wrote another four which concerned her affairs. One of the letters asked Elizabeth to send him her white greyhound, as he had a beautiful white greyhound himself, and had a 'great desire to have puppies from them'. Possibly Elizabeth complied with this request immediately, as the prince wrote to her husband the earl of Hereford just a day later, thanking him for the greyhounds which Humphrey had sent him. Edward sent two pregnant mares, and foals which they had previously borne, to Elizabeth from his stud-farm as a gift. Another letter written on 1 July 1305 was addressed to the prince's *treschere soer* or 'dearest sister', though which sister is unclear.[6]

It is unfortunate that Edward of Caernarfon's letters only survive for the year 1304/05, though it seems reasonable to assume that the prince kept in touch with his sisters in other years as well just as frequently as he did in 1304/05. Elizabeth was pregnant for the third time during the summer of 1305 when her brother wrote to her, and on 23 November 1305 at Pleshey in Essex, three years after her wedding, she bore her third child and second son, John de Bohun. John was Elizabeth and Humphrey's oldest child who lived into adulthood, and succeeded his father as earl of Hereford and Essex. Elizabeth's eldest child Margaret de Bohun, still alive when her brother John was born, died on 7 February 1306.[7]

The unwilling nun Mary of Woodstock was with her father in East Anglia on 14 February 1305 and probably with him again at Westminster on 29 March and 1 April, and between 27 June and 4 October 1305, visited her little half-brothers Thomas of Brotherton and Edmund of Woodstock no fewer than eleven times, staying with them for up to five days on each occasion (Thomas turned 5 years old in June 1305 and Edmund's fourth birthday fell in August that year). The accounts of Thomas and Edmund's household reveal purchases of various types of sugar, dill, dried ginger and sandalwood from apothecaries of London and Florence before one of Mary's visits. On 12 May 1305, Mary was said to be 'dwelling at Ambresbury' for once, but by 20 October that year was at court with her father yet again.[8] Mary's remarkably frequent visits to see Thomas and Edmund show how close she was to her half-brothers and how affectionate she felt towards them, and Elizabeth obviously felt the same: her daughter Margaret lived in the two boys' household between 1303 and 1305. Although little Margaret de Bohun sadly died at the age of only 2, Elizabeth was to name another of her daughters 'Margaret', more evidence of her closeness to her stepmother.

Sometime before 8 May 1306, Queen Marguerite gave birth to her third and youngest child, and her only daughter, Eleanor. The child's date and place of birth are, unlike those of her older brothers Thomas and Edmund, not known for certain, though the chronicler of Westminster Abbey says that she was born on 6 May 1306. The king was now almost 67 years old, and the little girl was half a century younger than his eldest daughter, the child assumed to have been born prematurely to Leonor of Castile on 29 May 1255. Little Eleanor was perhaps named in honour of the late Queen Leonor, and it would be interesting to know whether this was Edward I's own idea or Marguerite's. It may be, however, that the child's name was chosen to honour the memory of her late half-sister, the countess of Bar (1269–98), or her late Provençal grandmother.

If the Westminster chronicler gives young Eleanor's date of birth correctly, she was only 2 days old when her father opened negotiations for her future marriage on 8 May 1306. The intended bridegroom was Robert of Burgundy (b. *c.* 1300), heir to his mother Mahaut (d. 1329), countess of Artois in her own right, and to his late father Othon (d. 1302), the count palatine of Burgundy.[9] In the end this marriage did not take place because Eleanor died young, and Robert also died in 1315 at the age of about 15, unmarried and childless, leaving his elder sister Jeanne as his heir. In August 1306, the king bound himself and his son Edward of Caernarfon to provide 10,000 marks for Eleanor's marriage and 5,000 marks for her trousseau, to be paid within seven years, 'and to find her proper sustenance according to her estate until she is married'. The king also bound himself and his son to provide lands for Eleanor's brothers Thomas of Brotherton and Edmund of Woodstock.[10] On 31 August 1306, the king assigned a further 1,000 marks (£666) to pay for the wedding of 'our dear daughter Eleanor' (*nostre chere file Alianore*).[11]

Also on 8 May 1306, King Edward arranged another marriage when he wrote to Agnès, dowager duchess of Burgundy, suggesting his grandson Édouard of Bar (now about 10 or 12 years old) as a possible husband for one of her daughters. He also sent a letter to Édouard's uncle Thibaut of Bar, bishop of Liège and former bishop of Metz, asking him to promote the marriage.[12] Duchess Agnès was born *c.* 1260 as the youngest child of Louis IX of France and Marguerite of Provence, and hence was King Edward's much younger first cousin. Her husband Robert, duke of Burgundy, had died a few weeks earlier on 31 March 1306, and she was regent of the large and wealthy duchy for her eldest son Duke Hugues V until he came of age in 1311. Agnès agreed that this marriage was an excellent idea, and matters progressed remarkably quickly: on 13 June 1306, just a few weeks after the king of England dictated his letter, the young Duke Hugues of Burgundy issued a charter referring to the 'marriage which shall be made between our dear and beloved cousin Édouard, of the county of Bar, and Marie, our dear sister'.[13] Marie of Burgundy was the youngest daughter of Duke Robert and Duchess Agnès, born probably in the late 1290s, and her grandfather Louis IX been canonised shortly before she was born. She might have been the child with whom Agnès was pregnant when Duke Robert made his will on 25 March 1298, as she was, unlike her older siblings, not named in it, though Robert did mention his wife's pregnancy.[14] Her older sisters Marguerite (b. *c.* 1290) and Jeanne (b. *c.* 1293) married two of their royal French cousins, and both became queens.[15]

Chapter 29

Three Weddings and a Death

Edward of Caernarfon, prince of Wales, earl of Chester, count of Ponthieu and now duke of Aquitaine as well, was knighted at Westminster on Sunday, 22 May 1306, the feast of Pentecost. Well over 250 other men were knighted on the same, splendid occasion, and two of Edward's nieces married within a few days of their uncle's knighting. The late Eleanor of Windsor's only daughter Jeanne de Bar, who was no more than 11 years old and perhaps even younger, wed John de Warenne, born on 30 June 1286 and hence almost 20 at the time of his wedding. John was the heir to the earldoms of Surrey and Sussex formerly held by his late grandfather; his father William de Warenne was killed jousting in late 1286 when John was just a few months old. After John's grandfather John the elder died in 1304, John became a ward of the king until he came of age at 21, and an account where Edward I paid for his household expenses and necessities still exists.[1] John's sister Alice de Warenne, born a few months after their father's death, married Edmund Fitzalan, earl of Arundel, probably also in May 1306, though at first he refused to marry her.[2] Jeanne de Bar received almost £170 from her grandfather at the time of her wedding, to purchase robes, coffers, horses and carriages for herself. Young though she was, Jeanne already employed her own minstrels: among the many dozens of performers hired by Edward I to entertain the new knights during the banquet in Westminster Hall after the mass knighting on 22 May, shortly before Jeanne's wedding, was *Mahu qui est oue la Dammoisele de Baar*, 'Mahu who is with the Damsel of Bar'. He probably played the tabor, i.e. a small, portable snare drum.[3]

In February 1307 a few months after Jeanne's wedding to John de Warenne, her grandfather did the young man a remarkably generous favour by pardoning all his ancestors' debts to the treasury. The debts amounted to an enormous £6,693, the equivalent of a few years' income for John.[4] Probably the king intended to get the couple's marriage off on the right foot, but unfortunately, the Bar-Warenne match proved to be an unhappy and childless disaster. By May 1313 when Jeanne was still only in her teens, and probably well before, the couple lived apart. Jeanne's uncle, who by then had succeeded his father as Edward II, sent his servant William Aune to John de Warenne's castle of Conisbrough to bring Jeanne to him.[5] Their marriage might have been on the rocks as early as August 1309, most probably before Jeanne was even old enough for it to have been consummated, when Edward II gave the earl of Surrey permission 'to make whom he please heir to the lands he holds' as long as the earl gave him surety that 'he will not disinherit any heir he may have by the king's niece Joan, his wife'.

A letter from Pope Clement VI dated late February 1344 states that John and Jeanne had then 'lived together for thirty-two years'. This might mean that the couple had consummated their marriage and begun living together around early 1312 or a little before, and if this is accurate, it might indicate that Jeanne was the younger of Eleanor of Windsor's two children, born perhaps in 1296 and therefore 15 or 16 when she began living with her husband. It seems unlikely that she was born in 1294 if she only began cohabiting with her husband in early 1312. John de Warenne already had an illegitimate son, whom he named William after his father, by 24 August 1310, and by August 1316 he had fathered two more sons named Thomas and John with his mistress Maud Nerford. He ultimately had two illegitimate sons called William, one who became a knight and the other who became the prior of Horton in Kent and of Castle Acre in Norfolk. The prior, Master William de Warenne, was said in 1338/39 to have been born in his father's castle of Conisbrough, and he was already a prior then and therefore was already an adult. If Jeanne was also living in the castle of Conisbrough when one of her husband's mistresses was bearing his children there, this would certainly go a long way to explaining her unwillingness to continue to live with him, and her uncle's sending a man there to fetch her.[6]

The other royal marriage of May 1306 proved much more successful. Joan of Acre's eldest daughter Eleanor de Clare, aged 13 and a half, married Hugh Despenser the Younger, who was about 17 or 18. He was a grandson of the late earl of Warwick, William Beauchamp (d. 1298), and his paternal grandmother Aline Basset, Lady Despenser (d. 1281) married Roger Bigod (d. 1306), earl of Norfolk, as her second husband and his first wife. Hugh's older half-sister Maud Chaworth had married Edward I's nephew Henry of Lancaster some years before, and Hugh had some impressive family connections, though he would not himself inherit an earldom. His father Hugh Despenser the Elder was still alive, and Hugh held no lands of his own at all. It is possible that Joan of Acre felt that her eldest daughter was somewhat disparaged by her marriage given that she would not become a countess, though as Joan and her sister Eleanor of Windsor had sent a letter about an ongoing feud between Despenser the Elder and 'John Lovel the bastard' in *c.* 1287, she must have known the family for a long time. Edward I clearly deemed the young man to be a suitable husband for his eldest granddaughter, and he certainly thought very highly of the abilities of Hugh the Younger's father: he often sent Hugh the Elder on important diplomatic missions abroad, to the pope, the kings of France and Germany, the Guardians of Scotland, and others. King Edward paid Hugh the Elder £2,000 for his son and heir's marriage, gave his granddaughter Eleanor £29 to buy jewels for her wedding and £10 to buy robes for her attendants, and hired two harpers to perform for the wedding guests.[7] On their wedding day, Hugh the Younger was given letters of protection to go on the king's latest military campaign to Scotland.[8] The Clare/Despenser marriage lasted for just over twenty years until November 1326, when Hugh the Younger was executed, and produced at least ten children.

Edward I had fumed over his daughter's marriage to Ralph de Monthermer in 1297, but with little other choice had come to accept it, and in the early 1300s pragmatically realised that he could use the marriage of one of Joan's Monthermer daughters to his own advantage. On 7 October 1306, he asked the pope to issue a dispensation for Joan and Ralph's eldest child Mary de Monthermer to marry Duncan MacDuff, earl of Fife (*Duncan de Fyf*) as they were related in the fourth degree of kindred.[9] Mary was barely 9 years old, and Duncan was a few years older, born in 1289. Most confusingly, Duncan was the grandson of Joan of Acre's first husband Gilbert 'the Red' de Clare, earl of Gloucester, via his mother Joan de Clare (b. *c.* 1264/65), Gilbert's younger daughter from his first marriage to Alice de Lusignan. Duncan never knew his father, also called Duncan, as he had been murdered before he was born, and his mother married her second husband Gervase Avenel some years later; Duncan grew up in England. Pope Clement V finally issued the required dispensation for consanguinity a year later on 3 November 1307, by which time both King Edward and Mary's mother were dead.[10] Joan of Acre's feelings about her daughter's marriage to her late husband's Scottish grandson are unrecorded.

Joan of Acre, countess of Gloucester and Hertford, died at Clare Castle in Suffolk on 23 April 1307. She was 35 or almost, and it may be, given her age and the pattern of her pregnancies over the years, that she died during a difficult pregnancy or after childbirth. This is only speculation, however, and there is no direct evidence to prove it, and if Joan did give birth to a child in 1307, s/he certainly did not live long. Three hundred miles away in Carlisle, Edward I heard of his daughter's death on or a little before 6 May. He asked all the bishops of England and the abbots of Westminster, Waltham, St Albans, Evesham and St Augustine's Priory in Canterbury to 'cause the soul of Joan, countess of Gloucester and Hertford, the king's daughter, who has just died, to be commended to God by all the men of religion' within their diocese 'by the singing of masses and other pious works'.

On the other hand, Joan might have been seriously ill for some time and in March 1307 was believed to be dead, as on 1 April 1307 in Carlisle, the king told his chancellor to order 'all archbishops, bishops, abbots, priors, chapters of cathedrals and collegiate churches, universities, friars preachers [Dominicans] and minor [Franciscans] and other religious of the realm' to sing masses 'for the soul of the king's daughter Joan, countess of Gloucester, who is commanded to God'. This was just over three weeks before Joan did in fact die, so unless the king's letter of 1 April was dated incorrectly, it seems that false news of Joan's passing had been carried from Suffolk to her father in Carlisle. 'Commanded to God' or 'called to God' was a typical contemporary and politely euphemistic idiom for stating that someone had died ('on whom God has worked His will' was another). Edward referred to her as *Johanne nostre chiere fille*, 'Joan, our dear daughter' in the order of 1 April, which was issued in French; the order of 6 May was written in Latin and called Joan *Johannam ... filiam nostram carissimam*, 'our dearest daughter'. Her eldest child Gilbert de Clare was with his grandfather at Carlisle in the spring of 1307, and must have heard the news of his mother's death (as well as, presumably, the false news) at the same time as the king.[11]

Joan chose to be buried at the Augustinian priory in Clare, Suffolk, which had been founded by her first husband's father Richard de Clare, earl of Gloucester, in 1248. She specifically requested to be interred in the chapel dedicated to Saint Vincent of Zaragoza (died *c.* 304) which she herself had established in the priory, a request which perhaps reveals her awareness of her Spanish heritage. Although not a particularly popular saint in England in the Middle Ages, there was an awareness of St Vincent in certain quarters: Abingdon Abbey, a few miles from Oxford, obtained some of his relics in the twelfth century. Perhaps Joan's long stay in childhood with her maternal grandmother the dowager queen of Castile had fostered her knowledge of and interest in the Spanish part of her ancestry more than was the case with her sisters, and given her interest in St Vincent, she would surely have been delighted to know that her own Spanish grandfather King Fernando III would be canonised as San Fernando centuries later. At an uncertain date before 1284, Joan had received a letter from Suger, bishop of Cadiz, commending two Castilian envoys, 'Peter Arnold de Vico' and 'Peter Reymund de Ardir', to her. Bishop Suger was a chaplain of Joan's uncle Alfonso X of Castile, and one of Alfonso's envoys both to England and to the pope.[12] This also reveals Joan's interest in and association with her mother's homeland, and perhaps that she maintained a correspondence with her learned Castilian uncle.

Joan's inquisition post mortem was held in June 1307, and reveals that she owned castles, lands, manors and tenements in Oxfordshire, Berkshire, Wiltshire, Somerset, Devon, Dorset, Kent, Cambridgeshire, Huntingdonshire, Buckinghamshire, Northamptonshire, Essex, Hertfordshire, Sussex, Surrey, Hampshire, Norfolk, Suffolk, Gloucestershire, Worcestershire, Monmouthshire and Glamorgan as her enormous dower from Gilbert 'the Red'. Among much else, she held Tonbridge ('Thonebregg') Castle in Kent, Clare Castle in Suffolk, Hanley Castle in Worcestershire, and the Welsh castles of Usk, Caerleon, Tregruk, Caerphilly, Cardiff, Dinas Powys, Kenfig, Neath, Newport, Llantrisant and Llanbethian. She also held various lands and castles in Ireland including Kilkenny Castle.[13]

Joan's eldest child and heir, Gilbert, was not quite 16 when she died, and the youngest of her eight children, Edward de Monthermer, was barely 3. The village of Clare, and the priory where Joan was buried on 26 April 1307, passed into the ownership of her third daughter Elizabeth de Burgh, née de Clare, in 1317, and Elizabeth held the manor for the remaining forty-three years of her life and spent a lot of time there; she often referred to herself as 'Lady of Clare'.[14] Ralph de Monthermer lived as a widower for more than eleven years, and married Isabella, Lady Hastings, one of the sisters of Joan of Acre's son-in-law Hugh Despenser the Younger, in or soon before November 1318. With Joan's death, Ralph lost his right to call himself earl of Gloucester, and although Edward I had briefly granted Ralph the Scottish earldom of Atholl in October 1306, he soon changed his mind. Edward executed his kinsman the earl of Atholl, John de Strathbogie, as an adherent of his enemy Robert Bruce in early November 1306, but shortly after granting the earldom to Ralph, he decided to allow Strathbogie's son David to have it. He gave Ralph 10,000 marks (£6,666) instead to purchase lands 'to support himself and his children by the late countess of Gloucester, the king's daughter' in June 1307.[15]

As early as 18 August 1307, Ralph's brother-in-law Edward of Caernarfon, by then king of England for a few weeks, allowed Ralph's stepson Gilbert de Clare to have possession of his inheritance and to claim his rightful title even though he was still a few years under age; Gilbert did not turn 21 until late April or early May 1312.[16] At some point during the eighteen years between Joan of Acre's death and his own in 1325, Ralph de Monthermer received a petition from Juliana Everard, widow of the London goldsmith William Everard. The distraught Juliana claimed that she and her children were 'entirely impoverished' because her late husband had made a number of loans to Joan of Acre, but she had never paid them back. As a result, William and Juliana had been forced to sell some of their property in London.[17]

Chapter 30

Death of the King

On 7 July 1307, two and a half months after Joan of Acre's death, Edward I died in a remote corner of his kingdom, at Burgh-by-Sands near Carlisle, close to the Scottish border. He was 68 years old and died of dysentery on his way to campaign against Robert Bruce, who had been crowned king of Scotland the previous year against Edward's wishes. King Edward had made his will in Acre on Saturday, 20 June 1271, while on crusade in the Holy Land, and although he lived for another three and a half decades, he never updated it (or at least if he did, the newer version has never been found). His father Henry III was still alive at the time, and in the will Edward talked about the dower that would fall to 'our dear wife Alianore' in case of his death and made arrangements for the guardianship of his underage children, John of Windsor, who died a few weeks later, Henry of Windsor, and Eleanor of Windsor.[1]

Edward of Caernarfon, now 23, succeeded as Edward II. The new king was in or near London when he heard the news of his father's demise 300 miles away, and swiftly travelled north to Carlisle, where he was proclaimed king of England and lord of Ireland 'by descent and heritage' on 20 July. Edward I's body was taken south, and on 27 October 1307, he was laid to rest in Westminster Abbey with his first wife Leonor of Castile and his father Henry III. Queen Marguerite outlived him by eleven years, and rather than returning to her native France, spent the rest of her life in her stepson's kingdom. She never remarried.

Edward I was outlived by only seven of the many, at least seventeen and perhaps nineteen or twenty, children he had fathered: Margaret, Mary, Elizabeth and Edward from his first marriage, and Thomas, Edmund and Eleanor from his second. On 1 November just days after his father's funeral, Edward II attended the wedding of his niece Margaret de Clare at Berkhamsted Castle. The bridegroom was Sir Piers Gaveston, whom Edward had recalled from the exile the old king had imposed on him earlier in the year as soon as he knew that his father was dead, and whom he had created earl of Cornwall on 6 August 1307. Joan of Acre's second daughter Margaret, just 13, became a countess on marriage to a man who was involved in an intense and perhaps sexual relationship with her uncle. If Joan had been alive, one wonders whether her brother would have dared to marry off her daughter to his lover, and Joan had perhaps shared her father's disquiet over Edward II's passion for the Gascon nobleman and how it might, and indeed did, affect Edward's relations with his earls and barons.

The young king purchased a 'roan-coloured palfrey' for £20 as a wedding gift for his niece, and spent £30 on expensive silk cloth and pearls for Margaret and her attendants. Edward also provided the large sum of £7, 10*s* and 6*d* in coins to be thrown over the couple's head 'at their entrance into the said church'.[2] Margaret almost certainly was too young to live with Gaveston as his wife or to consummate their marriage, and marrying the king's niece made little difference to Gaveston's relationship with Edward II. Gaveston held a jousting tournament at his castle of Wallingford in early December 1307 to celebrate the marriage that made him a member of the royal family. Margaret's uncle-in-law Humphrey de Bohun, earl of Hereford, was one of the noblemen the new earl of Cornwall and his band of young knights defeated, to the rage and humiliation of Hereford himself and, especially, Guy Beauchamp, earl of Warwick, soon to emerge as the royal favourite's most deadly enemy.

According to the cartulary of Walden Abbey in Essex, where Elizabeth of Rhuddlan and some of her children were buried, Elizabeth gave birth to her son Humphrey – her second son who bore this name – at Lochmaben Castle, an English outpost in southern Scotland, sometime in 1307.[3] Humphrey's exact date of birth, or even the month, is not recorded in the cartulary, but he must have been born at least nine months plus forty days (the period after giving birth before a woman was purified or 'churched') after his older brother John was born on 23 November 1305, so January 1307 is the earliest possible date. John de Bohun's inquisition post mortem taken in February 1336, however, indicates that his brother and heir Humphrey was born later than 1307. Almost all of the jurors thought that Humphrey was either 26 or 27 years old in February 1336; the London jurors said he was 24; and one Welsh jury said he was 25. None of them stated that he was 28 or 29. Two other juries in Wales said very specifically on 12 and 19 February 1336 that Humphrey was 'aged

26 years on the feast of St Nicholas last', which gives him a date of birth of *c.* 6 December 1309.[4]

Most unusually for a medieval nobleman, Humphrey de Bohun never married, and he did not take part in his cousin Edward III's wars in Scotland and France from the 1330s onwards, unlike his younger brothers Edward and William and unlike almost every other English nobleman of the era. Humphrey, therefore, perhaps suffered from some kind of disability or long-term illness, though he lived until 1361 when he was about 52 or 54. His elder brother John married twice but had no children either, and died at age 30. The de Bohun siblings' cousin Edward III gave John de Bohun permission on 24 October 1330 to allow his younger brother Edward to 'discharge the duties of his office as constable of England, while he is unable to do so by reason of bodily infirmity'.[5] It seems as though both of Elizabeth of Rhuddlan's eldest surviving sons might have suffered from a disability, or from a long-term illness that occasionally flared up; Edward III's statement that Edward de Bohun could fulfil his brother's duties 'while he is unable to do so' implies that John was expected to recover.

It is extremely difficult to work out the correct dates of birth of Elizabeth of Rhuddlan's many children. The Ford Abbey Cartulary says that her daughter Margaret de Bohun II was born on 3 April 1311, and the Llanthony Abbey Cartulary says that Margaret was her eighth child.[6] It is certain that Elizabeth's sons Edward and William were twins, but even so, fitting all the dates of birth of her other children into the necessarily narrow timeframe is problematic. Her eldest surviving son John, earl of Hereford, was, according to his uncle Edward II, who took John's homage for his earldoms in October 1326 a few weeks before he turned 21, born on 23 November 1305, and we somehow have to fit in the births of Humphrey, the twins Edward and William, and Eleanor between John in November 1305 and Margaret in April 1311.

The Llanthony Abbey Cartulary gives the birth order of the de Bohun children as Margaret I (died young), Humphrey I (died young), John, Humphrey II, Edward and William the twins, Eleanor, Margaret II, Aeneas and Isabella, and specifically states that Eleanor was the elder daughter. There is other evidence, however, which states that Margaret was older than Eleanor, and she married in 1325, several years before Eleanor did. On the other hand, Humphrey de Bohun's will of 1319 names his daughter Eleanor before his daughter Margaret, and the 1361 will of his son Humphrey II, earl of Hereford, also names Eleanor, countess of Ormond, before Margaret, countess of Devon.[7] This indicates that Eleanor was indeed older than her sister. Isabella was certainly the youngest de Bohun child and was born on 5 May 1316 shortly before Elizabeth of Rhuddlan died. The youngest son, Aeneas, was probably born *c.* 1312/14, and the twins Edward and William were certainly born before 2 February 1313 (the feast of the Purification in the sixth year of their uncle Edward II's reign) when their father acquired the manor of 'Rothyng Marcii' for himself, to pass eventually to 'William de Bohoun his son'.[8] It is also certain that Humphrey II was older than the twins, as he was their elder brother John's heir on John's death in 1336.

Although Elizabeth gave birth at least nine times in the thirteen and a half years of her second marriage, her sister Duchess Margaret is not known to have become pregnant again after bearing her son Jan in *c.* October 1300. Given, however, that Elizabeth certainly died after giving birth and that the same fate might, given Eleanor of Windsor and Joan of Acre's ages when they passed away, have befallen them as well, Margaret surely did not shed too many tears over her lack of pregnancies. Little is known of her life as duchess as Brabant. Judging by the evidence of his charters, Jan II spent most of his time in Brussels, where he issued sixty-seven of his 137 charters whose place of issue is specified. He issued another five in Leuven, six in Tervuren, three in Antwerp, six in Mechelen, three in Maastricht, four in Keulen, and twelve in Nijvel. Assuming that the couple did not lead completely separate lives, this reveals the towns that Margaret would have known. One Dutch chronicler, Lodewijk van Velthem, stated that Edward I once visited his daughter in Brussels, though looking at Edward's itinerary, it is hard to see when this visit might have taken place.[9]

Chapter 31

Coronation

On 10 November 1307, Edward II ordered the sheriffs of Essex and Herefordshire to give Humphrey de Bohun and Elizabeth of Rhuddlan the money his late father had granted to them (£40, 10*s* 10*d* yearly from Essex and £20 yearly from Herefordshire) in November in the thirty-first year of his reign, ie. in November 1302, just after their wedding. Apparently the sheriffs were reluctant to do so, as Edward had to repeat the order to them eighteen months later.[1] Humphrey, almost certainly with Elizabeth in his company, spent much time with her brother between the autumn of 1307 and the spring of 1308: he witnessed twelve of Edward II's thirty-eight charters issued in the first year of his reign, all of them between September 1307 and March 1308.[2]

Mary of Woodstock was probably away from Amesbury and with her brother at Langley in Hertfordshire – Edward II's favourite residence – on or just before 14 November 1307, when the king granted a favour to a man named Robert Martyn of Bristol at Mary's request. Just a few days later, Edward gave his first nurse, Mary Maunsel of Caernarfon, seventy-three acres of land of Caernarfon rent-free for life.[3] His favours to his sisters Mary and Elizabeth and to his former nurse in November 1307 reveal Edward's affection for his family and for those who had looked after him in childhood, and also that he was, like his father, willing to allow his sisters to intercede with him on behalf of others and to enjoy a measure of influence. He took over from his father the responsibility for his three young half-siblings Thomas, Edmund and Eleanor, and on 9 October 1307 paid £53, 6*s* 8*d* for the children's expenses.[4] Thomas of Brotherton, who turned 7 years old a month before his father's death, was now heir to the English throne and would hold that position until Edward II's son was born in November 1312.

King Edward left England for France on 22 January 1308, and married his long-term fiancée, Philip IV of France and the late Queen Juana of Navarre's 12-year-old daughter Isabella, three days later in

Boulogne. His sister Margaret and Duke Jan II travelled the 140 miles from Brussels to attend the great royal wedding, and it was the first time Margaret had seen her little brother since the summer of 1297 when he was 13. Also present were their stepmother Queen Marguerite and her mother Marie of Brabant, the dowager queen of France; Philip IV, the bride's father, who was Marguerite's half-brother and Marie's stepson; Philip's eldest son Louis, king of Navarre since the death of his mother Juana in 1305; Charles of Salerno, king of Sicily and Naples and titular king of Jerusalem, who was Edward I's cousin; and Albrecht von Habsburg, King of the Romans, older brother of Joan of Acre's first fiancé, who attended with his wife Elisabeth of Carinthia and their son Leopold, duke of Austria. Albrecht would be murdered by his nephew Johann later the same year. The counts of Flanders, Namur, Hainault and Holland, Nevers, St Pol, Dreux and Savoy were there too.[5]

The bridal couple arrived at Dover on 7 February 1308, and Edward's two sisters who still lived in England, Mary and Elizabeth, were among the welcoming party who greeted them. Their cousin Henry of Lancaster, second son of Edward I's brother Edmund and the younger brother of the earl of Lancaster, also travelled to Dover.[6] Jan II and Margaret of Brabant sailed across the Channel to England to attend King Edward and Queen Isabella's coronation in Westminster Abbey on 25 February, as did Amadeus, count of Savoy, who would probably have married Joan of Acre in or shortly after 1297 if she had not secretly wed Ralph de Monthermer. Also present were Duke Jan of Brabant's brother-in-law Henry, count of Luxembourg, elected King of the Romans later in 1308 after Albrecht von Habsburg's murder and promoted to Holy Roman Emperor in 1312, and Arthur II, duke of Brittany (b. 1262), first cousin of Edward I's children, who had succeeded his long-lived father in 1305.[7] It was the first time, as far as is known, that Margaret of Windsor had seen her sister Mary of Woodstock since she departed from England in 1297, and again as far as is known, 1308 would be the last time she would ever see Mary, Elizabeth and Edward II in person. The siblings did exchange letters over the next few years, however. Margaret and Jan had brought Edward a precious gift: a vial of the holy oil of St Thomas Becket of Canterbury, which they intended the king to use for his anointing at the coronation. Edward and his council decided against it, however, and a few years later the oil would cause him some political embarrassment (see below).[8]

Edward II gave Piers Gaveston a prominent role during the coronation ceremony, and discourteously talked only or mostly to him at the banquet held afterwards in Westminster Hall. His excessive favouritism, his giving the regency to Gaveston in early 1308 when one of his little half-brothers should have been appointed as nominal regent, as was customary, angered much of his baronage. During a parliament held shortly after the coronation, a large group of earls and barons, led by Henry de Lacy, earl of Lincoln, demanded Gaveston's exile. Edward refused for months, and the kingdom teetered on the brink of war. Finally, in June 1308, he was forced to give in, and sent Gaveston to Ireland as his lord lieutenant. Gaveston, deprived of his earldom of Cornwall but compensated with numerous lands and money by the infatuated king, lived there for a year with Margaret de Clare.

Elizabeth of Rhuddlan was described in a letter of 1308 as one of those who were 'close to the queen' (*familiares regine*), and might even have brought Isabella into the baronial opposition to Gaveston, though the two women's attitude towards the earl of Cornwall is uncertain. The letter of 1308 was sent by Brother Roger de Aldenham of Westminster Abbey, an enemy of Gaveston who resented the royal favourite's interference in the abbey's affairs, so Aldenham's claim that both Queen Isabella and Countess Elizabeth hated Gaveston should probably be taken with a pinch of salt.[9] Humphrey de Bohun witnessed his last charter of Edward II's on 22 March 1308 and his next on 2 August that year, so he and Elizabeth seem to have left court for a while.[10] Possibly this reveals Elizabeth's hostility to the man who was her niece Margaret de Clare's husband and her brother's probable lover, or perhaps simply that the de Bohuns judged it politic to depart from the fevered atmosphere of court for a while. It might also be that Elizabeth, who was pregnant numerous times between 1303 and 1316, gave birth to another child this year.

Chapter 32

Downfall of a Royal Favourite

In November 1308, Edward II ordered the sheriffs of Hampshire and Wiltshire to provide firewood for Mary of Woodstock, in line with a grant made to her by their father. She was called 'the king's sister Mary, nun of Fontevraud', and the firewood was to be sent to her 'when staying at Amesbury'. This is a revealing statement which shows that Mary frequently did not stay at the priory. In the same month, a servant of Mary's called Michael Aune or Anne was referenced, when the king appointed him lifelong keeper of the forest of Kingswood ('Kyngeswode') in Gloucestershire. This almost certainly means that Mary had requested her brother to make this appointment, and therefore was with him or at least in contact with him.[1] Michael Aune worked for Mary for a long time; he took news to Edward II of the birth of one of their great-nieces at Amesbury in 1317.[2]

A few months later in the spring of 1309, the prioress of Amesbury died, and 'our lady, Madam Mary' wrote to her brother on the matter on 9 May. Typically, she was not at the priory at the time but in Swainston on the Isle of Wight, 7 miles from the manor of Freshwater ('Freskwatre') which her father had granted to her a few years before and which she was presumably visiting at the time. Mary's letter began, conventionally, 'To the very high and noble prince, her very dear lord and brother, my lord Edward, his sister Mary sends health and all manner of honour and reverence', and she named the deceased prioress as 'Dambert'. The 'convent of Aumbresbury' also sent a letter to the king in which they begged him to ask his and Mary's cousin the abbess of Fontévrault, Eleanor of Brittany, not to appoint an 'alien prioress', which would cause 'discord and great destruction of our temporal goods'. Both they and Mary asked Edward to request that the abbess appoint instead their own choice, 'Dame Isabel de Geinville' or de Geneville, and apparently they were successful; Isabel de Geneville was named as prioress of Amesbury in 1337 and had probably held the position since 1309. Edward responded to his sister two and a half weeks later on 27 May, and evidently was happy to do her bidding. Mary's letter reveals that she was annoyed with their cousin the abbess of Fontévrault, who wished to impose 'a prioress from beyond the sea' on the convent of Amesbury against the sisters' wishes. Mary remarked that Eleanor was bound to consider the request to appoint Isabel de Geneville, as Eleanor 'was brought up and veiled amongst us'.[3] Mary was either with her brother, or at the very least in contact with him again, around 5 June 1309, when Edward ordered a commission of *oyer et terminer* ('hear and determine') to look into Mary's complaint that a Robert Neuman and others broke into her close at her manor of Sherston, Wiltshire, drove away her cattle, destroyed her grass and corn, and assaulted her servants.[4]

Elizabeth of Rhuddlan probably gave birth in 1309, though which of her children was born is not clear. It was perhaps her second oldest surviving son Humphrey II, if he had not been born in 1307, or her twins Edward and William, who, according to the Walden Abbey Cartulary, were born in Caldicot Castle in Monmouthshire, one of the Welsh castles that belonged to their father. Edward was named before William in the cartulary, so was almost certainly the older twin, and must have been named in honour of Elizabeth's late father or her brother; perhaps Edward II was the boy's godfather. William was perhaps also named after a godfather, as the name was unknown in the royal family and was not common in the de Bohun family either.

On 25 February 1310, Edward II wrote to his sister Duchess Margaret of Brabant, enclosing documents concerning her dower, as she had asked him to do (though her letter to her brother on this subject has not survived). Part of the king's letter has been destroyed, and what remains is not particularly illuminating, except that Edward told Margaret that he was sending her transcripts of the documents rather than the originals for fear that they might be lost at sea.[5] Sometime that year, the wedding of Edward and Margaret's nephew took place: as planned by Edward I some years earlier, Eleanor of Windsor's son Édouard, count of Bar, married Marie of Burgundy, granddaughter of King/Saint Louis IX, and daughter and sister of dukes of Burgundy. In the autumn of 1310, King Edward set off on a long but ultimately fruitless journey to the far north of England and Scotland, attempting unsuccessfully to deal with King Robert Bruce. Two of his nieces, Édouard of Bar's sister Jeanne, countess of Surrey, and Joan of Acre's second daughter Margaret de Clare Gaveston, countess of Cornwall, visited their uncle at Berwick-on-Tweed on 19 April 1311.[6] Countess Margaret became pregnant by Piers Gaveston around this time.

In the same month that the two countesses visited the king, on 3 April 1311, Jeanne and Margaret's aunt Elizabeth of Rhuddlan bore another daughter, Margaret de Bohun, a future countess of Devon and mother of an archbishop of Canterbury. Margaret was perhaps born not too long after her sister Eleanor de Bohun, future countess of Ormond, who is sometimes thought to have been born in 1310 though the date is not known for certain. Also in 1311, possibly on 9 July, another wedding took place: Duchess Margaret's only son Duke Jan III of Brabant married Marie of Évreux, one of the daughters of Louis, count of Évreux (1276–1319), a younger half-brother of Philip IV of France. Jan was almost certainly only 10 years old in the summer of 1311, and Marie was several years younger, perhaps 8 or so. Their first child, Johanna, was not born until 24 June 1322.

Sometime not long before 28 August 1311, the royal sisters' little half-sister Eleanor, youngest child of Edward I and Marguerite of France, passed away; she was only 5 years old. Edward II paid £113 for the girl's burial and funeral at Beaulieu Abbey in Hampshire, which had been founded in the early 1200s by their great-grandfather King John.[7] Young Eleanor's fiancé Robert of Burgundy died in 1315 at the age of about 15, having never married. His heir to the counties of Burgundy and Artois was his older sister Jeanne, countess of Poitiers, who became queen-consort of France in 1316 when her husband, second brother of Edward II's queen, Isabella, took the throne as Philip V.

In early November 1311, Joan of Acre's son-in-law Piers Gaveston was exiled from England, Wales, Ponthieu and even his native Gascony for the third time. Although it is not entirely clear whether he ever truly left England and he might simply have gone into hiding in the west country, Edward II mulled over the possibility of sending him to Brabant, to be looked after by Margaret of Windsor and Duke Jan. He sent letters to the ducal couple asking them to provide a safe haven for Gaveston, and it is possible that they did, though nothing is known about the few months the royal favourite might have spent outside England in late 1311 and early 1312.[8] Margaret de Clare was pregnant when her husband was exiled and hence did not accompany him wherever he went abroad, as she had to Ireland in 1308/09. Gaveston returned to England in early 1312, possibly only for a short time to see his wife and their newborn daughter, born in York in January 1312, whom Margaret named Joan after her mother. Edward II, however, as infatuated with and dependent on Piers as he always had been, restored him to the earldom of Cornwall and revoked his exile, to the utter fury of the English barons. Eleanor of Windsor's son-in-law John de Warenne, earl of Surrey, was one of the noblemen who besieged Gaveston in Scarborough, and on 19 June 1312, Humphrey de Bohun, earl of Hereford, was present at the execution (or murder, depending on one's perspective) of his wife's nephew-in-law in Warwickshire.

It is apparent that many people in England rejoiced at the downfall and death of the loathed royal favourite, though what Elizabeth of Rhuddlan thought about it, and about her husband's role in Gaveston's death, cannot be known. Edward II, by the law and custom of the time, was now the legal guardian of Gaveston's daughter and heir Joan, his great-niece and Joan of Acre's granddaughter. He sent her to Amesbury Priory to be with his sister Mary and with his niece Eleanor de Bohun, one of Elizabeth's two surviving daughters, who was probably about 2 years old in 1312. The king granted the two children a joint annual allowance of 100 marks (£66.66).[9] Neither of the two royal girls was intended to become a nun, but Amesbury was a safe place for them, and possibly Joan of Acre's daughters had also all grown up there, at least partly. In 1316, Edward II arranged a marriage for Joan Gaveston with Thomas, Lord Wake (b. 1298), which did not work out as he married the earl of Lancaster's niece Blanche of Lancaster instead without royal permission that same year. In 1317, the king negotiated another future marriage for Joan Gaveston with Lord Multon's heir John Multon (b. 1308), though this did not work out either as Joan died in Amesbury Priory in January 1325, a day or two before her thirteenth birthday. Eleanor de Bohun would marry in 1328, and become a countess in Ireland.

All of Joan of Acre's four de Clare children became parents in 1312. Margaret gave birth to Joan Gaveston in January; Elizabeth gave birth to her and her husband's son and heir William de Burgh, future earl of Ulster, in September; Eleanor gave birth to her eldest daughter Isabella Despenser probably sometime in 1312, as she was said to be 8 years old in early 1321; and Gilbert de Clare's wife Maud de Burgh gave birth to their son John in April. John de Clare would have been heir to the vast Clare fortune, but died in infancy and was buried at the family's mausoleum in Tewkesbury Abbey.[10] Joan's fourth daughter Mary MacDuff, née de Monthermer, still lived in England, as did her Scottish husband Duncan, the English-raised earl of Fife, and as Mary turned 15 in *c.* October 1312 they might have begun to live together as husband and wife that year. Mary's sister Joan de Monthermer perhaps already lived at Amesbury with her aunt and her cousins Joan Gaveston and Eleanor de Bohun.

Chapter 33

The Knight of the Swan

Joan of Acre's children were now producing children of their own, and so was Joan's youngest sister Elizabeth of Rhuddlan, ten years her junior: Elizabeth's youngest son Aeneas or Eneas de Bohun was born sometime between *c.* 1312 and 1314. Aeneas was a very unusual name in the Middle Ages, and Elizabeth and Humphrey took their inspiration from a poem called *The Knight of the Swan*, whose protagonist was named Aeneas. The de Bohuns' emblem was a swan, and the family claimed descent from the mythical 'Knight of the Swan'. In her will of August 1399, Humphrey and Elizabeth's great-granddaughter and co-heir, Eleanor de Bohun, duchess of Gloucester and countess of Buckingham (*c.* 1366–99), bequeathed a manuscript of a 'poem called The History of the Knight and the Swan in French' to her son Humphrey (who in fact died a few weeks before she did), and the tale of Aeneas was well-known in the de Bohun family.[1] Nor was this the only example of a medieval English family naming a child after a literary hero. William Beauchamp (d. 1298) and Maud FitzJohn (d. 1301), earl and countess of Warwick, named their son and heir Guy Beauchamp (*c.* 1271/75–1315) after Guy of Warwick, the protagonist of a number of popular romances written in England and France in the Middle Ages.[2]

Aeneas de Bohun is very obscure; he was named in his father's will of August 1319 when he was at least 5 years old and perhaps more, but seems never to have married and certainly he had no children, and died in his late teens in 1331. In 1330, 'Enee de Bouhon' – evidently scribes struggled to spell his unusual first name – was a squire in the household of his cousin Edward III, who was very close to his own age. Aeneas was named second in the list of many dozens of young squires in the royal household, after his kinsman Henry of Grosmont, heir to his royal father Henry of Lancaster and born around 1310/12, and just before Richard Fitzalan, heir to the earldom of Arundel and born *c.* 1313. Aeneas's older brother Edward de Bohun was also a member of the royal household, and was a knight banneret by June 1328 when he cannot have been more than about 19 years old.[3]

Despite spending most, or at least much, of her time in Amesbury Priory, Mary of Woodstock retained her interest in the secular world and in the lives, births and deaths of her peers, the English nobility. Edmund Benstede, son and heir of John Benstede, was born in a place in Middlesex called 'Rosamunde' on 2 July 1312, and was baptised in Westminster on the same day. At Edmund Benstede's proof of age in July 1333 (when he demonstrated that he was now 21 and was thus eligible to enter his late father's lands), one of the twelve jurors who confirmed his date of birth was Thomas Barber. Thomas's testimony stated that in July 1312, 'he was with Lady Mary, sister of King Edward II, at Amesbury, and was sent thence by her to the said John de Benstede, father of the said heir'. Thomas 'immediately returned to the said Lady Mary, informing her of the birth of the said heir', and Mary rewarded him with 30 shillings for his journey and for bringing her the news. This money, Thomas said, was enough to set him up in his profession as a barber the following year.[4] Mary, despite being cloistered, knew that John Benstede's wife was about to give birth in the summer of 1312, and obviously kept herself well-informed of events in the secular world. This also reveals that Mary had at least one male servant at the priory (the expression 'he was with' means that Thomas Barber served in her household), and there were others, including Michael Aune, whom she often sent to her brother with her messages.

On 27 October 1312, in his hall at Tervuren Castle, Duke Jan II of Brabant passed away at the early age of 37. According to the nineteenth-century writer Mary Anne Everett Green, Tervuren was rebuilt on a magnificent scale, with gardens and groves, by Margaret of Windsor after she was widowed.[5] The castle was demolished in 1782. Duke Jan was succeeded by his and Margaret's son Jan III, who was 12 or almost. Margaret, as the mother of the underage duke of Brabant, stayed in the duchy for the rest of her life, and did not return to England as her widowed and then childless sister Elizabeth had done in 1300. There are no extant personal letters by Margaret so it is impossible to know how she felt about her husband's death, but as noted, it does not appear that their marriage had ever been a happy or close one.

In November and December 1312, Mary of Woodstock spent a long time away from Amesbury and with the king. On 8 November, while staying at Windsor Castle, Edward granted a favour to the prioress and nuns to Amesbury at her request (Edward I and Edward II's willingness to heed Mary's requests and to grant favours to Amesbury Priory was, of course, a key reason for the prioress's willingness to tolerate Mary's frequent absences).[6] Queen Isabella was just about to give birth to her and the king's first child, and bore a son, named Edward after his father and grandfather, at Windsor Castle on 13 November 1312. On 1 January 1313, Edward II ordered the sheriff of Wiltshire to pay £12, 7*s* 3*d* to Mary of Woodstock 'which the king owes her for hay, oats, litter, farriery and the wages of her grooms, whilst staying at Wyndesore [Windsor] in December', and for her expenses in travelling to and from Amesbury.[7] It seems therefore that Mary spent most, or perhaps all, of November and December with her brother and sister-in-law, and almost certainly remained with them for the festive season of 1312/13. She probably made her way back to Amesbury at the beginning of 1313. Elizabeth of Rhuddlan seems also to have been at Windsor in early November 1312 shortly before her nephew was born, or at least, her husband was: Humphrey de Bohun witnessed one of Edward II's charters at Windsor on 2 November.[8] Given Humphrey's role in Piers Gaveston's recent death, and given that he and his allies took their armies to within a few miles of London in early September and for a while it seemed that civil war was inevitable, it is surprising to find him in his brother-in-law's company. Perhaps Elizabeth did her utmost behind the scenes to reconcile her husband and her brother.

Mary and Edward's stepmother Queen Marguerite was also in Windsor Castle, as was Marguerite's brother Louis, count of Évreux, who had travelled from France at the request of his half-brother Philip IV to negotiate between Edward II and the barons who killed Gaveston, and who stayed in England for a few months. Their first cousin John of Brittany, the earl of Richmond, their kinsman Aymer de Valence, the earl of Pembroke, and Hugh Despenser the Elder, a wealthy baron who was a close friend and ally of Edward II, also stayed with the king and queen and Mary at Windsor. The festive season of 1312/13 was a rare period of calm and happiness during Edward's turbulent reign, and two chroniclers commented that the king's joy at the birth of his son and heir went some way to assuaging his terrible grief for Gaveston.[9]

In May 1312 at Tynemouth, Edward and Piers Gaveston had fled from Thomas, earl of Lancaster, who marched there with an armed force and came close to capturing Gaveston. The two men left a large number of their possessions behind at Tynemouth, which Lancaster seized, inventoried, and finally returned to his cousin the king in February 1313. The many precious and valuable items included a brooch given to Edward by 'my lady Isabell, the sister', which means Elizabeth of Rhuddlan, and Edward II had also received three gold clasps from his sister Margaret, duchess of Brabant.[10] Later in 1313, the king and queen of England spent two months in France, and Jeanne de Bar, though not her estranged husband the earl of Surrey, accompanied her uncle Edward to her and Queen Isabella's homeland.[11]

Chapter 34

Defeat in Scotland

One of the defining features of Edward II's disastrous reign was his inability to impose his authority on Scotland, of which both he and his father believed themselves to be the rightful overlords, or to defeat Robert Bruce, who had had himself crowned king in 1306 and who proved to be a great leader both politically and militarily. Edward II was no match for Bruce, and a previous long campaign there which he undertook in 1310/11 proved pointless and fruitless. In June 1314, Edward decided to try to deal with Robert Bruce and with the Scottish situation once and for all, and marched the largest army ever assembled in England to the vicinity of Stirling Castle. The English king's dire relations with his earls meant that only three of them accompanied him to Scotland: his nephew Gilbert de Clare of Gloucester, his cousin Aymer de Valence of Pembroke, and surprisingly, given his role in the death of Piers Gaveston two years earlier, his brother-in-law Humphrey de Bohun of Hereford, constable of England. The possessions Humphrey took with him on the Scottish campaign required an entire ship, and King Edward organised a travelling wine cellar at Newcastle-upon-Tyne on the way.[1]

Elizabeth of Rhuddlan must have accompanied her husband and her brother to the north: a letter of protection for Katherine de Halliwell, going to Scotland with the countess of Hereford, was issued on 13 April 1314.[2] Queen Isabella also travelled north with the king, and stayed in the port of Berwick-on-Tweed; almost certainly, the two royal women travelled and stayed together. On 9 June 1314, on their way north, Elizabeth handed her brother a petition she had received from some of the people of her town of Dordrecht in Holland, who had been robbed, beaten and killed in Harwich. The king sent it to the archbishop of Canterbury to deal with.[3]

The two-day battle of Bannockburn near Stirling Castle on 23 and 24 June 1314 has gone down in history as one of England's worst and most humiliating military defeats ever. A knight called Sir Henry de

Bohun was killed by Robert Bruce in person with an axe after challenging him to single combat; although usually called Earl Humphrey's nephew, Henry was in fact the earl of Hereford's cousin. Humphrey himself sought refuge after the battle in Stirling Castle, where he was taken prisoner by the Scots. King Edward, meanwhile, galloped to Dunbar on the coast surrounded by 500 knights, and managed to return to Berwick-on-Tweed safely, albeit humiliatingly, in a fishing-boat. Joan of Acre's eldest child, 23-year-old Gilbert de Clare, fell at Bannockburn; he forgot to put on the surcoat that would have identified him as a great nobleman, and was killed. Had they known who he was, the Scottish soldiers would have captured him for ransom instead. Bizarrely, Gilbert's widow Maud, daughter of the earl of Ulster, claimed to be pregnant with his son and heir for as long as three years after his death. In reality, Gilbert's heirs were his three full sisters, Eleanor Despenser, Margaret Gaveston and Elizabeth de Burgh.

Elizabeth of Rhuddlan was still with Edward II and Queen Isabella in York on or a little before 21 July 1314, when at her request, the king gave Thomas Storgeon of Norfolk his goods and chattels back. Storgeon had been indicted for the death of John Tovy also of Norfolk, and had accompanied Humphrey de Bohun to Scotland and did 'good service' there during the Bannockburn expedition.[4] For his sister's sake, Edward agreed to return all the fifteen Scottish hostages in England, captured by his father in 1306/07, in exchange for Humphrey de Bohun. The Scottish hostages included Robert Bruce's wife Elizabeth de Burgh, queen of Scotland, whose sister Maud was Gilbert de Clare's widow, two of Bruce's sisters, and his daughter Marjorie.

In Edward II's eighth regnal year, which ran from 8 July 1314 to 7 July 1315, he paid for Mary of Woodstock to visit him at Westminster, and the following year, Mary made at least two more journeys to see her brother at court. The king paid for the expenses of Mary's horses and carriages travelling from Amesbury.[5] Edward reminded the treasurer and barons of the exchequer on 23 February 1315 that Mary was entitled to an allowance of £200 a year, in line with his father's grant to her of that amount on 4 October 1300.[6]

On 28 February 1315, Elizabeth of Rhuddlan's daughter Margaret de Bohun, not yet 4 years old, was betrothed to Hugh Courtenay, son and heir of Hugh Courtenay the elder, baron of the west country.[7] Margaret was most probably a goddaughter of the dowager queen Marguerite, her step-grandmother, and perhaps it was Queen Marguerite who decided on her marriage to Courtenay and who certainly helped to arrange it. It is rather odd, however, that Margaret de Bohun, who seems to have been the younger sister, was betrothed before Eleanor. The agreement ran:

> On Friday after the feast of St Mathias the apostle in the eighth year of the reign of our lord King Edward son of King Edward, the agreement was made between the very noble lady, Lady Margaret queen of England, and Sir Humphrey de Bohun earl of Hereford and Lady Elizabeth his wife on one side, and Sir Hugh de Courtenay on the other. It was agreed that Hugh, son of Sir Hugh, should take as his wife Margaret, daughter of the earl and countess.

Hugh Courtenay was eight years his fiancée Margaret's senior, born in 1303, and his father (1276–1340) would become earl of Devon a few years later. The Bohun-Courtenay marriage would be an extremely fruitful one, producing as many as seventeen children, and was an extremely long one: Hugh lived until 1377 and Margaret until 1391. Elizabeth and Humphrey also took care of the future of one of their sons in 1315: on 1 May, they granted William, the younger of the twins, two manors in Bedfordshire and Huntingdonshire plus a messuage (a dwelling with outbuildings and some land) and 140 acres of land and 4 acres of meadow in another manor.[8]

Elizabeth of Rhuddlan was still experiencing endless difficulties in being paid her rightful dower from her short marriage to the count of Holland. Edward II sent a frustrated letter to Count Willem on 10 July 1315, requesting that Willem pay 'at once' the arrears of Elizabeth's rightful dower in Holland. The king reminded the count that Willem's sister Alix or Alicia, dowager countess of Norfolk and the widow of Roger Bigod (d. 1306), lived in England, and stated that he should treat Edward's sister as he would wish the king to treat his own sister. On the same day, Edward inspected and confirmed an agreement made between Count Willem and Elizabeth and Humphrey de Bohun, 'touching payment of the dower settled on the said countess' by Count Jan I and dated the Sunday before the Nativity of St John the Baptist in 1308 (i.e. 23 June 1308) in The Hague.[9]

Chapter 35

Death in Childbirth

By July 1315, thirteen months after Bannockburn, it was obvious that Edward II and Elizabeth of Rhuddlan's niece-in-law Maud, dowager countess of Gloucester, could not possibly be pregnant by Earl Gilbert, and their nieces Eleanor Despenser and Margaret Gaveston appointed attorneys to seek their rightful inheritance (the widowed Elizabeth de Burgh was still in Ireland).[1] Edward, however, who was enjoying the late earl's vast income and had no mind to give it up to Joan of Acre's daughters, fond of his nieces though he surely was, continued to pretend that Maud might bear Gilbert's son. As late as December 1316, two and a half years after Gilbert's death, he stated that Gilbert's lands were still in his own hands 'by reason of the minority of the heir'.[2]

Around mid-August 1315 or thereabouts, Elizabeth of Rhuddlan became pregnant again for at least the ninth, and last, time. She was probably with her brother in Lincoln on or just before 1 September 1315, when Edward wrote to the abbess and convent of 'Elnestowe', i.e. Elstow in Bedfordshire, requesting that they pay a yearly pension to John Houton, one of Elizabeth's clerks. This strongly suggests that Elizabeth had asked him to do this, and it was common for servants in royal or noble households to retire to an abbey or priory. On 29 September 1315 at Ditton in the Fens, on a month-long swimming and rowing holiday with 'a great company of common people', Edward II wrote to his chancellor. Elizabeth had nominated a new abbess of Elstow, and Edward had backed her up, but, he said, the convent 'has done nothing, in contempt of the king's commands' and declared himself 'much annoyed'.

Earlier in 1315, the election of a new abbess of Elstow had been fraught with division, with some nuns electing Elizabeth Beauchamp, one of their fellow nuns, and others Joan Wauton, previously the prioress of Elstow. Elstow Abbey, a house of Benedictine nuns, had been established in the eleventh century by William the Conqueror's niece Judith, countess of Huntingdon, and hence was considered a royal foundation. A petition sent to

Edward II in *c.* 1315 by the abbess and convent of Elstow (their scribe spelt it 'Aunestowe') reveals that they were well aware of their house's history, and commented to Edward that 'the said abbey is of the foundation of Judit, late countess of Huntingdon'.[3] The matter was still not resolved by 10 November 1315, when Edward II sent another angry letter claiming that the abbey of Elstow was 'trying to impugn' his own right and his sister Elizabeth's.[4]

The 28th of November 1315 marked the twenty-fifth anniversary of Queen Leonor's death, punctiliously commemorated by her son and doubtlessly by her three surviving daughters as well.[5] In the same year, Edward II paid a man named Nicholas Percy five pounds for compiling a book about the life and times of his father for him, and in 1324, paid his painter Jack St Albans to create scenes from Edward I's life on the walls of the Painted Chamber of the Palace of Westminster.[6]

Elizabeth of Rhuddlan gave birth to a daughter, Isabella de Bohun, her tenth child and fourth daughter, on 5 May 1316. Sadly, something went badly wrong during labour or shortly afterwards, and Elizabeth died on the same day; little Isabella soon died too. The countess of Holland, Hereford and Essex was 33 years old when she passed away. One of her household attendants looking after her at the time of her death was Joan Mereworth, who had previously worked for Queen Leonor. On 17 June 1316, Edward II granted Joan an income of £40 annually because of the 'great labour' she had performed for his mother and sister for many years. This was an extremely generous income for a woman of Joan's status, as £40 was the annual income necessary for a man to qualify for knighthood, and speaks to Edward's affection for his sister and his gratitude to a woman who served her and their mother. Elizabeth's husband Humphrey had witnessed a charter issued by the king at the royal hunting-lodge of Clipstone not far from Nottingham on 13 January 1316, which, assuming she accompanied him, was perhaps one of the last occasions when Elizabeth saw her brother. Humphrey was back at court in Westminster by 12 May 1316, a week after Elizabeth's death, when he witnessed three more royal charters.[7]

Elizabeth's other children were still very young in May 1316 when they lost their mother. John the eldest and his father's heir was 10, Humphrey was 8 or 9, the twins Edward and William perhaps 7, Eleanor perhaps 6, Margaret had recently turned 5, and Aeneas probably still a toddler. Of the ten children Elizabeth bore, only three were to have children of their own: Eleanor, countess of Ormond, Margaret, countess of Devon, and William, earl of Northampton. Her sons John and Edward both married but had no children, Humphrey II lived into his fifties but never married, Aeneas died in his teens, and the others had died in infancy in Elizabeth's lifetime. Elizabeth's second eldest surviving son Humphrey II, his brother John's successor as earl of Hereford and Essex in 1336, made his will on 15 October 1361 shortly before he died. He left money for a chaplain to travel to Jerusalem on pilgrimage on behalf of his parents and their souls. To his sister Margaret, countess of Devon, Humphrey left a brass basin he had used for washing his head and which had once belonged to Elizabeth, *Madame ma miere* ('my lady, my mother').[8] Margaret, countess of Devon, was the last surviving grandchild of Leonor of Castile, and died at the age of 80 in December 1391, having outlived her mother by three-quarters of a century; one of her many children was William Courtenay (d. 1396), bishop of London and archbishop of Canterbury.[9]

Elizabeth's funeral took place on 23 May 1316 at Walden Abbey in Saffron Walden, Essex, 20 miles from Pleshey, where she had spent much of her married life.[10] Her brother attended; King Edward stayed the night before and the night of the funeral itself in Bishop's Stortford 12 miles from Saffron Walden, and the staff of his wardrobe, one of the divisions of his enormous household, remained there while he travelled to Walden Abbey. He was back at Westminster on 27 May, with Elizabeth's widower Humphrey de Bohun in his company.[11] Even in February 1317, nine months after Elizabeth of Rhuddlan's death, Edward II was still trying to persuade Willem, count of Hainault and Holland, to pay the arrears of Elizabeth's rightful dower in Holland to Humphrey.[12]

Edward sent a letter to Clemence of Hungary, the second wife of his brother-in-law Louis X of France and Navarre, on 17 May 1316, twelve days after Elizabeth of Rhuddlan's death and six days before her funeral. One of his absent-minded clerks addressed the letter to 'the most excellent lady, Lady Elizabeth, by the grace of God queen of France and Navarre' by mistake. This surely reveals that the recent death and impending funeral of Edward's sister the countess of Holland and Hereford were on the clerk's mind, and he might well have caused a major diplomatic incident; to write the name of the queen of France incorrectly in a letter sent to her in the king of England's name was a howling error. As it happened, Louis X died suddenly and unexpectedly on 5 June 1316 at the age of only 26, leaving Queen Clemence four months pregnant.[13]

Chapter 36

Maud Nerford and the Court Christian

Now, only two of Edward I and Queen Leonor's many daughters were still alive, Margaret in Brabant, and Mary at Amesbury Priory. Edward II received letters from his sister Margaret and her 16-year-old son Duke Jan III of Brabant on 24 June and 4 December 1316. They requested that a number of merchants in the port of Ipswich paid the large debts they owed to an English-born burgess of Antwerp, Geoffrey of Ely (in Cambridgeshire).[1] Mary was at court with her brother at Clipstone, where the king spent much time in the mid-1310s, and Nottingham during the festive season of 1316, and went back to Amesbury Priory with some generous gifts from him: fifteen tapestries, which the king had purchased at a cost of 40 marks (£26, 13s and 4d). They were provided by Richard of Horsham, a mercer of London.[2]

Mary's niece Elizabeth de Burgh, Joan of Acre's third daughter, may have travelled to Amesbury with her after Christmas, and Elizabeth spent at least part of the final trimester of her second pregnancy at the convent. She gave birth to her second husband Theobald de Verdon's daughter Isabella de Verdon on 21 March 1317, eight months after Theobald's death on 27 July 1316. Elizabeth named her daughter after the queen, the little girl's godmother: the under-sheriff of Wiltshire escorted Queen Isabella from the royal palace of Clarendon on the day of Isabella de Verdon's baptism. Mary herself was the other godmother of her latest great-niece, and sent news of little Isabella's birth to King Edward via a servant who worked for her for many years, Michael Aune or Anne.[3]

Eleanor of Windsor's daughter Jeanne de Bar had lived apart from her husband John de Warenne, earl of Surrey, since at least 1313 and probably earlier, and John lived with his mistress Maud Nerford and had several children with her. In 1316, he began the first of his decades-long attempts to annul his marriage to Jeanne so that he could marry Maud instead, and make their sons John and Thomas his heirs. Edward II gave Surrey permission on 24 February 1316 to 'bring his suit for a divorce against Dame Joan de Bars, the king's niece, in the Court Christian'. Surrey had in fact already begun proceedings, and he and Maud Nerford had decided that their best course of action was to claim a 'pre-contract of matrimony' between them before Surrey married Jeanne (which was, of course, untrue).[4] It was, unfortunately for Jeanne, a simple fact that the earl of Surrey was a more important political figure than the countess, and Edward II, one of the most disastrously unsuccessful kings in English history, needed all the allies he could get. On the other hand, Edward paid all his niece's expenses (300 marks, or over £166) when she went on an extended visit to her native county of Bar towards the end of 1316, and paid all her legal costs in regard to the attempted annulment. He hired and paid for an Italian lawyer named Master Aymon de Jovenzano 'to prosecute in the Arches in London and elsewhere in England' on Jeanne's behalf. As for John de Warenne's long-term and intense relationship with Maud Nerford, which produced at least two and perhaps as many as five or six children, it was over by *c.* 1320, when John stated that he had 'removed Maud de Nerforde from his heart and expelled her from his company'.[5]

On or soon before 3 May 1317, Edward II arranged the wedding of Elizabeth de Burgh to his latest infatuation, Sir Roger Damory, a knight of Oxfordshire, mere weeks after she had borne her second husband's posthumous daughter. Elizabeth's sister Margaret Gaveston married their uncle's other infatuation, a young knight named Sir Hugh Audley, at Windsor Castle on 28 April. Before and after the two weddings, Mary of Woodstock went on pilgrimage to various sites around the country with Elizabeth and their kinswoman Isabella of Lancaster. Isabella was the second of the six daughters of Henry of Lancaster, who was the younger brother and heir of Thomas, earl of Lancaster and Leicester, and Mary's first cousin. Isabella, born around 1305 or 1308, was a child in 1317, and herself entered Amesbury Priory as a nun in 1327 and became its prioress in 1343. Edward II paid the ladies' expenses of £40.[6]

On 6 May 1317, still at Windsor Castle after attending his nieces' weddings, Edward wrote to Master Thomas Deuart, dean of Angers, thanking him for assisting his (Edward's) clerk Master John de Hildesle. The king had sent Hildesle to the abbess of Fontévrault, asking her to commission his sister Mary to 'visit and correct the houses of that order in England'. Edward requested the dean to remind the abbess of his letter as she had not yet acted on it, 'at which the king is surprised'. He added 'the king does not believe that any other lady of religion of that order in England or anyone else could execute the office more usefully than his sister'. This letter suggests that Mary was still in her brother's company on 6 May after the weddings of their two Clare nieces, or that she had been very recently before she and Elizabeth de Burgh resumed their pilgrimage.[7]

Edward I's widow Marguerite of France, the dowager queen, died at her castle of Marlborough on 14 February 1318, probably not yet 40 years old. Her stepson Edward II appointed her two sons Thomas of Brotherton and Edmund of Woodstock, aged 17 and 16, as her executors.[8] The dowager queen's body arrived in the conventual church of St Mary's, Southwark, on 13 March 1318, and she was buried at the Greyfriars' church in London on 15 March. Her stepdaughter Mary attended the funeral with her brother, and, one assumes, with their half-brothers. Edward II bought six pieces of Lucca cloth for himself and two pieces each for his sister and Sir Roger Damory, who was now his and Mary's nephew-in-law.[9] A few weeks later, the king stayed with his niece Elizabeth de Burgh, née de Clare, in the village of Clare – Elizabeth was about seven months pregnant with her third child, Roger Damory's daughter – and surely took the opportunity to visit his sister Joan of Acre's tomb while he was there.[10]

Chapter 37

Holy Oil and Simplicity

The nineteenth-century historian Mary Anne Everett Green believed that Margaret of Windsor, duchess of Brabant, died in 1318, and this erroneous date has often been copied ever since, despite the multiple pieces of evidence which prove conclusively that Margaret was alive many years after that date.[1] Edward II wrote to his sister fairly often, including as late as September 1326 not long before the revolution which swept him from his throne, and it is obvious that the king of England would have known if his own sister had been dead for eight years at that point.[2]

It is, unfortunately, almost impossible to say anything very much about Margaret's life in Brabant, as she rarely came to the attention of chroniclers. In 1317/18, however, the dowager duchess inadvertently caused problems for her brother when she sent her confessor, Friar Nicholas of Wisbech, to England. (Wisbech lies in Cambridgeshire, so this reveals that at least some of Margaret's attendants and servants were English, many years after she left her homeland.) Nicholas was a Dominican friar, the order much favoured by the late Queen Leonor and several of her children, and in March 1317 Edward II sent Nicholas to Pope John XXII in Avignon on his business. Ten months later, Edward sent him again to the pope.[3]

So far, so good, but Edward II was in dire straits in 1318: an impostor called John of Powderham was executed that year after claiming to be the true son of Edward I and the rightful king of England, the 1310s saw terrible famine across Northern Europe, Edward was also engaged in a power struggle with his despised cousin the earl of Lancaster, and the royal clerk who wrote the *Vita Edwardi Secundi* stated rather sarcastically but also truthfully that 'Neither has our King Edward, who has reigned eleven years and more, done anything that ought to be preached in the market-place or upon the house-tops.'[4] Edward decided that being anointed with the holy oil of St Thomas Becket would, with its miraculous properties, put an end to his political troubles, and Nicholas of Wisbech persuaded him to take up the matter with the pope. Duchess Margaret and Duke Jan II had brought the oil, which supposedly had once been used by Thomas Becket, the archbishop of Canterbury murdered in 1170 and subsequently revered by the English royal family, to England in early 1308 to be used at Edward's coronation, but he had not done so. Now Edward raised the matter with John XXII, supposedly on hearing from Wisbech that the holy oil had healed Duke Jan II's sister the countess of Luxembourg of a severe and dangerous knife wound while she was visiting Jan and Margaret of Windsor in their duchy. Edward subsequently came to his senses, and sent an astonishingly candid letter to John XXII in which he spoke of his regret for his own 'imbecility', 'dove-like simplicity' and weakness in believing Friar Nicholas of Wisbech's blandishments. Nicholas was imprisoned in England but escaped, and thereafter disappeared from history; perhaps he returned to Brabant and continued to serve Duchess Margaret.[5]

The holy oil reappeared later in the fourteenth century. Supposedly, Henry of Grosmont, made first duke of Lancaster in 1351, the son and heir of Edward II and Duchess Margaret's cousin Henry of Lancaster (b. 1280/81), found it in France in the 1340s or 1350s, and presented it to the prince of Wales, the eldest son of Edward III. It was then forgotten again until 1399 when the prince of Wales's son Richard II came upon it in the Tower of London, locked in a chest. Richard, who, like the great-grandfather Edward II he closely resembled in many ways, had numerous political problems, decided that being anointed with the oil would solve them all. However, he was forced to abdicate his throne some months later to his cousin Henry IV, who became the first king of England to be anointed with the miraculous oil during his coronation in October 1399.[6] Whether or to what extent any of this is true is unclear, nor is it clear how the apparently accidental discovery of the holy oil in France by an English nobleman in the middle of the fourteenth century can be reconciled with Duke Jan and Duchess Margaret's visit to England with it a few decades earlier.

On 11 August 1319, Elizabeth of Rhuddlan's widower Humphrey de Bohun was with his brother-in-law the king at Gosforth near Newcastle-upon-Tyne, about to take part in the siege of Berwick-upon-Tweed, an important port which Robert Bruce, king of Scotland, had captured the year before. (Not surprisingly, given Edward II's utter lack of military aptitude, the siege failed utterly, and Berwick remained in Scottish hands until the king's son Edward III retook it in 1333.) Humphrey de Bohun made his will on that date, calling himself 'Humfrai', the typical fourteenth-century spelling of his name.[7] The will reveals how wealthy Humphrey was: he left the astonishingly large sum of £8,000 to his sons, another £666 went to Sir Hugh Courtenay, he left £333 for his two daughters' wedding clothes, and there were numerous other bequests as well. In modern values, £8,000 or £10,000 is a good few million pounds, perhaps tens of millions.

Humphrey asked to be buried at Walden Abbey with Elizabeth, and the will shows that the count of Hainault and Holland still owed him money from Elizabeth's unpaid dower, despite all Edward I and Edward II's letters to Count Willem and his father Jan II on the subject over the years. The earl bequeathed a pot and a gold cup, which Elizabeth had given to him, to her brother the king; left to each of his four younger sons, Humphrey, Edward, William and Aeneas, £2,000 'to buy lands or marriages'; and he gave £200 to his daughter Eleanor to buy wedding clothes. He also left 200 marks (£133) to his other daughter Margaret for her wedding clothes, and 1,000 marks (£666) to Sir Hugh Courtenay (b. 1276) for the marriage between Margaret and Hugh's son and heir Hugh (b. 1303). Humphrey left no money to his eldest son John, but John was his heir who would inherit all the lands and income of his father's two earldoms, and did receive all of Humphrey's armour and a green bed embroidered with swans, the Bohun emblem. The youngest de Bohun son, Aeneas, who was still a young child in 1319, was sent to live in the custody of Sir Robert Haustede and 'Dame Margerie his wife', and Humphrey left the couple £100 for the boy's expenses.[8]

Eleanor de Bohun's *maistresse*, the woman in charge of her household, was Philippa Wake, and Margaret's was Katherine Boklaunde. The unusually-named Huard de Soyrou was the tutor of Humphrey and Elizabeth's second son Humphrey, who was 10 or 12 in 1319, and Robert Swan, 'who is with my son John and his brothers', received £20. Huard also appears on record in 1303 as 'Huward de Seyru' when Elizabeth sent him as a messenger to her father to inform him of the birth of her first child, and he is probably the same person as the 'Hugh Soyrn' (this may be a modern misreading of 'Soyru') whom Elizabeth sent to the county of Holland on her affairs in the early 1300s. Humphrey left £40 to his sister Maud Baskerville, 'towards her marriage', by which he must, given that he called her by the name Baskerville and not de

Bohun, have meant a second marriage. His barber was named Poun, one of his falconers was Berthelet (a nickname for men called Bertelmew, or Bartholomew in modern spelling) and his cooks were Master William and Roger. Few wills survive from England in the early fourteenth century – though there are far more from later in the century – so we are lucky to have Humphrey's detailed will that reveals much about his family and his household, most or all of whom had certainly served Elizabeth of Rhuddlan as well.

Chapter 38

Mary and the Chronicler

In June 1319, Duke Jan III of Brabant sent a letter to his uncle Edward II, in French, promising that Robert Bruce, king of Scotland, would receive no aid from him or from any of his territories. Addressing King Edward as 'our dearest and beloved uncle' and calling himself 'Jehans', Jan told him that he knew of the 'harm, damage and defiance' done by Robert and his adherents to Edward II and to 'my lord the king, your father and our grandfather' (*nostre tayon*). Whether he truly believed this or not, Jan was willing to take a pro-English stance, at least in public and in letters to his uncle, and must have heard all about the English claims to overlordship of Scotland from his mother.[1] Later in 1319, Margaret of Windsor and Duke Jan contacted her brother on behalf of a group of merchants from Brabant. Four merchants 'and their fellows' had laden two ships with 166 sacks of wool and other merchandise in the port of Boston, Lincolnshire, to take back to Brabant. The two ships sailed down the coast of England, and when they reached Essex, thirteen named men and others 'boarded the said ships sailing off the coast of Essex, drove their men and servants out of the ships, and carried off the wool and merchandise to diverse places on the sea coasts of the counties of Essex, Kent, Sussex, Surrey, Southampton [i.e. Hampshire], Somerset and Dorset.' Edward II ordered a commission of *oyer et terminer* on 31 December 1319 to investigate what had happened.[2]

At an unknown date perhaps in *c.* 1320 or rather earlier, Mary of Woodstock became the patron of the chronicler and historian Nicholas Trivet or Trevet, who wrote several works about the kings of England. Nicholas Trivet, about ten or twenty years older than Mary, was born into a noble English family, studied at the universities of Oxford and Paris, and ultimately became a Dominican friar. In patronising and perhaps commissioning a chronicle about her family, Mary probably took inspiration from Juana, queen of Navarre and France: Queen Juana commissioned Jean de Joinville to write the *Life of Saint Louis*, an account of Louis IX of France's first crusade in Egypt between 1248 and 1254. The very long-lived Joinville (*c.* 1224–1317) came from a noble family of Champagne, and his daughter Alix de Joinville married Mary of Woodstock's rather obscure cousin John of Lancaster (before 1286–1317). He was the third and youngest son of her uncle Edmund, earl of Lancaster and Blanche of Artois, and was the younger half-brother of Queen Juana.

Jean de Joinville's brother, usually known nowadays as Geoffrey de Geneville (d. 1314), spent much of his career in England, Wales and Ireland, and his granddaughter and heir Joan de Geneville (1286–1356) married the famous English nobleman Roger Mortimer, lord of Wigmore and first earl of March, who was executed by Mary of Woodstock's nephew Edward III in 1330. In 1309, Mary did her utmost to persuade the abbess of Fontévrault to appoint Isabel de Geneville, another member of the Joinville/Geneville family, as prioress of Amesbury (see above). Given her connections to the family, it seems highly likely that she was aware of Jean de Joinville's writings about Louis IX and of Queen Juana's patronage of Joinville, and also that she decided to promote a similar kind of text about her own family and her ancestors.

In *c.* 1320, Trivet wrote a work in Latin titled *The Annals of Six Kings of England* (*Annales Sex Regum Angliae*), covering the period from 1135 to 1307 and the reigns of King Stephen, Henry II, Richard I Lionheart, John, Henry III and Edward I. A few years later, he also wrote *Les Cronicles*, in French (or rather, Anglo-Norman), and the four earliest manuscripts of this work begin with the dedication *Ci comencerent les cronicles qe Frere Nichol Trivet escrit a ma dame Marie la fillie moun seignour le Roi d'Engleterre Edward le filtz Henri*, 'Here begin the chronicles which Brother Nicholas Trivet wrote for my lady Mary, daughter of my lord the king of England, Edward son of Henry'.[3] The fact that this text was in French and not in Latin as Trivet's earlier work had been tends to confirm that it was indeed intended for Mary, who would not have been able to follow a complex text in Latin but who spoke and understood French fluently. Unfortunately, it seems likely that Mary died before the completion of this work and therefore did not have a chance to read it, or to have it read to her. (This was also the case with Queen Juana, who died at only 33 years old in 1305, several years before Jean de Joinville completed the book about Saint Louis IX's crusade which she had commissioned.)

One manuscript of Nicholas Trivet's *Cronicles*, now held in the Bibliothèque Nationale de France (the National Library of France) in Paris, is believed to have been the copy originally intended to be presented to Mary of Woodstock. Almost certainly, this manuscript later belonged to Philip 'the Bold', duke of Burgundy (1342–1404), youngest son of King John II of France (r. 1350–64), and his wife Margaretha, countess of Flanders in her own right (1350–1405).[4] In this context, it is interesting to note that the heiress Margaretha of Flanders, duchess of Burgundy and countess of Flanders, was the great-granddaughter of Margaret of Windsor, duchess of Brabant, and thus was Mary of Woodstock's great-great-niece. Duchess Margaretha was named after her mother and ultimately after her English great-grandmother, and would certainly have been aware of her royal English ancestors and relatives, including Mary of Woodstock.

In 1318, Joan of Acre's son-in-law Hugh Despenser the Younger had been appointed as Edward II's chamberlain by some of the magnates, apparently against the wishes of Edward himself, as, despite their close family connections, he had never liked or trusted Hugh. Once the two men came to spend much time together, however, Edward's feelings towards his nephew-in-law underwent a massive change, and he seems to have fallen in love with Hugh and become infatuated with him, or at the very least grew highly dependent on him personally and politically. The king's favouritism pushed some of the important English barons into opposition, as had happened with Piers Gaveston earlier in the reign. One of Hugh and Edward's chief opponents was Humphrey de Bohun, earl of Hereford, one of the Marcher lords who were threatened by Hugh's upsetting the balance of power as the new lord of Glamorgan. Perhaps Elizabeth of Rhuddlan's death in 1316 weakened the ties between Humphrey and Edward II, and in March 1322 Humphrey was killed fighting against the royal army at the battle of Boroughbridge in Yorkshire. His and the other Marchers' chief ally was Thomas, earl of Lancaster and Leicester, and Thomas's royal birth and enormous wealth did not save him: Edward II had his cousin beheaded outside one of his own castles six days after Boroughbridge.

Margaret of Windsor, dowager duchess of Brabant, now 47 years old, became a grandmother on 24 June 1322 when her daughter-in-law Marie of Évreux gave birth to her first child, Johanna. Two more daughters, Margaretha and Marie, and three sons, Jan, Henryk and Godfrey, were to follow. Of the six Brabant children born to Duke Jan III and Marie of Évreux, only the second eldest, Margaretha, had a surviving child. Via Margaretha of Brabant (1323–80), countess of Flanders, and her daughter Margaretha of Flanders (1350–1405), duchess of Burgundy and countess of Flanders (and most probably the owner of a manuscript of Nicholas Trivet's *Les Cronicles*), Margaret of Windsor was an ancestor of the dukes of Burgundy, Bavaria, Austria, Brittany, Cleves, Savoy, and numerous others. Margaret's son Duke Jan III also fathered numerous illegitimate children, apparently as many as twenty-one or twenty-two.[5] Although he almost certainly never saw her again after 1308, and despite the fiasco with the holy oil brought to him by Margaret's confessor, Edward II kept in touch with Duchess Margaret, and wrote to her from Westminster on 9 June 1324; he was planning to send an envoy to her and her son in Brabant, though for what purpose was not stated.[6]

In and after 1322, everything went badly wrong for Edward II and for his kingdom. His last campaign in Scotland that summer proved an utter disaster, and the Scots launched a counter-invasion of England and almost captured him at Rievaulx Abbey in Yorkshire; in 1324 he went to war against his brother-in-law Charles IV of France, the third and last of Queen Isabella's brothers; and he allowed his chamberlain, nephew-in-law and perhaps his lover Hugh Despenser the Younger to extort money and lands from a large number of victims, both male and female, both nobly-born and of more humble origin. One of Despenser's chief victims was his own sister-in-law, Joan of Acre's daughter Elizabeth de Burgh, who lost her valuable Welsh lordship of Usk, once held by her father Gilbert 'the Red' de Clare, to the greedy Despenser. Elizabeth's older sister Margaret spent four and a half years in captivity at Sempringham Priory in Lincolnshire on the orders of their vindictive uncle the king after her second husband Hugh Audley joined the Marcher rebellion of 1321/22. Although Edward paid Margaret generous living expenses, he kept all her lands in his own hands.

In 1324/25, Margaret de Bohun had her own chamber at her much older cousin Elizabeth de Burgh's castle of Clare in Suffolk, so must have spent a lot of time with her.[7] Margaret turned 14 in April 1325, and married Hugh Courtenay on 11 August that year; he had recently turned 22. The first of their many children was born on 22 March 1327 shortly before Margaret turned 16, and was a son, inevitably named Hugh Courtenay, the eldest grandchild of Elizabeth of Rhuddlan.[8] Margaret's eldest brother also wed in the 1320s: John de Bohun's marriage to a daughter of Edmund Fitzalan, earl of Arundel (b. 1285), was planned by 22 February 1324, when Pope John XXII in Avigon issued a dispensation for John to marry 'one of the daughters of the said Edmund'.[9] John was 18 at this time, and his future wife, Alice Fitzalan, somewhat younger; her parents probably married in or shortly before May 1306. Surprisingly, given that he had been present at Piers Gaveston's death in June 1312, the earl of Arundel had become a staunch ally of Edward II and Hugh Despenser, and in early 1321 his 7-year-old son and heir, Richard, married Despenser's 8-year-old daughter Isabella, Joan of Acre's eldest granddaughter.

Chapter 39

Estrangement and Invasion

After *c.* 1322, it seems that Mary of Woodstock and her brother had fallen out. Even when Edward travelled to Wiltshire and Gloucestershire in May 1326 and hence was very close to Mary at Amesbury Priory, there is no record that he visited his sister or invited her to court, or even that the siblings sent each other letters or oral messages. Curiously, Mary does not appear even once in the king's extant chamber accounts of 1324–1326; neither does she appear in the chancery rolls after 1322, whereas she had frequently done so before.[1] It may be that Mary was distressed or angry about the king's shabby treatment of their de Clare nieces Margaret Audley and Elizabeth de Burgh. Her lack of contact with her brother may even speak to the hold her nephew-in-law Hugh Despenser the Younger had over the king, and perhaps indicates that Hugh and his wife Eleanor dominated and maybe even manipulated Edward. By 1326 the king was so extraordinarily close to his eldest niece Eleanor and her husband Hugh Despenser that one English annalist called Edward and Hugh 'the king and his husband', while a Continental chronicler stated that Edward and Eleanor were involved in an incestuous relationship. Eleanor's sister Margaret Audley, née de Clare was still held in captivity at Sempringham Priory, where she lived from May 1322 until December 1326 on the king's orders, and Hugh Despenser was still threatening and persecuting his sister-in-law Elizabeth in 1326.[2]

Between 1322 and 1325, Edward II became estranged from almost all his family members to whom he had once been close: his sister Mary; his half-brothers Thomas and Edmund; his wife Isabella; his eldest child Edward of Windsor; his first cousins John of Brittany, earl of Richmond, and Henry of Lancaster; and his niece Margaret Audley (he had never been particularly fond of or close to Margaret's sister Elizabeth de Burgh, and Edward's three younger children, John of Eltham, Eleanor of Woodstock and Joan of the Tower, were only 10, 8 and 5 years old in 1326, so were too young to have much, if any, awareness of what was happening). Mary of Woodstock did keep in touch with her niece Elizabeth de Burgh: there is a record of messages Elizabeth sent to 'Lady Maria' in August, September and October 1326. The two women probably kept in touch regularly, though Elizabeth's accounts do not survive before the autumn of 1326, so it is impossible to say for sure.[3]

Edward II sent letters to his other surviving sister the dowager duchess of Brabant and to her son Jan III, on 25 and 26 September 1326.[4] One of the letters concerned the arrest of Master William Weston, Edward's envoy to Pope John XXII in Avignon, who had been imprisoned in Antwerp on his way back to England, 'whereby he [Edward II] is much disturbed'. The other related to an act of piracy in the Channel. Four 'merchants of Almain', i.e. Germany or somewhere close to it, who were perhaps subjects of Duke Jan, had complained that while they were travelling from Waterford in Ireland to Bruges in Flanders, having loaded their ship with wool, hides and other goods, they passed near the Isle of Wight. Here, Alisandre Keu of Winchelsea and Thomas of London, with numerous armed accomplices, boarded their ship by force on the sea and stole forty-two sacks of wool, twelve sackes of hides, three containers full of salmon and two of cheese, and cloth, jewels and bowls. This theft had become something of a political hot potato, and Edward ordered the sheriff of Kent to arrest the men responsible and to force them to restore all the stolen goods to the merchants.

Edward's infatuation with Hugh Despenser the Younger alienated him from his wife as much as from his sister Mary, and after Queen Isabella travelled to her homeland in 1325 to negotiate a peace settlement between her husband and her brother Charles IV, she refused to return. The queen sent Edward an ultimatum: to send Despenser away from him, or she would not come back to England nor permit her and Edward's teenage son and heir Edward of Windsor, in her custody in France, to do so either. Edward II refused the ultimatum, and so Isabella remained in France and formed an alliance with the remnant of the rebellious baronial faction of 1321/22 who had escaped from England and fled to the Continent. Their leader was Roger Mortimer, baron of Wigmore and Ludlow, who had escaped from the Tower of London in August 1323. The queen and the barons formed another alliance with Willem, count of Hainault on France's northern border, who provided ships and mercenaries for an invasion of England in exchange for his third daughter Philippa's future marriage to Edward of Windsor.

The queen's invasion force landed in Suffolk on 24 September. Elizabeth de Burgh, who spent much of her time at her castle of Clare 40 miles away in the same county, heard of the arrival the same day, and sent messengers 'in haste' to her manor of Cranbourne in Dorset to inform them.[5] Edward II's support simply collapsed; few men were willing to fight against their future king Edward of Windsor on behalf of the present king's powerful, loathed and despotic favourite Hugh Despenser the Younger. Edward and Hugh fled from London towards South Wales, most of which Hugh owned. They left Despenser's father Hugh the Elder, earl of Winchester, to hold Bristol, but it soon fell to the queen and her army, and Winchester was hanged on 27 October. The earl of Arundel, the only remaining important supporter of the king and Despenser, whose son and heir was married to Joan of Acre's eldest granddaughter, was captured and beheaded in Hereford.

On 31 October 1326, John de Bohun must have been with his uncle Edward II at Caerphilly Castle, which belonged to Hugh Despenser. He performed homage to the king for his inheritance on this day, and was allowed to take possession of his father's lands. John, born on 23 November 1305, was not quite 21. His brother Edward, aged either about 13 or about 16 or 17, was there too: on 10 November, the king appointed the teenager as one of his five envoys to the queen, though almost certainly they never left.[6] Edward II, Hugh Despenser the Younger and the handful of men who remained with them were captured near Llantrisant on Sunday, 16 November, and the reign of Leonor of Castile and Edward I's son ended in all but name at that moment.

Hugh Despenser the Younger was executed by hanging, drawing and quartering in Hereford on 24 November. One of the many charges against him, which he was not allowed to answer, stated: 'many other magnates you had sent to hard prison, such as ... the children of [the earl and countess of] Hereford, who were the nephews of our lord the king'.[7] Elizabeth's sons, or at least some of them, had indeed been temporarily held at Windsor Castle after the death of their father at the battle of Boroughbridge in March 1322, with some of the sons of Roger Mortimer of Wigmore.

Chapter 40

Depositions and Deaths

At a parliament held in London in early 1327, it was decided that Edward II must be forced to abdicate his throne to his 14-year-old son, whose reign as Edward III began on 25 January. The former king was held in captivity at Kenilworth Castle in Warwickshire, then, from early April, at Berkeley Castle in Gloucestershire. John de Bohun, earl of Hereford and Essex, was one of the many noblemen who attended his cousin Edward III's coronation at Westminster Abbey on 1 February 1327.[1] As the new king was still well underage, his mother Isabella and her allies ruled in his name, though Isabella was never appointed as regent and mostly ignored the council of magnates and prelates who in fact were appointed to rule the kingdom until her son came of age.

There is no way of knowing how Mary of Woodstock felt about the forced abdication of her brother and the subsequent accession of her teenage nephew, or about the news, taken to Edward III at Lincoln during the night of 23/24 September, that Edward II had died in captivity at Berkeley Castle in Gloucestershire on the 21st. Edward III wrote on 24 September to his cousin John de Bohun to tell him that 'our very dear lord and father has been commanded to God'.[2] Edward II's funeral took place in St Peter's Abbey, Gloucester, later Gloucester Cathedral, on 20 December 1327. Presumably Mary attended; her niece Elizabeth de Burgh and her half-brother Edmund of Woodstock, earl of Kent, were certainly there, and most probably her other half-brother Thomas of Brotherton, earl of Norfolk, as well.

In 1327, Joan de Bohun, née Plucknett (or Plokenet) passed away. She was the heir of her brother Alan Plucknett (*c.* 1276–1325), and the widow of Henry de Bohun, who was killed at the battle of Bannockburn in 1314 and was the cousin of the late Humphrey de Bohun (d. 1322), earl of Hereford and Essex. Joan left some of her lands and castles to Eleanor de Bohun, Elizabeth of Rhuddlan's daughter, out of 'affection' for her. These included Kilpeck Castle in Herefordshire, and the hereditary keeping of the forest of Haye, now Haywood, in the same county.[3] Eleanor married the Anglo-Irish nobleman James Botiller or Boteler between 14 February 1328 and 21 November 1328; he was made earl of Ormond at a parliament held in Salisbury in the autumn of 1328.[4] James was an ally of the powerful Roger Mortimer, the real ruler of England with Queen Isabella during Edward III's minority, and Mortimer created the grandiose earldom of March for himself during the same parliament. The regime of the dowager queen and her favourite, Mortimer, was by now almost as unpopular as Edward II's and Hugh Despenser's had been some years earlier.

Joan of Acre had only two grandchildren from her second marriage to Ralph de Monthermer: Mary's daughter Isabella MacDuff, countess of Fife in her own right, was born *c.* 1320 and lived until 1389, but had no children from her four marriages, and Thomas's daughter Margaret de Monthermer was born at his manor of Stokenham in Devon on 18 October 1329. Thomas celebrated his daughter's birth by hunting two does in his park at Stokenham.[5] All three of Joan's de Clare daughters had grandchildren and numerous descendants, though, of Joan's two granddaughters from her second marriage, only Margaret de Monthermer had descendants: her son John Montacute was born *c.* 1350, and succeeded his elderly uncle as earl of Salisbury in 1397. In 1329/30, Joan's youngest child, Edward de Monthermer, became involved in a bizarre plot by his half-uncle Edmund, earl of Kent, to free the supposedly dead Edward II from captivity. Kent was beheaded in March 1330; Edward de Monthermer was imprisoned in Winchester, as were many other men who seemingly shared his belief that Edward II was not dead after all.[6]

Edward III and Queen Philippa's first child was born at the palace of Woodstock on 15 June 1330. It was a boy, who was named after his father, grandfather and great-grandfather, and who immediately became heir to the English throne. On the day his son and heir Edward of Woodstock was born, Edward III granted his aunt Mary of Woodstock permission to appoint two attorneys, John Spakeman and Stephen Gissyng, to act on her behalf for two years.[7] Having fathered a son and secured the succession to his throne, Edward III overthrew his mother Isabella and her chief counsellor Roger Mortimer in October 1330, had Mortimer executed and confined Isabella to temporary house arrest, and took over the governance of his own kingdom (and freed his kinsman Edward de

Monthermer and others from prison). The king lived until June 1377 when he was 64, and his reign of half a century was a mostly glorious one, and certainly extremely dramatic.

Mary, the reluctant nun of Amesbury Priory, saw very little of her nephew's reign: she died on 29 May 1332 at the age of 53.[8] A few years later in the early 1340s, her nephew-in-law John de Warenne, earl of Surrey, trying again to annul his marriage to Mary's niece Jeanne de Bar, claimed that he had had an affair with Mary ('had carnally known' her) before he married Joan. He hoped that this would persuade Pope Clement VI to annul his marriage on the grounds of incest.[9] Divorce in the modern sense of ending a marriage was impossible; an unhappy spouse could only claim that the marriage had never been valid in the first place, which required a pre-existing impediment, such as consanguinity which had not received the required papal dispensation; or that the bridegroom had been intimate with a close member of his wife's family before marriage, and had therefore committed incest. In 1316, John had tried to annul the marriage by claiming that he was already contracted to marry his mistress Maud Nerford before his wedding to Jeanne in 1306; this was a new tactic.

For numerous reasons, although Mary of Woodstock was certainly an unconventional nun, an affair with her nephew-in-law seems extremely unlikely. Surrey, without any legitimate children and heirs from his long marriage to Jeanne and wishing to marry his latest mistress Isabelle Holland and legitimise his children (or future children) with her, had grown desperate, and Mary was conveniently closely related to his wife, conveniently dead and unable to gainsay the claim, and conveniently had no children to take offence at his claims. Had the story been true, Surrey would surely have tried to use it on a much earlier occasion, when Mary was alive and could have been questioned on the matter, perhaps in 1316 when he first attempted to annul his marriage. The earl's ploy failed and the pope warned him to treat his wife 'with marital affection', having also dismissed John's secondary claim that the dispensation for consanguinity issued by Clement V in 1305/06 was invalid. The queen-consorts of England and France, Philippa of Hainault and Jeanne of Burgundy, took a sympathetic interest in Countess Jeanne's plight, and their intercession on her behalf might have gone some way to persuading Clement VI to reject Surrey's claims. When John de Warenne died in late June 1347 the day before his sixty-first birthday, Jeanne de Bar was still his wife and had been for over forty years. His heir was his late sister Alice's son, Richard Fitzalan, earl of Arundel, although he had fathered at least six illegitimate sons and three illegitimate daughters with various mistresses.[10]

Only one of Mary's numerous sisters outlived her. Margaret, dowager duchess of Brabant, was still alive on 8 October 1331 and apparently also on 11 March 1333, when her nephew Edward III sent a letter to her son Duke Jan III and stated that he (Edward) had granted 'the bailiwick of Hastyng Rope' to one Francis Rauland 'at the request of Margaret the king's aunt and at that of the duke'.[11] She was either still alive in March 1333 or had been alive until fairly recently, when she made this request of her nephew the king. The date of Margaret's death is, unfortunately, unknown. The website of the Cathedral of St Michael and Ste Gudule in Brussels, where Margaret and her husband were buried, states that her funeral took place there in July 1330. However, it wrongly calls her 'Margaret of York', apparently a confusion with Edward IV of England's sister of this name (1446–1503) who married Duke Charles 'the Bold' of Burgundy in 1468.[12] Edward III's letters of 8 October 1331 and 11 March 1333 referring to Margaret do not say 'the duchess of Brabant, the king's aunt, whom God absolve' or 'the king's late aunt', as one would generally expect if she were dead.

Born in February or March 1275, Margaret turned 58 years old in early 1333, and was a grandmother to the six legitimate children of her son Jan III and to his numerous illegitimate offspring. Assuming that her brother Edward II was dead, though, given the wealth of evidence that he did not die at Berkeley Castle in September 1327 as usually assumed but lived on for years past that date, this is by no means certain, Margaret was the last surviving child of Leonor of Castile. The only sibling who certainly outlived her was her much younger half-brother Thomas of Brotherton, earl of Norfolk, the elder son of Edward I and his second wife Marguerite of France, who died in August 1338 at the age of 38. It is sad that we do not know the date of Margaret's death, given that she was the last surviving daughter of a prolific and powerful king.

Epilogue

Four of the daughters of Edward I and Leonor of Castile had children, and they had and have numerous illustrious descendants. Elizabeth of Rhuddlan was a great-great-grandmother of Henry V (b. 1386, r. 1413–22) via her son William de Bohun, earl of Northampton, whose granddaughter Mary de Bohun, countess of Derby (*c.* 1370–94), was King Henry's mother. Joan of Acre was an ancestor of Edward IV (r. 1461–83) and his brother Richard III (r. 1483–85) via her third daughter Elizabeth de Burgh, née de Clare and Elizabeth's great-granddaughter Philippa of Clarence (1355– *c.* 1379), countess of March and Ulster. Via her son Édouard of Bar, Eleanor of Windsor was an ancestor of Louis XI, king of France (r. 1461–83), Henri IV, the first Bourbon king of France (r. 1589–1610), and René of Anjou (d. 1480), titular king of Naples, Sicily, Jerusalem and Majorca, whose daughter Marguerite of Anjou (d. 1482) married Henry VI of England in 1445. Margaret of Windsor was a great-great-grandmother of John 'the Fearless', duke of Burgundy (assassinated in 1419), and through him was an ancestor of Charles V, Holy Roman Emperor (d. 1558) and Charles's son Philip II of Spain (d. 1598). Like her older sister Eleanor, Margaret was an ancestor of the Bourbons, kings of Navarre and France.

Both Joan of Acre and Elizabeth of Rhuddlan were ancestors of Henry VIII's second, fifth and sixth wives, Anne Boleyn, Katherine Howard and Katherine Parr. Margaret of Windsor was an ancestor of Henry's fourth wife Anne of Cleves via her granddaughter Margaretha of Brabant, countess of Flanders, and Margaretha's grandson John 'the Fearless' of Burgundy. Joan of Acre, though not her sisters, was an ancestor of Henry's third wife Jane Seymour, via her second and third daughters Margaret and Elizabeth de Clare. Katherine of Aragon was the only wife of Henry VIII not descended from one of Edward I's daughters, though she was descended from their brother Edward II, via his grandson John of Gaunt and John's daughters Philippa, queen of Portugal and Catalina, queen of Castile. All four daughters of Edward I and Queen Leonor who had children are ancestors of the present British royal family, in multiple different ways, and ancestors of huge numbers of people around the world.

Three (and possibly four) of the five sisters were buried in England, and Margaret of Windsor was buried with her husband in the church of Sainte Gudule, now the Cathedral of Saint Michael and Sainte Gudule in central Brussels. Joan of Acre's burial site of Clare Priory, near the River Stour in Suffolk, was founded in 1248 by her first husband's father Richard de Clare as the first Augustinian house in England, and still exists. It is now a mixed house of Augustinian friars and lay people, and is also a retreat centre which is open to visitors. Mary of Woodstock was buried at Amesbury Priory, which was dissolved in 1539 and pulled down, though the parish church of St Mary and St Melor in the village of Amesbury is believed by some authorities to have been the church that was attached to the priory and is, perhaps, the location where Mary's remains still lie. Amesbury Abbey, a mansion currently in operation as a nursing home, stands on or near the site of the medieval priory and was built in the 1830s. Walden Abbey in Essex, where Elizabeth of Rhuddlan, her husband and several of her children and her de Bohun descendants were buried, was dissolved in 1538. Henry VIII gave the site to his chancellor, Sir Thomas Audley, who built a home there, and the palatial Audley End House can still be visited. Finally, the tombs and effigies of the royal sisters' parents Edward I and Leonor of Castile are still in Westminster Abbey, where Eleanor of Windsor might also have been buried. The tomb of their brother Edward II can be seen in Gloucester Cathedral, formerly St Peter's Abbey.

Appendix 1

Brief Biographical Details of Edward I's Daughters

For ease of reference, the key dates in the women's lives, with their brothers interspersed to show the birth order of the royal children.[1]

1) Possibly **a daughter**, name unknown, died in Bordeaux on 29 May 1255; not a full-term pregnancy.
2) **Katherine**, born sometime before 16 June 1264, perhaps as early as *c*. 1261; died 5 September 1264, buried in Westminster Abbey.
3) **Joan**, born December 1264 or January 1265; died shortly before 7 September 1265, buried in Westminster Abbey.
   John of Windsor, born 13/14 July 1266, died 3 August 1271.
   Henry of Windsor, born *c*. 6 May 1268, died 14/17 October 1274.
4) **Eleanor**, born at Windsor Castle on 17 or 18 June 1269; betrothed to Alfonso III, king of Aragon (4 November 1265–18 June 1291) in 1273, but married Henri III, count of Bar (*c*. 1255/60–1302), in Bristol on 20 September 1293; died 29 August 1298, possibly buried in Westminster Abbey.
5) **A daughter**, name unknown, born in the Holy Land sometime in 1270/71, died not long after birth.
6) **Joan of Acre**, born in the Holy Land in the spring of 1272; married (1) Gilbert de Clare, earl of Gloucester and Hertford (b. 2 September 1243), on 30 April 1290, widowed 7 December 1295; married (2) Ralph de Monthermer (b. *c*. 1262, d. 5 April 1325) sometime in early 1297; died 23 April 1307 and buried in Clare Priory, Suffolk.
   Alfonso of Bayonne, born 24 November 1273, died 19 August 1284.
7) **Margaret**, born *c*. 15 March (or possibly mid-February) 1275, almost certainly at Windsor Castle; married Jan of Brabant (b. 27 September 1275), later Duke Jan II of Brabant, on 3 July 1290, widowed 27 October 1312; apparently still alive on 11 March 1333;

date of death unknown, buried in the church of Sainte Gudule in Brussels with her husband.[2]

8) **Berengaria**, born at Kempton *c.* 1 May 1276, died before 27 June 1278.
9) **A daughter**, name unknown, born 3 January 1278, died shortly afterwards.
10) **Mary**, born at the palace of Woodstock near Oxford on 11 or 12 March 1279; entered Amesbury Priory, Wiltshire on 15 August 1285 and later veiled as a nun; died 29 May 1332 and probably buried at Amesbury.

    Possibly **a son**, name unknown, born *c.* the early months of 1281.
11) **Elizabeth**, born *c.* 7 August 1282 in Rhuddlan, North Wales; married (1) Jan I, count of Holland (b. 1283/84), in Ipswich on 7 or 8 January 1297, widowed 10 November 1299; married (2) Humphrey de Bohun, earl of Hereford and Essex (b. *c.* 1276, d. 16 March 1322) in Westminster Abbey on 14 November 1302; died 5 May 1316, buried in Walden Abbey, Essex.

    Edward of Caernarfon, born 25 April 1284 in North Wales; King Edward II of England 8 July 1307 to 24 January 1327; reportedly died 21 September 1327.

    Thomas of Brotherton, earl of Norfolk and Earl Marshal, eldest child of Edward I and his second wife Marguerite of France, born 1 June 1300, died shortly before 25 August 1338.

    Edmund of Woodstock, earl of Kent, second child of Edward and Marguerite, born 5 August 1301, executed 19 March 1330.
12) **Eleanor**, Edward I's youngest child, born to Marguerite of France on 6 May 1306, according to a chronicler. Betrothed on 8 May 1306 to Robert, heir to the French counties of Burgundy and Artois, but died young in *c.* August 1311 and buried in Beaulieu Abbey, Hampshire.

Appendix 2

The Children of Edward I's Daughters

Eleanor of Windsor, countess of Bar (1269–98)

1) **Édouard I**, count of Bar (*c*. 1294/95 – November 1336). Succeeded his father Henri III as count of Bar in 1302, and in or after 1306 married Marie of Burgundy, a granddaughter of Saint Louis IX of France, daughter and sister of dukes of Burgundy, and sister of two queens of France.[1] Their son and heir Henri IV was born in 1321; Édouard's uncle Edward II of England gave 10 marks to a messenger on 21 May that year for bringing him news of the birth.[2] Count Édouard drowned off the coast of Famagusta, Cyprus, in November 1336, in his early forties. His son Count Henri IV's second son, Robert, first duke of Bar (1344–1411), continued the Bar line; Robert's son Henri, who would have succeeded him but died before his father, married Edward III of England's granddaughter Marie de Coucy (1366–1405).
2) **Jeanne de Bar**, countess of Surrey (*c*. 1295/96 – 29 August 1361). Moved to England in 1305 some years after the death of her father, and known as the Damsel of Bar in her mother's homeland. She married John de Warenne, earl of Surrey (b. 30 June 1286) on 25 May 1306 when she was no more than about 11 years old and perhaps younger, but by 1313 and probably well before, they lived apart. John spent much of their forty-year marriage trying to persuade various popes to annul the marriage, but failed. He did not even mention Jeanne in his will of 1347, though pointedly referred to his current mistress Isabelle Holland as his *compaigne*, a word that meant 'wife' or 'consort'. Jeanne was left a 'gold image of St John the Baptist in the desert' by her cousin Elizabeth de Burgh, Joan of Acre's third daughter, when Elizabeth died in November 1360, though she outlived Elizabeth by only a few months.[3] Jeanne had no children.

Joan of Acre, countess of Gloucester and Hertford (1272–1307)

1) **Gilbert de Clare**, earl of Gloucester and Hertford (*c.* 23 April/10 May 1291 – 24 June 1314). Edward I's eldest grandchild, and his parents' heir. Married Maud de Burgh, one of the many daughters of the earl of Ulster and sister-in-law of Robert Bruce, king of Scotland, on 29 September 1308, but they had no surviving children. Killed during his uncle Edward II's defeat at the battle of Bannockburn, aged 23; his heirs were his three younger full sisters. Gilbert's body was returned to England, and he was buried at the Clares' mausoleum, Tewkesbury Abbey in Gloucestershire, with his father and grandfather. His heart, however, as was common in the royal family of the era, was interred separately at the conventual church of Shalford, Nottinghamshire, and Gilbert's uncle the king distributed oblations there in memory of his soul and because Gilbert's 'heart lies there inhumed' in August 1317.[4]
2) **Eleanor de Clare**, Lady Despenser (*c.* 14/24 October 1292 – 30 June 1337). Married Hugh Despenser the Younger (executed 24 November 1326) on 26 May 1306, and William Zouche (d. 1337) soon before 26 January 1329, when his abduction of her from Hanley Castle in Worcestershire and their (possibly forced) marriage was recorded in the chancery rolls. She gave birth to at least eleven children between *c.* 1308 and *c.* 1330, of whom ten lived into adulthood; her heir to her third of the earldom of Gloucester was her eldest son Hugh Despenser, called 'Huchon', born 1308 or early 1309. Eleanor was, like her father and her elder brother Gilbert, buried at Tewkesbury Abbey, as were both of her husbands and many of her Despenser descendants including her eldest son and heir Huchon (d. 1349), grandson Edward (d. 1375), great-grandson Thomas, earl of Gloucester (d. 1400), and great-great-granddaughter and heir Isabelle Despenser, countess of Worcester and Warwick (d. 1439).
3) **Margaret de Clare**, countess of Cornwall and Gloucester (*c.* 1293/94 – 2 April 1342). Married to two of her uncle Edward II's favourites, Piers Gaveston, earl of Cornwall (d. 1312), and Hugh Audley, made earl of Gloucester in 1337. Her only surviving child and heir, Margaret Audley, born *c.* early 1320s, was abducted by and forcibly married to Ralph Stafford, later the first earl of Stafford, in

1336, and was an ancestor of the Stafford dukes of Buckingham and of many kings of France and Spain. Margaret de Clare was buried at Tonbridge Priory in Kent with her second husband Hugh, earl of Gloucester (d. 1347).

4) **Elizabeth de Clare** (16 September 1295 – 4 November 1360). Married the earl of Ulster's son and heir John de Burgh on 30 September 1308, secondly Theobald Verdon on 4 February 1316, and thirdly Roger Damory between *c.* 30 April and 3 May 1317. Her heir on her death was her granddaughter Elizabeth de Burgh, countess of Ulster and later duchess of Clarence (1332–63), her only son William's only child. Elizabeth the elder was buried at the convent of the Minoresses, often called the Minories, near the Tower of London. Her will and many of her household accounts still survive and reveal much about her life, and she is perhaps most famous for her endowment of a college at the University of Cambridge in 1338, originally called Clare Hall and later Clare College.
5) **Mary de Monthermer**, countess of Fife (*c.* October 1297 – *c.* 1371). Married Duncan MacDuff, earl of Fife (1289–1353) in 1307. Her only child, Isabella MacDuff (*c.* 1320–89), countess of Fife in her own right, was married four times but had no children, and so Mary and Duncan's line ended with Isabella's death.
6) **Joan de Monthermer**, nun of Amesbury Priory in Wiltshire. Probably born in 1299, though the year and even the decade of her death were not recorded, and nothing at all is known about her life except that she joined her aunt Mary in becoming a nun of Amesbury.
7) **Thomas de Monthermer** (4 October 1301 – 24 June 1340), his father Ralph's heir. Thomas's only child and heir was Margaret de Monthermer (b. 1329), who was the mother of John Montacute, earl of Salisbury (*c.* 1350–1400). Margaret was the only grandchild of Joan of Acre and her second husband Ralph de Monthermer who had descendants. Thomas was killed at the naval battle of Sluys, his cousin Edward III's great victory over the French, in June 1340.
8) **Edward de Monthermer** (*c.* 11 April 1304 – late 1339). Never married and had no children, and is rather obscure; his half-sister Elizabeth de Burgh buried him with their mother at Clare Priory in Suffolk around 12 December 1339.[5]

Margaret of Windsor, duchess of Brabant

1) **Jan III**, duke of Brabant (*c.* late October/early November 1300 – 5 December 1355). Married Marie of Évreux (1303–35) in 1311; she was one of the daughters of Louis (1276–1319), count of Évreux, a younger half-brother of King Philip IV of France.[6] Duke Jan III's three sons Jan, Henryk and Godfrey died before him, and his heir was his eldest child Johanna, duchess of Brabant and Luxembourg (1322–1406). Jan is believed to have fathered more than twenty illegitimate children. Of his six legitimate children, only his second daughter, Margaretha, countess of Flanders, had descendants.

Elizabeth of Rhuddlan, countess of Holland, Hereford and Essex

For the following, I am indebted to Brad Verity's article 'The Children of Elizabeth, Countess of Hereford, Daughter of Edward I of England' in the journal *Foundations*, though the birth order of Elizabeth's children is not absolutely clear, and some of their dates of birth are impossible to ascertain.

1) **Margaret de Bohun I** (September 1303 – 7 February 1306).
2) **Humphrey de Bohun I** (10 September 1304 – 28 October 1304).
3) **John de Bohun**, earl of Hereford and Essex (23 November 1305 – 20 January 1336); married firstly to the earl of Arundel's daughter Alice and secondly to Margaret Basset, but had no children, and his younger brother Humphrey II was his heir.[7]
4) **Humphrey de Bohun II**, earl of Hereford and Essex (1307 or *c.* 9 December 1309 – 16 October 1361); his brother John's successor as earl in 1336, but never married and had no children, and his heir was his younger brother William's son Humphrey (b. 1342).
5) **Edward de Bohun** and **6) William de Bohun**, earl of Northampton. Twins, with Edward the elder, born perhaps 1309 or *c.* 1312/13. Edward married Margaret Ros but had no children, and drowned in Scotland shortly before 8 November 1334. His heir on his death was his eldest brother, John, earl of Hereford.[8] William was made earl of Northampton by their cousin Edward III in 1337, and married

Elizabeth Badlesmere, widow of Edmund Mortimer of Wigmore (d. 1331/32), mother of Roger Mortimer, second earl of March (1328–60), and co-heir of her brother Giles, Lord Badlesmere (1314–38). William de Bohun and Elizabeth Badlesmere's son Humphrey de Bohun (1342–73) was earl of Hereford, Essex and Northampton, and their daughter Elizabeth (*c.* mid-1340s–1385) was countess of Arundel and Surrey. William de Bohun, earl of Northampton, died on 16 September 1360, thirteen months before his elder brother Humphrey, earl of Hereford. His son Humphrey the younger inherited the earldoms of Northampton, Hereford and Essex when he came of age, 21, in 1363.

7) **Eleanor de Bohun**, countess of Ormond (*c.* 1310 – 7 October 1363). A cartulary compiled in her own lifetime states that Eleanor was the elder of the two surviving Bohun daughters, though a petition presented to parliament in 1425 says that Eleanor was the younger Bohun daughter. The 1319 will of the sisters' father Humphrey names Eleanor before Margaret, as does the 1361 will of their brother Humphrey, which would tend to prove that Eleanor was indeed older than her sister.[9] If she was the elder daughter, as seems likely, it is rather odd and unusual that her sister Margaret married several years before she did. Eleanor married James Botiler or Butler, first earl of Ormond, sometime between 14 February 1328 and 21 November 1328. He died in early 1338 and Eleanor married secondly Sir Thomas Dagworth (d. 1350), and had children from both her marriages. Her eldest surviving son, James Botiller the younger, earl of Ormond, was born in Ireland in the autumn of 1331.[10] Eleanor inherited lands in Herefordshire in 1327 from Joan Plucknett, widow of her father's cousin Henry de Bohun (d. 1314). She wrote her will on 20 August 1363 and died at the Botiller manor of Shere ('Shiere Vachery') in Surrey on 7 October; in her will, she left £6 for alms and masses to 'soothe the soul of our most dear aunt Lady Mary, nun of Amesbury', and £10 for the soul of her cousin Jeanne de Bar, countess of Surrey.[11]

8) **Margaret de Bohun II**, countess of Devon (3 April 1311 – 27 December 1391). She married Hugh Courtenay, later earl of Devon (1303–77), on 11 August 1325, and had sixteen or seventeen children, including William Courtenay, archbishop of Canterbury

(d. 1396). Margaret and Hugh were married for fifty-two years, and Margaret died at age 80, the last surviving grandchild of Leonor of Castile.[12]

9) **Aeneas de Bohun** (*c*. 1312/14–29 September 1331), died unmarried at Kimbolton Castle in Huntingdonshire, and buried in Walden Abbey with his mother and younger sister Isabella.
10) **Isabella de Bohun**, born 5 May 1316 and died on the day of her birth or shortly afterwards. Elizabeth died soon after giving birth to Isabella, and they were both buried in Walden Abbey.

Abbreviations

C	Chancery (National Archives)
CCR	Calendar of Close Rolls
CChR	Calendar of Charter Rolls
CFR	Calendar of Fine Rolls
CIPM	Calendar of Inquisitions Post Mortem
CLR	Calendar of Liberate Rolls
CPR	Calendar of Patent Rolls
DL	Duchy of Lancaster (National Archives)
E	Exchequer (National Archives)
IPM	Inquisition Post Mortem
ODNB	Oxford Dictionary of National Biography
SC	Special Collections (National Archives)
TNA	The National Archives

Bibliography

Primary Sources

'Account of the Expenses of John of Brabant and Thomas and Henry of Lancaster, 1292–3', *Camden Miscellany,* 2nd volume, ed. J. Burtt (1853), pp. 2–11

Adae Murimuth Continuatio Chronicarum, ed. E.M. Thompson (1889)

Annales Londonienses 1195–1330, in ed. W. Stubbs, *Chronicles of the Reigns of Edward I and Edward II*, vol. 1 (1882)

Annales Monastici, vol. 4, ed. H.R. Luard (1869)

Annales Paulini 1307–1340, in ed. Stubbs, *Chronicles of the Reigns*, vol. 1

The Anonimalle Chronicle 1307 to 1334, from Brotherton Collection MS 29, ed. W.R. Childs and J. Taylor (1991)

The Antient Kalendars and Inventories of the Treasury of His Majesty's Exchequer, vol. 1, ed. F. Palgrave (1836)

The Brut or the Chronicles of England, part 1, ed. F.W.D. Brie (1906)

Calendar of the Close Rolls, eighteen vols., 1251–1333 (1898–1927)

Calendar of the Charter Rolls, four vols., 1226–1341 (1903–12)

Calendar of Chancery Warrants, one vol., 1244–1326 (1927)

Calendar of Documents Relating to Scotland, vols. 2 and 3, 1272–1357, ed. J. Bain, and vol. 5, Supplementary, ed. G.G. Simpson and J.D. Galbraith (1881–7)

Calendar of the Fine Rolls, four vols., 1272–1337 (1912–15)

Calendar of Inquisitions Miscellaneous (Chancery), two vols., 1219–1348 (1916)

Calendar of Inquisitions Post Mortem, six vols., 1235–1327 (1904–10)

Calendar of the Liberate Rolls, six vols., 1226–72 (1916–64)

Calendar of Entries in the Papal Registers Relating to Great Britain and Ireland: Papal Letters, two vols., 1198–1341, ed. W.H. Bliss (1893–5)

Calendar of Memoranda Rolls (Exchequer): Michaelmas 1326–Michaelmas 1327 (1968)

Calendar of the Patent Rolls, fourteen vols., 1247–1334 (1893–1908)

Calendar of Wills Proved in the Court of Husting, London, part 1, 1258–1358 (1889)

Cartulaire de Hugues de Chalon (1220–1319), ed. B. Prost and S. Bougenot (1904)

Cartulary of the Augustinian Friars of Clare, ed. C. Harper-Bill (1991)

The Chronicle of Lanercost 1272–1346, ed. H. Maxwell (1913)

The Chronicle of Pierre de Langtoft in French Verse, From the Earliest Period to the Death of King Edward I, vol. 2, ed. T. Wright (1868)

The Chronicles of the Mayors and Sheriffs of London, 1188–1274, ed. H.T. Riley (1863)

Chronique de Ramon Muntaner, Traduite pour la Première Fois du Catalan, vols. 1 and 2, ed. J.A. Buchon (1827)

A Collection of All the Wills Now Known to be Extant of the Kings and Queens of England, Princes and Princess of Wales, and Every Branch of the Blood Royal, From the Reign of William the Conqueror to That of Henry the Seventh, ed. J. Nichols (1780)

Flores Historiarum, vol. 3, ed. H.R. Luard (1890)

The Flowers of History, Especially Such As Relate to the Affairs of Britain, From the Beginning of the World to the Year 1307, Collected by Matthew of Westminster, vol. 2, ed. and trans. C.D. Yonge (1853)

Foedera, Conventiones, Litterae et Cujuncunque Generis Acta Publica, two vols., 1272–1327 (1816–18)

Gesta Edwardi de Carnarvon Auctore Canonico Bridlingtoniensi, in ed. W. Stubbs, *Chronicles of the Reigns of Edward I and Edward II*, vol. 2 (1883)

Groot Charterboek der Graaven van Holland en Zeeland en Heeren van Vriesland, vol. 1, ed. F. van Mieris (1753)

The Household Book of Queen Isabella of England for the Fifth Regnal Year of Edward II, 8th July 1311 to 7th July 1312, ed. F.D. Blackley and G. Hermansen (1971)

Issues of the Exchequer: Being a Collection of Payments Made Out of His Majesty's Revenue, ed. F. Devon (1837)

Johannis de Trokelowe et Henrici de Blaneforde Chronica et Annales, ed. H.T. Riley (1866)

Letters of Royal and Illustrious Ladies of Great Britain, from the Commencement of the Twelfth Century to the Close of the Reign of Queen Mary, ed. M.A.E. Wood, vol. 1 (1846)

Le Livere de Reis de Brittaniae e le Livere de Reis de Engletere, ed. J. Glover (1865)

List of Diplomatic Documents, Scottish Documents and Papal Bulls Preserved in the Public Record Office (Reprinted 1963; originally published 1923)

Monasticon Anglicanum, ed. W. Dugdale, vols. 2, 4 and 5 (1819–25)

National Archives records, especially SC 1 (Ancient Correspondence), SC 8 (Ancient Petitions), C 53 (Charter Rolls), E 100 (Accounts Various)

The Parliament Rolls of Medieval England 1275–1504, ed. C. Given-Wilson, P. Brand, S. Phillips, M. Ormrod, G. Martin, A. Curry and R. Horrox (2005)

The Parliamentary Writs and Writs of Military Summons, ed. F. Palgrave, vol. 1 (1827)

Polychronicon Ranulphi Higden, Monachi Cestrensis, ed. J.R. Lumby, vol. 8 (1865)

The Roll of Arms of the Princes, Barons and Knights who Attended King Edward I to the Siege of Caerlaverock, in 1300, ed. T. Wright (1864)

A Roll of the Household Expenses of Richard de Swinfield, Bishop of Hereford, During Part of the Years 1289 and 1290, ed. The Rev. J. Webb (1854)

Royal Charter Witness Lists for the Reign of Edward II 1307–1326, ed. J.S. Hamilton (2001)

Rymkronyk van Jan van Heelu betreffende den Slag van Woeringen van het Jaer 1288, ed. R. van Breugel Douglas (1836)

*Scalacronica: The Reigns of Edward I, Edward II and Edward III, as Recorded by Sir Thomas Gray of Heton, Knigh*t, ed. H. Maxwell (1907)

Stapleton, T., 'A Brief Summary of the Wardrobe Accounts of the Tenth, Eleventh and Fourteenth Years of King Edward the Second', *Archaeologia*, 26 (1836), pp. 318–45

Testamenta Vetusta: Being Illustrations from Wills, ed. N.H. Nicholas, vol. 1 (1826)

Vaderlandsche Chronyk, of Jaarboek van Holland, Zeeland en Friesland, van de Vroegste Tijden af tot op 1404, ed. P. van der Eyk and D. Vygh (1784)

Vita Edwardi Secundi Monachi Cuiusdam Malmesberiensis, ed. N. Denholm-Young (1957)

The War of Saint-Sardos (1323–1325): Gascon Correspondence and Diplomatic Documents, ed. P. Chaplais (1954)

Secondary Sources

Altschul, M., *A Baronial Family in Medieval England: The Clares, 1217–1314* (1965)

Andrews-Reading, M., 'The Will of Humphrey de Bohun, Earl of Hereford and Essex, 1319', *Foundations*, vol. 6 (2006), pp. 11–12

Barefield, L., 'Lineage and Women's Patronage: Mary of Woodstock and Nicholas Trevet's *Les Cronicles*', *Medieval Feminist Forum*, 33 (2002), pp. 21–30

Bennett, M., 'Edward III's Entail and the Succession to the Crown, 1376–1471', *English Historical Review*, 113 (1998), pp. 580-609

Benz St John, L., *Three Medieval Queens: Queenship and the Crown in Fourteenth-Century England* (2012)

Bigelow, M.M., 'The Bohun Wills', *The American Historical Review*, vol. 1 (1896), pp. 414–35

Bigelow, M.M., 'The Bohun Wills, II', *The American Historical Review*, vol. 1 (1896), pp. 631–49

Bridgeman, G.T.O., *History of the Princes of South Wales* (1876)

Bullock-Davies, C., *Menestrellorum Multitudo: Minstrels at a Royal Feast* (1978)

Bullock-Davies, C., *A Register of Royal and Domestic Minstrels 1272–1327* (1986)

Cavanaugh, S., 'Royal Books: King John to Richard II', *The Library,* 5th series, 10 (1988), pp. 304–16

Chaplais, P., *English Medieval Diplomatic Practice, Part 1: Documents and Interpretation*, 2 vols. (1982)

Chaplais, P., *Piers Gaveston: Edward II's Adoptive Brother* (1994)

Cockerill, S., *Eleanor of Castile: The Shadow Queen* (2014)

Correale, R.M., 'Chaucer's Manuscript of Nicholas Trevet's "Les Cronicles"', *The Chaucer Review*, 25 (1991), pp. 238–65

Davies, J.C., *The Baronial Opposition to Edward II: Its Character and Policy* (1918)

Dean, R.J., 'Nicholas Trevet, Historian', in ed. J.J.G. Alexander and M.T. Gibson, *Medieval Learning and Literature: Essays Presented to Richard William Hunt* (1976), pp. 328–51

De Boer, D.E.H., E.H.P. Cordfunke and H. Sarfatij, eds., *1299, Één Graaf, Drie Graafschappen: De Vereniging van Holland, Zeeland en Henegouwen* (2000)

De Ridder, P., 'Brussel, Residentie der Hertogen van Brabant onder Jan I (1267–1294) en Jan II (1294–1312)', *Revue Belge de Philologie et d'Histoire*, 57 (1979), pp. 329–41

Dek, A.W.E., *Genealogie der Graven van Holland* (1969)

Doubleday, S., *The Wise King: A Christian Prince, Muslim Spain, and the Birth of the Renaissance* (2015)

Estow, C., *Pedro the Cruel of Castile, 1350–1369* (The Medieval Mediterranean: Peoples, Economies and Cultures, 400–1453, number 6, 1996)

Estow, C., 'Royal Madness in the Crónica del Rey Don Pedro', *Mediterranean Studies*, 6 (1996)

Fairbank, F.R., 'The Last Earl of Warenne and Surrey, and the Distribution of his Possessions', *Yorkshire Archaeological Journal*, 19 (1907), pp. 193–264

Farris, C.H.D.C., 'The Pious Practices of Edward I, 1272–1307', Univ. of London PhD thesis, 2013

Folger, R., *Generaciones Y Semblanzas: Memory and Genealogy in Medieval Iberian Historiography* (2003)

Gee, L.L., *Women, Art and Patronage from Henry III to Edward III* (2002)

Gibbs, V., and H.A. Doubleday, *The Complete Peerage of England, Scotland, Ireland, Great Britain and the United Kingdom*, 14 vols. (1910–40)

Gough, H., *Itinerary of King Edward the First Throughout his Reign*, vol. 1, 1272–1285, and vol. 2, 1286–1307 (1900)

Green, M.A.E., *Lives of the Princesses of England from the Norman Conquest*, vols. 2 and 3 (1850–51)

Gue, E., 'The Education and Literary Interests of the English Lay Nobility, *c*. 1150–*c*. 1450', Univ. of Oxford DPhil thesis (1983)

Haines, R.M., *King Edward II: His Life, His Reign, and Its Aftermath, 1284–1330* (2003)

Hallam, E.M., *The Itinerary of Edward II and his Household, 1307–1327* (1984)

Hamilton, J.S., 'The Character of Edward II: The Letters of Edward II Reconsidered', in eds. G. Dodd and A. Musson, *The Reign of Edward II: New Perspectives* (2006), pp. 5–21

Hamilton, J.S., *Piers Gaveston, Earl of Cornwall 1307–1312: Politics and Patronage in the Reign of Edward II* (1988)

Holmes, G.A., 'The Judgement on the Younger Despenser, 1326', *English Historical Review*, 70 (1955), pp. 261–7

Howell, M., 'The Children of King Henry III and Eleanor of Provence', in eds. P. R. Coss and S. D. Lloyd, *Thirteenth Century England IV* (1991), pp. 57–72

Howell, M., *Eleanor of Provence: Queenship in Thirteenth-Century England* (1998)

Huffman, J.P., *The Social Politics of Medieval Diplomacy: Anglo-German Relations (1066–1307)* (2000)

Johnstone, H., 'The County of Ponthieu, 1279–1307', *English Historical Review*, 29 (1914), pp. 435–52

Johnstone, H., *Edward of Carnarvon 1284–1307* (1946)

Johnstone, H., *Letters of Edward, Prince of Wales, 1304–5* (1931)

Johnstone, H., 'The Wardrobe and Household of Henry, Son of Edward I', *Bulletin of the John Rylands Library*, 7 (1920), pp. 384–420

Jolly, M., ed., *Encyclopedia of Life Writing: Autobiographical and Biographical Forms* (2013)

Köhler, R., *Die Heiratsverhandlungen zwischen Eduard I. von England und Rudolf von Habsburg* (1969)

Levelt, S., *Jan van Naaldwijk's Chronicles of Holland: Continuity and Transformation* (2011)

Linehan, P., 'The English Mission of Cardinal Petrus Hispanus, the Chronicle of Walter of Guisborough, and News from Castile at Carlisle (1307)', *English Historical Review*, 117 (2002), pp. 605–21

Lucas, H.S., 'The Problem of the Poems Concerning the Murder of Count Floris V of Holland', *Speculum*, 32 (1958), pp. 283–98

Lutkin, J., and J. Mackman, 'Will of Eleanor, Countess of Ormond, 1363', *Foundations*, 8 (2016), pp. 73–74

Lysons, S., 'Copy of a Roll of the Expenses of King Edward the First at Rhuddlan Castle', *Archaeologia*, 16 (1812), pp. 32–79

Maddicott, J.R., *Simon de Montfort* (1994)

Marshall, A., 'The Childhood and Household of Edward II's Half-Brothers, Thomas of Brotherton and Edmund of Woodstock', in eds. G. Dodd and A. Musson, *The Reign of Edward II: New Perspectives* (2006), pp. 190–204

McFarlane, K.B., *The Nobility of Later Medieval England* (1973)

McKisack, M., *The Fourteenth Century 1307–1399* (1959)

Mitchell, L.E., 'Joan de Valence and Her Household: Domesticity, Management, and Organization in Transition from Wife to Widow', in ed. T. Earenfight, *Royal and Elite Households in Medieval and Early Modern Europe* (2018), pp. 95–114

Mitchell, L.E., *Portraits of Medieval Women: Family, Marriage and Politics in England 1225–1350* (2003)

Moor, C., *Knights of Edward I*, 5 vols. (1929–32)

Morris, M., *A Great and Terrible King: Edward I and the Forging of Britain* (2008)

Nusbacher, A., *Bannockburn 1314* (2005)

Oostrom, F.P. van, for the Commissie Ontwikkeling Nederlandse Canon, *A Key to Dutch History: The Cultural Canon of the Netherlands. Report by the Committee for the Development of the Dutch Canon* (2007)

Orme, N., *From Childhood to Chivalry: The Education of the English Kings and Aristocracy, 1066–1530* (1984)

Orme, N., *Medieval Children* (2003)

Oxford Dictionary of National Biography, online edition, available at https://www.oxforddnb.com

Pagan, H., 'Trevet's *Les Cronicles*: Manuscripts, Owners and Readers', in eds. J. Rajsic, E. Kooper and D. Hoche, *The Prose Brut and Other Late Medieval Chronicles: Books Have Their Histories. Essays in Honour of Lister M. Matheson* (2016), pp. 149–64

Parsons, J.C., 'Of Queens, Courts, and Books: Reflections on the Literary Patronage of Thirteenth-Century Plantagenet Queens', in ed. J.H. McCash, *The Cultural Patronage of Medieval Women* (1996), pp. 175–202

Parsons, J.C., *Eleanor of Castile: Queen and Society in Thirteenth-Century England* (1995)

Parsons, J.C., 'The Year of Eleanor of Castile's Birth and Her Children by Edward I', *Mediaeval Studies*, 46 (1984), pp. 245–65

Peltzer, J., 'The Marriages of the English Earls in the Thirteenth Century: A Social Perspective', in eds. J. Burton, P. Schofield and B. Weiler, *Thirteenth Century England XIV* (2013), pp. 61–85

Pérez de Guzmán, F., *Pen Portraits of Illustrious Castilians* (2003)

Phillips, J.R.S., 'Edward II and the Prophets', in ed. W. M. Ormrod, *England in the Century: Proceedings of the 1985 Harlaxton Symposium* (1986), pp. 189–201

Phillips, J.R.S., 'The Place of the Reign of Edward II', in eds. G. Dodd and A. Musson, *The Reign of Edward II: New Perspectives* (2006), pp. 220–33

Phillips, S., *Edward II* (2010)

Prestwich, M., *Documents Illustrating the Crisis of 1297–98 in England* (1980)

Prestwich, M., *Edward I* (1988)

Prestwich, M., 'Royal Patronage under Edward I', in eds. P. R. Coss and S. D. Lloyd, *Thirteenth Century England I* (1986), pp. 41–52

Pugh, R.B., 'A Fragment of an Account of Isabel of Lancaster, Nun of Amesbury, 1333–4', *Festschrift zur Feier des zweihundertjährigen Bestandes des Haus-, Hof- und Staatsarchivs*, vol. 1, ed. L. Santifaller (1949), pp. 487–98

Pugh, R.B., ed., *The Victoria History of Wiltshire*, vol. 3 (1953)

Rady, M., *The Habsburgs: The Rise and Fall of a World Power* (2020)

Redlich, O., *Rudolf von Habsburg. Das Deutsche Reich nach dem Untergange des Alten Kaisertums* (1903, reprinted 2012)

Reese, P., *Bannockburn: Scotland's Greatest Victory* (2000)

Roche, T.W.E., *The King of Almayne: A Thirteenth-Century Englishman in Europe* (1966)

Salvador Martínez, H., translated into English by O. Cisneros, *Alfonso X, The Learned: A Biography* (2010)

Salzman, L.F., *Edward I* (1968)

Sandquist, T.A., 'The Holy Oil of St Thomas of Canterbury', in eds. T.A. Sandquist and M.R. Powicke, *Essays in Medieval History Presented to Bertie Wilkinson* (1969), pp. 330–44

Smit, J.G., 'De Verblijfplaatsen van de Graven van Holland en Zeeland in de Late Middeleeuwen', *Regionaal-Historisch Tijdschrift*, 24 (1992), pp. 113–29

Underhill, F.A., 'Elizabeth de Burgh: Connoisseur and Patron', in ed. J.H. McCash, *The Cultural Patronage of Medieval Women* (1996), pp. 267–88

Underhill, F., *For Her Good Estate: The Life of Elizabeth de Burgh* (1999)

Vale, M., *The Origins of the Hundred Years War: The Angevin Legacy 1250–1340* (1990)

Vale, M., *The Princely Court: Medieval Courts and Culture in North-West Europe* (2001)

Verbruggen, J.F., ed. K. DeVries, trans. into English by D.R. Ferguson, *The Battle of the Golden Spurs (Courtrai, 11 July 1302): A Contribution to the History of Flanders' War of Liberation, 1297–1305* (first published in Dutch 1952; English translation 2002)

Verity, B., 'The Children of Elizabeth, Countess of Hereford, Daughter of Edward I of England', *Foundations*, vol. 6 (2014), pp. 3–10

Verity, B., 'Descendants to the Third Generation of Eleanor, Countess of Ormond (*c*. 1310–1363)', *Foundations*, vol. 8 (2016), pp. 75–89

Verkaik, J.W., *De Moord op Graaf Floris V* (1996)

Vincent, N., 'A Forgotten War: England and Navarre, 1243–4', *Thirteenth Century England XI*, ed. B. Weiler, P. Schofield and K. Stöber (2007), pp. 109–46

Wade Labarge, M., *Mistress, Maids and Men: Baronial Life in the Thirteenth Century* (1965; republished 2003)

Ward, J., *Elizabeth de Burgh, Lady of Clare (1295–1360)* (2014)

Ward, J.C., *Women of the English Nobility and Gentry 1066–1500* (1995)

Warner, K., 'The Adherents of Edmund of Woodstock, Earl of Kent, in March 1330', *English Historical Review*, 126 (2011), pp. 779–805

Warner, K., *Edward II: The Unconventional King* (2014)

Warner, K., *Hugh Despenser the Younger and Edward II: Downfall of a King's Favourite* (2018)

Warner, K., *Isabella of France: The Rebel Queen* (2016)

Warner, K., *Powerful Pawns of the Crown: The Clare Sisters, Nieces of Edward II* (2020)

Wilkinson, L.J., 'Royal Daughters and Diplomacy at the Court of Edward I', in ed. A. King and A.M. Spencer, *Edward I: New Interpretations* (2020), pp. 84–103

Wilson-Lee, K., *Daughters of Chivalry: The Forgotten Children of Edward I* (2019)

Wodderspoon, J., *Memorials of the Ancient Town of Ipswich in the County of Suffolk* (1850)

Woolgar, C.M., *The Great Household in Later Medieval England* (1999)

Woolgar, C.M., *The Senses in Late Medieval England* (2006)

Wurstemberger, J.L., *Peter der Zweite, Graf von Savoyen, Markgraf in Italien, sein Haus und seine Lande: Ein Charakterbild des Dreizehnten Jahrhunderts*, vol. 4 (1858; reprinted 2013)

Endnotes

Introduction

1. K. Wilson-Lee, *Daughters of Chivalry: The Forgotten Children of Edward I* (2019), and L.J. Wilkinson, 'Royal Daughters and Diplomacy at the Court of Edward I', in ed. A. King and A.M. Spencer, *Edward I: New Interpretations* (2020), pp. 84-103.
2. M. Prestwich, *Edward I* (1988), p. 108; M. Morris, *A Great and Terrible King: Edward I and the Forging of Britain* (2008), p. 22; S. Cockerill, *Eleanor of Castile: The Shadow Queen* (2014), pp. 224-5.
3. C. Estow, 'Royal Madness in the Crónica del Rey Don Pedro', *Mediterranean Studies*, 6 (1996), p. 19; C. Estow, *Pedro the Cruel of Castile, 1350–1369* (The Medieval Mediterranean: Peoples, Economies and Cultures, 400–1453, number 6, 1996), pp. 30, 134; J. Pohl and G. Embleton, *Armies of Castile and Aragon 1370–1516* (2015), p. 44; M. Jolly, ed., *Encyclopedia of Life Writing: Autobiographical and Biographical Forms* (2013), p. 698; R. Folger, *Generaciones Y Semblanzas: Memory and Genealogy in Medieval Iberian Historiography* (2003), p. 187; F. Pérez de Guzmán, *Pen Portraits of Illustrious Castilians* (2003), p. 12.
4. One might also include the five sisters' great-great-niece Catalina of Lancaster (1372/73–1418), queen-consort of Castile and Leon, the daughter of Edward III's son John of Gaunt, Duke of Lancaster, and his second wife Constanza, daughter and heir of King Pedro I of Castile and Leon. Catalina was born in England and lived there until she was 13. Queen Mary I was the daughter of Henry VIII and his first wife Katherine of Aragon.

Chapter 1: A Spanish Wedding

1. Alfonso and Eleanor (1161/2–1214) were also Lord Edward's great-uncle and great-aunt, and Edward and Leonor were second cousins once removed: Edward was a great-grandson of Henry II of England and Eleanor of Aquitaine, and Leonor was their great-great-granddaughter. Leonor's grandmother Berenguela (b. 1180), queen of Castile in her own right and queen of Leon by marriage, had died almost exactly eight years before the wedding, and was buried at the abbey of Las Huelgas.
2. M. Howell, *Eleanor of Provence: Queenship in Thirteenth-Century England* (1998), pp. 10-11.
3. Alix or Alais, countess of Vexin (1160–*c.* 1220/21), was Louis VII's younger daughter from his second marriage to Constance of Castile (who died after giving birth to Alix), and was an older half-sister of Philip II 'Augustus' of France (b. 1165, r. 1180–1223). She was betrothed for many years to Richard Lionheart, king of England, but he refused to marry her, and in 1195 when she was almost 35, she wed Guillaume Talvas, count of Ponthieu, instead. He was almost twenty years her junior. Their only surviving child and Guillaume's heir, Marie, born in April 1199, was Jeanne de Dammartin's mother. Jeanne's first cousin Mahaut de Dammartin became queen of Portugal by marriage and was countess of Boulogne in her own right, so in addition to Jeanne's descent from the kings of France and Castile, her family was quite an important one. Jeanne's younger sister Philippa de Dammartin married Otto, count of Guelders in the modern-day Netherlands, and Philippa's grandson Reynald II of Guelders (b. *c.* 1295) married Jeanne's great-granddaughter Eleanor of Woodstock (b. 1318), daughter of Edward II of England, in 1332.
4. J. Carmi Parsons, 'The Year of Eleanor of Castile's Birth and Her Children by Edward I', *Mediaeval Studies*, 46 (1984), pp. 246-9; Parsons, *Eleanor of Castile: Queen and Society in Thirteenth-Century England* (1995), pp. 8-9, 260 note 10; Cockerill, *Eleanor of Castile*, pp. 39-41.
5. Parsons, 'Year of Birth', p. 246 note 5.

6. The county of Aumale, which Queen Jeanne inherited from her father Simon, passed to her grandson Jean, Don Fernando's son, who was killed in battle in 1302.
7. Eleanor of England (1161/2–1214) was the second daughter of Henry II and Eleanor of Aquitaine, and one of the sisters of Richard Lionheart and King John. For the Castilian claims to the duchy of Aquitaine (or rather Gascony, a part of it), see N. Vincent, 'A Forgotten War: England and Navarre, 1243–4', *Thirteenth Century England XI*, ed. B. Weiler, P. Schofield and K. Stöber (2007), pp. 111-17, 138.
8. *Calendar of Patent Rolls 1247–58*, pp. 219, 230, 279-81, 312, 323, 325, 362-4. *The Flowers of History, Especially Such As Relate to the Affairs of Britain, From the Beginning of the World to the Year 1307, Collected by Matthew of Westminster*, ed. and trans. C. D. Yonge (1853), vol. 2, p. 351.
9. *The Flowers of History*, p. 337; Howell, *Eleanor of Provence*, p. 126; *CPR 1247–58*, p. 55; *Calendar of Charter Rolls 1226–57*, pp. 345, 389; Morris, *A Great and Terrible King*, pp. 17-19.
10. *The Flowers of History*, p. 337; Parsons, *Eleanor of Castile*, p. 16; *CPR 1247–58*, p. 382. *Le Livere de Reis de Brittaniae e le Livere de Reis de Engletere*, ed. J. Glover (1865), p. 287, states wrongly that Henry III knighted his own son.
11. S. Doubleday, *The Wise King: A Christian Prince, Muslim Spain, and the Birth of the Renaissance* (2015), pp. 69-70.
12. *List of Diplomatic Documents, Scottish Documents and Papal Bulls Preserved in the Public Record Office* (Reprinted 1963; originally published 1923), p. 1.
13. Parsons, *Eleanor of Castile*, p. 16; *CPR 1247–58*, pp. 311, 351.
14. H. Salvador Martínez, *Alfonso X, The Learned: A Biography*, translated from Spanish by O. Cisneros (2010), pp. 132-3.
15. Salvador Martínez, *Alfonso X*, pp. 47, 58; J. C. Parsons, 'Of Queens, Courts, and Books: Reflections on the Literary Patronage of Thirteenth-Century Plantagenet Queens', in ed. J. H. McCash, *The Cultural Patronage of Medieval Women* (1996), p. 177.
16. Salvador Martínez, *Alfonso X*, pp. 38, 40. Beatriz of Swabia, queen of Castile, is also often known as Elisabeth von Hohenstaufen, and was the youngest of the four daughters of Eirene Angelina, daughter of Isaac Angelos, emperor of Byzantium, and Philipp of Swabia, king of Germany, the youngest son of Frederick Barbarossa, Holy Roman Emperor.

Chapter 2: Arrival in England

1. *Calendar of the Liberate Rolls*, vol. 4, 1251–60 (1959), p. 197. Louis IX of France was a first cousin of Fernando III of Castile (their mothers were sisters), and, like him, was canonised as a saint of the Catholic Church.
2. The manuscripts with the pictures of the elephant are now held in the Parker Library, Cambridge and in the British Library; see https://theparkerlibrary.wordpress.com/2013/05/08/matthew-paris-and-the-elephant-at-the-tower and https://britishlibrary.typepad.co.uk/digitisedmanuscripts/2013/05/the-elephant-at-the-tower.html, both accessed 24 July 2020. See also *Annales Paulini 1307–1340,* in ed. W. Stubbs, *Chronicles of the Reigns of Edward I and Edward II*, vol. 1 (1882), p. 48.
3. Parsons, 'Year of Birth', p. 257; Cockerill, *Eleanor of Castile*, pp. 89-90.
4. Alfonso and Violante's daughter Beatriz of Castile married Guglielmo, marquess of Montferrat in Italy, and her daughter Yolande of Montferrat, born *c.* 1273/74, married the Byzantine emperor Andronikus Palaiologus and was renamed Eirene. Alfonso and Violante's third child and first son, Fernando de la Cerda, was born in October 1255.
5. Cockerill, *Eleanor of Castile*, pp. 232-4; Carmi Parsons, *Eleanor of Castile*, pp. 51, 54.
6. Parsons, *Eleanor of Castile*, p. 9.
7. *Le Livere de Reis de Brittaniae*, p. 324; *Vita Edwardi Secundi Monachi Cuiusdam Malmesberiensis*, ed. N. Denholm-Young (1957), p. 40; P. Linehan, 'The English Mission of Cardinal Petrus Hispanus, the Chronicle of Walter of Guisborough, and News from Castile at Carlisle (1307)', *English Historical Review*, 117 (2002), p. 618.
8. Cited in T. W. E. Roche, *The King of Almayne: A Thirteenth-Century Englishman in Europe* (1966), pp. 127-8.
9. *The Chronicles of the Mayors and Sheriffs of London, 1188–1274*, ed. H. T. Riley (1863), p. 24, stating that Leonor arrived in London on 23 June 1255. *Annales Paulini*, p. 48, describes Leonor's reception at St Paul's.
10. *CLR 1251–60*, pp. 227-8, 234, 243-6, 249-50, 253-4.

11. Howell, *Eleanor of Provence*, pp. 101-2; *CLR 1251–60*, pp. 373, 375-6, 385, 448; F. Devon. ed., *Issues of the Exchequer: Being a Collection of Payments Made Out of His Majesty's Revenue* (1837), pp. 32, 42.
12. *CLR 1245–51*, pp. 65, 169; Howell, *Eleanor of Provence*, pp. 100-01.
13. *Calendar of the Close Rolls 1242–7*, p. 228; M. Howell, 'The Children of King Henry III and Eleanor of Provence', *Thirteenth Century England IV*, ed. P. R. Coss and S. D. Lloyd (1991), p. 63; H. Johnstone, 'The Wardrobe and Household of Henry, Son of Edward I', *Bulletin of the John Rylands Library*, 7 (1920), pp. 20-36.
14. Both these women died in their twenties, and King Henry, always a generous and compassionate giver of alms, fed large numbers of poor people on the anniversaries of his sisters' deaths every year. *CLR 1240–45*, p. 306; *CLR 1245–51*, p. 156.
15. *CLR 1251–60*, pp. 349-50, 445-7, 450, 452-3, 455, 463, 496, 500, 529. Devon, *Issues of the Exchequer*, pp. 68-9; *The Flowers of History*, p. 337.
16. *Chronicles of the Mayors and Sheriffs of London*, pp. 26, 44, 54, 240; *The Flowers of History*, p. 476.
17. Roche, *The King of Almayne*, pp. 148-9, citing Matthew Paris.
18. *CLR 1251–60*, pp. 336, 339, 353, 359, 378, 388, 469; Devon, *Issues of the Exchequer*, pp. 32, 38. In later years, Leonor and Edward did their utmost to have Enrique released from the Naples prison where he spent two decades, but failed: Parsons, *Eleanor of Castile*, pp. 30, 35.

Chapter 3: Two Battles

1. Parsons, 'Year of Birth', p. 258; *CPR 1258–66*, p. 325.
2. Joan of England was the eldest of Henry III's three younger full sisters, and died in 1238 in her late twenties, the year before Edward was born. Her widower, Alexander II of Scotland, married secondly the French noblewoman Marie Coucy and had a son with her in September 1241, Alexander III, who married Edward's sister Margaret in December 1251 when he was 10 and she was 11.
3. Parsons, 'Year of Birth', p. 258; *CCR 1264–8*, pp. 70-71 ('*uno bono et pulcro panno ad aurum*').
4. https://www.westminster-abbey.org/abbey-commemorations/royals/katherine-daughter-of-henry-iii, accessed 22 July 2020.

5. *Oxford Dictionary of National Biography*, 'Richard, first earl of Cornwall and king of Germany'.
6. *ODNB*, entry for Eleanor of Castile.
7. Cockerill, *Eleanor of Castile*, pp. 137-8.
8. *CPR 1258–66*, pp. 324-5. This child was perhaps Isabel de Valence, who married John, Lord Hastings (b. May 1262) and was old enough to give birth to her first son William Hastings in October 1282, or it may have been Joan Munchesni and William de Valence's first son William de Valence the younger, who was old enough to be killed fighting in Wales in June 1282. Joan Munchesni's mother was one of the five daughters and co-heirs of William Marshal and Isabella de Clare, earl and countess of Pembroke.
9. Henry III's reign of fifty-six years is the fourth longest in English history, after Elizabeth II (1952–present), Queen Victoria (1837–1901) and George III (1760–1820).

Chapter 4: Crusading

1. Parsons, 'Year of Birth', pp. 258-9; Morris, *A Great and Terrible King*, p. 77, for the celebrations.
2. Edward III's eldest sons were Edward of Woodstock, prince of Wales (1330–76), William of Hatfield, who died as an infant in 1337, and Lionel of Antwerp, duke of Clarence (1338–68). Edward of Woodstock left a son, Richard of Bordeaux, who was 9 years old when his father died in 1376 and succeeded his grandfather as King Richard II in 1377.
3. For example, *CPR 1272–81*, p. 130; *CPL 1198–1304*, p. 412.
4. M. A. E. Green, *Lives of the Princesses of England from the Norman Conquest*, vol. 2 (1850), p. 275, first made this error, which has often been perpetuated. Green noticed that the Peterborough chronicle (correctly) assigned Eleanor of Windsor's birth to 1269, but thought that as she was 'always designated the eldest daughter of Edward I', she must have been born in 1264, and that therefore the chronicler must have been mistaken.
5. *CPR 1266–72*, p. 349; *Le Livere de Reis de Brittaniae*, ed. Glover, p. 293.
6. See for example *CCR 1307–13*, p. 583 ('the king's mother Alice de Leygrave, who suckled him in his youth'); *CPR 1317–21*, p. 251 (Alice still alive). Alice and her daughter Cecily de Leygrave served

Edward II's queen Isabella of France (probably born in 1295) as damsels in 1311/12, and almost certainly in other years as well: *The Household Book of Queen Isabella of England for the Fifth Regnal Year of Edward II, 8th July 1311 to 7th July 1312*, ed. F. D. Blackley and G. Hermansen (1971), pp. xiv, 157, 193.

7. It was also reasonably common for kings to be addressed in correspondence as 'magnificent, most high and most puissant prince', but they did not address their own or each other's children this way. Edward of Caernarfon's fiancée Isabella of France, daughter of King Philip IV, was called *ma dame Yzabel* or 'my lady Isabella' before she married Edward; see for example W. E. Rhodes, 'The Inventory of the Jewels and Wardrobe of Queen Isabella (1307-8)', *English Historical Review*, 12 (1897), p. 521.
8. Johnstone, 'Wardrobe and Household of Henry', pp. 390, 396; M. Wade Labarge, *Mistress, Maids and Men: Baronial Life in the Thirteenth Century* (1965; republished 2003), pp. 26, 47, 77, 139, 160-1, 183; C. M. Woolgar, *The Great Household in Later Medieval England* (1999), p. 101; Cockerill, *Eleanor of Castile*, p. 250.
9. *List of Diplomatic Documents, Scottish Documents and Papal Bulls*, p. 2.
10. See W. Rhodes, 'Edmund, Earl of Lancaster', *English Historical Review*, vol. 10, no. 37 (1895), and Rhodes, 'Edmund, Earl of Lancaster (Continued)', *English Historical Review*, vol. 10, no. 38 (1895). Aveline's proof of age is in *CIPM 1272–91*, no. 44; she was born in Burstwick, Yorkshire on 20 January (the feast of St Fabian and St Sebastian) 1259.
11. Parsons, 'Year of Birth', p. 260. Leonor's next daughter was born in the spring of 1272, so was conceived around August or September 1271.
12. *Flores Historiarum*, vol. 3, ed. H. R. Luard (1890), p. 22 ('*maledictus a Domino, vagus fuit et profugus super terram*').

Chapter 5: The First Marital Alliance

1. L. E. Mitchell, 'Joan de Valence and her Household: Domesticity, Management, and organization in Transition from Wife to Widow', *Royal and Elite Households in Medieval and Early Modern Europe*, ed. T. Earenfight (2018), p. 106.

2. *Le Livere de Reis de Brittaniae*, ed. Glover, pp. 300-01, 308-9, 324; *The Brut or the Chronicles of England*, part 1, ed. F. W. D. Brie (1906), p. 178; *The Chronicle of Pierre de Langtoft in French Verse, From the Earliest Period to the Death of King Edward I*, ed. T. Wright (1868), vol. 2, pp. 160, 368.
3. *Chronicle of Pierre de Langtoft*, pp. 158-9; *Le Livere de Reis de Brittaniae*, p. 299; TNA E 101/333/15: '*Un cultell dount le Roi Edward estoit naufray en la terre seinte en Acres*'.
4. Devon, *Issues of the Exchequer*, p. 78.
5. Johnstone, 'Wardrobe and Household of Henry', p. (for Eleanor's illness). King Manfredi was killed at the battle of Benevento in 1266 fighting against Edward's uncle-in-law Charles of Anjou, husband of Beatrice of Provence, who subsequently became king of Sicily. Manfredi was a son of the Holy Roman Emperor Frederick II (1194–1250), born in 1232 to Frederick's mistress Bianca Lancia and thus illegitimate, but was a favourite son of his father. Constanza (d. 1302), wife of Pere of Aragon, was Manfredi's only child from his first marriage to the much older Beatrice of Savoy, and was born when her father was 16 or 17. Manfredi married secondly Helena Angelina Doukaina in 1259; she and their four sons died in captivity after Manfredi's defeat at Benevento, and, horribly, the four sons were all blinded. Helena and Manfredi's daughter Beatrice was eventually released and married the marquis of Saluzzo.
6. *List of Diplomatic Documents, Scottish Documents and Papal Bulls*, p. 2; *Chronique de Ramon Muntaner, Traduite pour la Première Fois du Catalan*, vol. 1, ed. J. A. Buchon (1827), pp. 438-9. Alfonso's younger sister Isabel of Aragon, b. 1271, became queen of Portugal by marriage, and was canonised as a saint of the Catholic Church in 1625. Alfonso's aunt Violante of Aragon (b. 1236), Infante Pere's eldest sister, was the queen of Alfonso X of Castile. Another of his aunts, Isabel of Aragon (b. *c.* 1247), married Philip III of France. Alfonso of Aragon was thus a first cousin of both Sancho IV of Castile (b. 1258, r. 1284–95) and Philip IV of France (b. 1268, r. 1285–1314).
7. Queen Juana of Navarre and King Philip IV of France's daughter Isabella would ultimately marry Edward I and Queen Leonor's youngest son in 1308. Blanche of Artois married Edward I's widowed brother Edmund of Lancaster in late 1275 or early 1276; his young first

wife Aveline de Forz died in November 1274. Blanche and Edmund were the parents of Thomas (executed by his cousin Edward II in 1322) and Henry (d. 1345), earls of Lancaster and Leicester.

8. Parsons, *Eleanor of Castile*, p. 31.
9. This error is perpetuated in A. Weir's *Britain's Royal Families* (1996), p. 83. Weir also repeats Mary Anne Everett Green's nineteenth-century error that Eleanor of Windsor was born in 1264, and muddles Edward I and Leonor's children, giving them children they did not have such as Juliana, Isabella, Beatrice and Blanche, and getting dates of birth and death wrong, including her erroneous statement that Margaret died in 1318, many years before she actually did. See John Carmi Parsons' article 'The Year of Eleanor of Castile's Birth' and his posts about the royal children in soc.genealogy.medieval, and his *Eleanor of Castile*, p. 267 note 73, for the statement about young Alfonso's name.

Chapter 6: Many Losses

1. *The Brut or the Chronicles of England*, pp. 179-80; *Chronicles of the Mayors and Sheriffs of London*, p. 237; Prestwich, *Edward I*, p. 90; Rhodes, 'Edmund, Earl of Lancaster (Continued)', p. 213.
2. Cited on the https://fmg.ac/Projects/MedLands website, accessed 20 June 2020; Cockerill, *Eleanor of Castile*, p. 186.
3. Wade Labarge, *Mistress, Maids and Men*, pp. 97, 102; Parsons, 'Year of Birth', pp. 259-60; Johnstone, 'Wardrobe and Household of Henry', p. 386 note 2. In 1276, Edward I paid off £77 of debts owed to various people on behalf of Henry and his elder brother John, calling them 'the king's late children' and stating that both boys had lived at Windsor for a time with their grandmother, Eleanor of Provence: Devon, *Issues of the Exchequer*, pp. 93-4. Perhaps Queen Eleanor and her grandson Henry moved to Guildford after the death of Henry's brother John at Wallingford in 1271.
4. Prestwich, *Edward I*, p. 126.
5. Parsons, *Eleanor of Castile*, p. 39; see A. Marshall, 'The Childhood and Household of Edward II's Half-Brothers, Thomas of Brotherton and Edmund of Woodstock', *The Reign of Edward II: New Perspectives*, ed. G. Dodd and A. Musson (2006), p. 197.

6. Morris, *A Great and Terrible King*, p. 195; Johnstone, 'Wardrobe and Household of Henry', p. 397 note 4; Cockerill, *Eleanor of Castile*, p. 250.
7. Cockerill, *Eleanor of Castile*, p. 247.
8. Cockerill, *Eleanor of Castile*, pp. 246-7; Morris, *A Great and Terrible King*, p. 22.
9. Johnstone, 'Wardrobe and Household of Henry', p. 393 note 4; *CCR 1272–9*, pp. 468, 539; Devon, *Issues of the Exchequer*, p. 79, which calls Pampelworth 'keeper of the king's boys', presumably meaning Edward's sons.
10. *CFR 1272–1307*, p. 35, says that Aveline died 'on the eve of St Martin', and the feast of St Martin is 11 November. See also *CIPM 1272–91*, nos. 130, 792.
11. *The Chronicle of Lanercost 1272–1346*, ed. H. Maxwell (1913), p. 9; *The Flowers of History*, ed. Yonge, p. 468..

Chapter 7: Eleanor at Court

1. Parsons, 'Year of Birth', p. 262; Cockerill, *Eleanor of Castile*, p. 249. In the nineteenth century, the historian Mary Anne Everett Green misread a chronicle and stated that Margaret was born on 11 September 1275. Given that Queen Leonor gave birth again on or about 1 May 1276, this is obviously impossible.
2. *Calendar of Chancery Warrants 1244–1326*, p. 169. The manor of Clewer, then spelt Cleware, was held by Richard Sifrewas, perhaps Cecile and Wygeyn's son, in 1321: *CPR 1321–24*, p. 43.
3. *CCR 1272–9*, pp. 296, 468; *CPR 1281–92*, p. 173. Alfonso's nurse was called Felicia Shorteford.
4. Cockerill, *Eleanor of Castile*, p. 247.
5. Cockerill, *Eleanor of Castile*, pp. 251-3, for this paragraph.

Chapter 8: A Marriage Proposal (1)

1. Ultimately, however, Hartmann's elder brother Albrecht would indeed succeed their father as king in 1291, but Hartmann was already dead by then. Although the correct title was 'King of the

Romans', Edward I also often referred to *le roi Dalemayne*, 'the king of Germany'; see for example M. Prestwich, *Documents Illustrating the Crisis of 1297–98 in England*, p. 162.

2. O. Redlich, *Rudolf von Habsburg. Das Deutsche Reich nach dem Untergange des alten Kaisertums* (1903, reprinted 2012), p. 413; see also R. Köhler, *Die Heiratsverhandlungen zwischen Eduard I. von England und Rudolf von Habsburg* (1969).
3. J. P. Huffman, *The Social Politics of Medieval Diplomacy: Anglo-German Relations (1066–1307)*, p. 303.
4. *Foedera 1272–1307*, p. 548; *List of Diplomatic Documents, Scottish Documents and Papal Bulls*, p. 2.
5. Redlich, *Rudolf von Habsburg*, pp. 13-14; *Foedera 1272–1307*, p. 1321.

Chapter 9: A Marriage Proposal (2)

1. Parsons, 'Year of Birth', p. 263.
2. *Foedera 1272–1307*, pp. 549-51, 550-52; *CPR 1272–81*, pp. 299, 302. The duke of Brabant's letter was dated 6 January 1278, the feast of the Epiphany (*le jour de la Tipheyne*).
3. Duke Jan I of Brabant was a grandson of Duke Hugh IV of Burgundy on his mother's side, and a great-great-grandson of two emperors, the Holy Roman Emperor Frederick Barbarossa and Isaac Angelos of Byzantium. He was married firstly to Louis IX of France and Marguerite of Provence's daughter Marguerite of France, but she died in 1271 when they were both still teenagers, and they had no surviving children together. Philip III of France's first wife Isabel of Aragon (d. 1271) was the mother of his sons Philip IV (b. 1268) and Charles de Valois (b. 1270), ancestor of the Valois dynasty of French kings.
4. *Foedera 1272–1307*, p. 550.
5. *Foedera 1272–1307*, p. 551 (Duke Jan's letter calling him 'our eldest son'); *CPR 1272–81*, pp. 299, 302. The Medieval Lands project on the Foundation for Medieval Genealogy site gives Godefroy's date of birth as 1273 or 1274, as does Duke Jan I's Wikipedia page, both accessed 12 July 2020. Cockerill, *Eleanor of Castile*, pp. 279, 393 note 27, also states that Jan was the younger Brabant son.

6. Godefroy's letter is cited in *Foedera*, p. 551. His and Jan's sister Margaretha married Henry, count of Luxembourg and became queen of Germany in 1309, and would have been Holy Roman Empress except that she died in 1311, six months before her husband's coronation.
7. *CPR 1272–81*, pp. 299, 302.

Chapter 10: Eleanor and Aragon

1. Jean of Aumale would, like countless other French noblemen, be killed at the battle of the Golden Spurs in 1302, an unexpected victory for the Flemish over the royal army of France during the Franco-Flemish War.
2. *CPR 1272–81*, p. 306, and for Leonor's possession of Ponthieu, see H. Johnstone, 'The County of Ponthieu, 1279–1307', *English Historical Review*, 29 (1914), pp. 436-8. Blanche of Artois (b. *c.* 1245/48) was the niece of Louis IX of France, the widow of King Enrique of Navarre, and the mother of Juana, b. 1273, queen-regnant of Navarre and later queen-consort of France.
3. For the possibility of a fifth royal son, see Parsons, 'Year of Eleanor of Castile's Birth', pp. 264-5, and Cockerill, *Eleanor of Castile*, pp. 247-8, 290. In July 1281, King Edward arranged the betrothal of his third and only living son Alfonso of Bayonne to Margaretha, daughter of Floris V, count of Holland.
4. *Foedera 1272–1307*, pp. 593, 602.
5. *Foedera 1272–1307*, p. 593 ('*Regina enim, mater sua, & karissima mater nostra, nolunt sustinere, propter teneritatem ejusdem filiae, quod antea traducator*'); *CPR 1281–92*, p. 10; Cockerill, *Eleanor of Castile*, pp. 252, 291.

Chapter 11: Sicilian Vespers

1. Huffman, *Social Politics of Medieval Diplomacy*, pp. 303-4; *Foedera 1272–1307*, p. 615, dated 17 August 1282; Cockerill, *Eleanor of Castile*, p. 293.
2. *Foedera 1272–1307*, pp. 602, 606, 613-15.

3. *Foedera 1272–1307*, pp. 609, 612. Edward's uncle-in-law Charles of Anjou, Louis IX's youngest brother, had reigned as king of Sicily after defeating and killing Manfredi in battle in 1266, but was hounded out of his kingdom. His son Charles of Naples, also sometimes called Charles of Salerno (b. 1254), Edward's first cousin, was taken as a hostage.
4. Cockerill, *Eleanor of Castile*, p. 297.
5. Parsons, 'Date of Birth', p. 265.
6. *Foedera 1307–27*, p. 203.
7. Cockerill, *Eleanor of Castile*, p. 253.
8. Cockerill, *Eleanor of Castile*, pp. 297, 299, stating 'with John de Vescy playing the part of the bride' (presumably in Aragon, where he and Anthony Bek had been sent as envoys).
9. See for example the Medieval Lands project on the www.fmg.ac site, accessed 16 June 2020.

Chapter 12: Leonor's Last Child

1. *Calendar of Papal Letters 1198–1304*, p. 476. King Pere's wife Constanza of Sicily was the daughter of King Manfredi of Sicily from his first marriage to Beatrice of Savoy (d. 1258/59), daughter of Count Amadeus of Savoy. Amadeus was the maternal grandfather of Queen Constanza, not her father; Pope Martin erred on that point. On the other hand, as both King Edward's maternal grandmother the countess of Provence (d. 1267) and Queen Constanza's mother the queen of Sicily were both called Beatrice of Savoy, and were aunt and niece, his confusion is understandable.
2. Cockerill, *Eleanor of Castile*, p. 304 (fire); *Lanercost*, ed. Maxwell, p. 55 (lightning).
3. C. H. D. C. Farris, 'The Pious Practices of Edward I, 1272–1307', Univ. of London PhD thesis, 2013, p. 266.
4. John Carmi Parsons' informative posts about Edward and Leonor's children in www.soc.genealogy.medieval discuss this issue.
5. *Scalacronica: The Reigns of Edward I, Edward II and Edward III, as Recorded by Sir Thomas Gray of Heton, Knigh*t, ed. H. Maxwell (1907), p. 45; *Polychronicon Ranulphi Higden, monachi Cestrensis*, ed. J. R, Lumby, vol. 8 (1865), p. 299; *Gesta Edwardi de Carnarvon Auctore Canonico Bridlingtoniensi*, ed. W. Stubbs, *Chronicles of*

the Reigns of Edward I and Edward II, vol. 2 (1883), p. 91; *The Anonimalle Chronicle 1307 to 1334, from Brotherton Collection MS 29*, ed. W. R. Childs and J. Taylor (1991), p. 80.

Chapter 13: Amesbury and Holland

1. *Account of the Expenses of John of Brabant and Thomas and Henry of Lancaster, 1292–3*, in the *Camden Miscellany*, 2nd volume, ed. J. Burtt (1853), p. iv; the ordinance for Jan of Brabant's household is printed in the original French in Vale, *The Princely Court*, pp. 347-8.
2. Cockerill, *Eleanor of Castile*, p. 252; Green, Lives of the Princesses, vol. 2, pp. 364-6.
3. *Lanercost*, ed. Maxwell, p. 51 (stating that Eleanor 'had already dedicated her own daughter to God', meaning granddaughter); Howell, *Eleanor of Provence*, pp. 300-02.
4. Parsons, *Eleanor of Castile*, pp. 37-8; Cockerill, *Eleanor of Castile*, pp. 252, 314; Howell, *Eleanor of Provence*, p. 300; Phillips, *Edward II*, p. 44..
5. *CCR 1288–96*, p. 25.
6. *CPR 1281–92*, p. 190.
7. Howell, *Eleanor of Provence*, pp. 300-01. Ela married Henry II's illegitimate son William Longespee, and carried her father's earldom of Salisbury to him.
8. R. B. Pugh, 'A Fragment of an Account of Isabel of Lancaster, Nun of Amesbury, 1333–4', *Festschrift zur Feier des zweihundertjährigen Bestandes des Haus-, Hof- und Staatsarchivs*, vol. 1, ed. L. Santifaller (1949), pp. 487-98.
9. Cockerill, *Eleanor of Castile*, 252.
10. *Foedera 1272-1307*, pp. 652, 658, 661.
11. J. W. Verkaik, *De Moord op Graaf Floris V*, pp. 96, 114-15, 212. Verkaik, citing the *Chronographia of Johannes de Beke*, names the daughters of Floris V of Holland and his wife Beatrijs of Flanders as Beatrijs the younger, Machtild, Elisabeth and Margaretha, and their sons as Theodric, Floris, Willem, Otto, Willem II, Floris II and Jan, born 1283/84 and the only son who survived childhood. Count Floris travelled to Westminster in 1281 to arrange the marriage of his daughter Margaretha and Edward I's son Alfonso of Bayonne.

12. F. P. van Oostrom for the Commissie Ontwikkeling Nederlandse Canon, *A Key to Dutch History: The Cultural Canon of the Netherlands. Report by the Committee for the Development of the Dutch Canon* (2007), p. 1.
13. *CCR 1279–88*, pp. 368-70; Devon, *Issues of the Exchequer*, pp. 99, 104.

Chapter 14: A Battle in Germany

1. Cockerill, *Eleanor of Castile*, pp. 317-18; TNA SC 1/10/133 is Eleanor and Joan's letter.
2. Vale, *The Princely Court*, pp. 288-9, for the English translation; the chronicle is printed in R. van Breugel Douglas, *Rymkronyk van Jan van Heelu betreffende den Slag van Woeringen van het Jaer 1288* (1836). Worringen is now a suburb of the city of Cologne, and its modern spelling is Woeringen.
3. Vale, *The Princely Court*, pp. 287-8, for the learning of French; P. De Ridder, 'Brussel, Residentie der Hertogen van Brabant onder Jan I (1267–1294) en Jan II (1294–1312)', *Revue Belge de Philologie et d'Histoire*, 57 (1979), p. 330, for the charters in Dutch; Green, *Lives of the Princesses*, vol. 2, p. 365, for the spindle and thread.
4. Johnstone, *Edward of Carnarvon*, pp. 23, 28; Parsons, *Eleanor of Castile*, pp. 39-40.
5. *Foedera 1272–1307*, pp. 722-3. On 10 January 1290, 'P. the infante', son of King Pere of Aragon, wrote to inquire about Edward I's health, p. 725.
6. Edward I sent a letter of condolence to Alexander III sometime before 20 April 1284, having heard of the death of his nephew Alexander, the elder son of King Alexander and Margaret of England: *Calendar of Documents Relating to Scotland 1272–1307*, no. 250.
7. *Foedera 1272–1307*, pp. 719-21, 730-31; *Calendar of Documents Relating to Scotland 1272–1307*, nos. 388-92, 416-17, 423.

Chapter 15: Books and Education

1. Parsons, *Eleanor of Castile*, p. 38; Cockerill, *Eleanor of Castile*, p. 253.

2. *A Roll of the Household Expenses of Richard de Swinfield, Bishop of Hereford, During Part of the Years 1289 and 1290*, ed. The Rev. John Webb (1854), p. 164.
3. *Foedera 1272–1307*, p. 721. On the same day, Pope Nicholas issued another dispensation for Edward of Caernarfon to marry Margaret, the 'Maid of Norway' and rightful queen of Scotland.
4. Cited in J. R. S. Phillips, 'The Place of the Reign of Edward II' in eds. G. Dodd and A. Musson, *The Reign of Edward II: New Perspectives* (2006), p. 224 note 26; see also Parsons, *Eleanor of Castile*, pp. 56 and 277 note 180.
5. *The Brut or the Chronicles of England*, part 1, ed. F. W. D. Brie (1906), pp. 264-7. Margaret's husband the earl of Kent attempted to free his supposedly long-dead half-brother Edward II from captivity at Corfe Castle in Dorset, and wrote Edward a letter; he asked Margaret to compose it for him, suggesting that he, at least, was not too comfortable with writing.
6. See Hugh's many letters of 1324/25 in P. Chaplais, ed., *The War of Saint-Sardos (1323–1325): Gascon Correspondence and Diplomatic Documents* (1954).
7. Cockerill, *Eleanor of Castile*, p. 253, states incorrectly that Richard II (r. 1377–99, Edward III's grandson) was the first English king who was able to write. In fact, he is the earliest king of England whose signature still exists.
8. Prestwich, *Edward I*, p. 6, states (though without citing a source) that Edward I spoke English. For Edward II, see for example my *Edward II: The Unconventional King* and my article '"Bought by the King Himself": Edward II, his Chamber, his Family and his Interests in 1325–26', *Fourteenth Century England X*, ed. G. Dodd (2018), pp. 1-23.
9. *Chronicle of Lanercost*, pp. 22-3, for Margaret of Scotland; J. R. S. Phillips, 'The Place of the Reign of Edward II' in ed. Dodd and Musson, *The Reign of Edward II: New Perspectives*, pp. 221-23, for Edward II and the 1317 letter; R. J. Dean, 'Nicholas Trevet, Historian', in ed. J. J. G. Alexander and M. T. Gibson, *Medieval Learning and Literature: Essays Presented to Richard William Hunt* (1976), p. 339, for Mary of Woodstock.
10. Cited in Johnstone, *Edward of Carnarvon*, p. 24.

Chapter 16: Eleanor, Possible Queen-Regnant of England

1. Edmund's third son John of Lancaster, who was born sometime before May 1286 and died in 1317, seems to have lived almost all of his life in his mother Blanche of Artois's native France, where he held lands and married, and he only very rarely appears on record in England. He had no children and his heir to his lands in France was his elder brother Henry; they ultimately passed to Henry's son Henry (d. 1361) and granddaughter Blanche (d. 1368) and were held by Blanche's widower John of Gaunt, Edward III's son.
2. The text is printed in the original French in *Foedera 1272–1307*, p. 742.
3. M. Bennett, 'Edward III's Entail and the Succession to the Crown, 1376–1471', *English Historical Review*, 113 (1998), pp. 583-5.

Chapter 17: Two Royal Weddings

1. *The Flowers of History*, p. 323; *ODNB*; Prestwich, *Edward I*, p. 348. For 'Alice de la Marche/de Marchia', see for example *CIPM 1300–07*, no. 435, and *CCR 1279–88*, p. 357 (the May 1285 agreement by Gilbert granting her six of his manors).
2. See Gilbert's entry in the *ODNB* for the date of birth.
3. L. E. Mitchell, *Portraits of Medieval Women: Family, Marriage and Politics in England 1225–1350* (2003), pp. 37-9, 42.
4. Though the exact date is not recorded, Maud died before 10 March 1289: *CCR 1288–96*, p. 6.
5. *Calendar of Papal Letters 1198–1304*, p. 570.
6. Cited in *ODNB*.
7. *CCR 1288–96*, pp. 138, 151-2, *CPR 1281–92*, pp. 359-60, and *CChR*, vol. 2, 1257–1300, pp. 350-1, for Gilbert's surrender of his lands and the re-grant. See *CIPM 1437–42*, no. 319, for an example of the confirmation of the 1290 re-grant and the identities and birth order of Gilbert's heirs 150 years later in 1440.
8. Wade Labarge, *Mistress, Maids and Men*, pp. 140, 143-4.
9. C. Bullock-Davies, *A Register of Royal and Domestic Minstrels 1272–1327* (1986), pp. 21, 51, 138, 154, 160.
10. Cockerill, *Eleanor of Castile*, p. 337.

11. *ODNB*; L. F. Salzman, *Edward I* (1968), pp. 92-3; Cockerill, *Eleanor of Castile*, p. 339.
12. Green, *Lives of the Princesses*, vol. 2, pp. 334-5; *CCR 1288–96*, p. 89; *The Flowers of History*, p. 485.
13. Bullock-Davies, *Register of Royal and Domestic Minstrels*, pp. 75, 160; H. Gough, *Itinerary of King Edward the First Throughout his Reign*, vol. 2, 1286–1307 (1900), p. 70.
14. Bullock-Davies, *Register of Minstrels*, p. 148.
15. Green, *Lives of the Princesses*, vol. 2, p. 370.
16. *Le Livere de Reis de Brittaniae*, p. 309; Green, *Lives*, vol. 2, pp. 370-72; Bullock-Davies, *Register of Minstrels*, pp. 4, 31, 136, 200; Prestwich, *Edward I,* p. 111.
17. *Foedera 1272–1307*, pp. 731, 734, 739; *CPR 1281–92*, p. 387.
18. *Calendar of Documents Relating to Scotland 1272–1307*, no. 185.
19. *Foedera 1272–1307*, pp. 735, 737; *Calendar of Documents Relating to Scotland 1272–1307*, nos. 446-50.
20. *Foedera 1272–1307*, p. 741; *Calendar of Documents Relating to Scotland 1272–1307*, no. 459.
21. *Foedera 1272–1307*, p. 738.

Chapter 18: The First Royal Grandchild

1. Cockerill, *Eleanor of Castile*, pp. 340-1.
2. J. R. S. Phillips, *Edward II*, p. 43.
3. Cockerill, *Eleanor of Castile*, pp. 339, 342.
4. Cited in Morris, *A Great and Terrible King*, p. 231, and Cockerill, *Eleanor of Castile*, p. 348.
5. *Chronicle of Lanercost*, p. 77, for the Henry Burg poem; *Flowers of History*, ed. Yonge, p. 486, for Ferrand.
6. Parsons, 'Year of Birth', p. 248; Cockerill, *Eleanor of Castile*, p. 40.
7. As noted in Cockerill, *Eleanor of Castile*, p. 360.
8. M. M. Bigelow, 'The Bohun Wills', *The American Historical Review*, vol. 1 (1896), p. 432.
9. *Foedera 1307–27*, pp. 203-4.
10. Cockerill, *Eleanor of Castile*, p. 252; Devon, *Issues of the Exchequer*, pp. 128-9; *CPR 1301–7*, p. 36.

11. See H. Johnstone, *Letters of Edward, Prince of Wales*, for the numerous letters Edward wrote on Maud's behalf; *Complete Peerage*, vol. 9, p. 265.
12. Cockerill, *Eleanor of Castile*, pp. 75, 134-5, 175, 225, 232, 237-8, 241, 244, 254.
13. F. A. Underhill, 'Elizabeth de Burgh: Connoisseur and Patron', in ed. J. H. McCash, *The Cultural Patronage of Medieval Women* (1996), p. 273; E. Gue, 'The Education and Literary Interests of the English Lay Nobility, *c.* 1150–*c.* 1450', Univ. of Oxford DPhil thesis (1983), pp. 171 notes 3 and 7, 185, for Margaret, countess of Devon.
14. N. Orme, *From Childhood to Chivalry: The Education of the English Kings and Aristocracy, 1066–1530* (1984), p. 91; S. Cavanaugh, 'Royal Books: King John to Richard II', *The Library*, 5th series, 10 (1988), pp. 305-9; Johnstone, *Edward of Carnarvon*, pp. 18, 86; M. McKisack, *The Fourteenth Century 1307–1399*, p. 2; Phillips, *Edward II*, p. 62; *Calendar of Chancery Warrants 1244–1326*, p. 463.
15. *CIPM 1291–1300*, no. 371, Gilbert the Red's inquisition post mortem of late 1295, says that his son Gilbert was born either at the feast of St George (23 April), or at St Mark (25 April), or at the Invention of the Holy Cross (3 May); or that he was aged 4 years and 9 months in late December 1295/early January 1296, or 4 and a half; or that he was (impossibly) 6 years old at the end of 1295; or that he was aged 5 at the next Whitsun, which fell on 13 May 1296. The Sussex jurors thought that he turned 5 at the feast of the Annunciation, 23 Edward I, which is 25 March 1295. This would place Gilbert's birth around 25 March 1290, over a month before his parents even married. *CIPM 1300–07*, no. 435, Joan of Acre's inquisition post mortem of June 1307, says that her son was '17 on 11 May last' or '16 on 1 May last' or '16 on 11 May last' or 'aged 18 and more' (this is impossible) or 'aged 16 on the first Friday in May last' (this was 5 May). Putting all this information together and bearing in mind Joan of Acre and Gilbert the Red's wedding date, Gilbert de Clare was 4 years and a few months old when his father died in December 1295 and had either just turned 16 or was shortly to do so when his mother died in April 1307, and was born sometime between 23 April and 13 May 1291.
16. *CCR 1288–96*, pp. 169-70.
17. Worcestershire Archive and Archaeology Service, manuscript no. 705:134/1531/65/6, from the National Archives website.

Chapter 19: The Death of Alfonso III

1. *Chronicle of Lanercost*, ed. Maxwell, p. 85, and see also *The Flowers of History*, p. 486; for the Provence-Savoy betrothal, see see J. L. Wurstemberger, *Peter der Zweite, Graf von Savoyen, Markgraf in Italien, sein Haus und seine Lande: Ein Charakterbild des Dreizehnten Jahrhunderts*, vol. 4 (1858; reprinted 2013), no. 49, pp. 22-3. Eleanor's parents Ramon-Berenger of Provence and Beatrice of Savoy were betrothed in June 1219, and her older sister Marguerite was born in 1220 or 1221 (and was about 13 when she married 20-year-old Louis IX in May 1234).
2. *Chronique de Ramon Muntaner*, vol. 2, ed. J. A. Buchon, pp. 58-9.
3. *Chronique de Ramon Muntaner*, vol. 1, pp. 438-9; vol. 2, p. 60. A few months after his accession, the new King Jaume II of Aragon married Isabel of Castile (b. 1283), eldest daughter of Queen Leonor's nephew Sancho IV (b. 1258) and the first of his four wives, but the marriage was never consummated, and after King Sancho's death in 1295 Jaume had it annulled and married Blanche of Anjou-Naples instead. She was a granddaughter of Queen Eleanor and Queen Marguerite's youngest sister Beatrice of Provence, queen of Sicily.
4. *CCR 1323–27*, p. 171; *CPR 1324–27*, p. 104; *CPR 1330–34*, p. 7; P. Chaplais, *English Medieval Diplomatic Practice*, part 1, vol. 1, pp. 64-6.
5. *Calendar of Chancery Warrants 1244–1326*, p. 30.
6. *CPR 1281–92*, p. 464.
7. *CPR 1281v92*, pp. 452, 454, 478, 489.
8. *CPR 1281v92*, p. 479.
9. *Annales Monastici*, vol. 4, ed. H. R. Luard (1869), p. 511; also in the *Annales de Wigornia*, cited in the *Complete Peerage of England, Scotland, Ireland, Great Britain and the United Kingdom*, ed. V. Gibbs (1916), vol. 4, p. 271 note e.
10. *CIPM 1307–17*, no. 66.
11. Maud was accused of poisoning her husband in 1304, and Edward of Caernarfon, now prince of Wales, wrote several letters on her behalf, calling her *nostre chere cosine Dame Maud de Mortimer du Chastel Richard*. See *Complete Peerage*, vol. 9, pp. 264-5, and Hilda Johnstone's edition of Edward's surviving letters of 1304/05.

12. TNA SC 1/22/156; Prestwich, *Edward I*, pp. 233-4. Gilbert's location on 7 November 1292 is given in his *ODNB* entry.

Chapter 20: Margaret and Jan's Marriage

1. *Issues of the Exchequer*, ed. Devon, pp. 107-8.
2. To give a couple of examples: on 14 January 1326 a Londoner named John Toly rose from his bed naked in the middle of the night to relieve himself, and fell out of his window and died while urinating. Even in the depths of winter, he slept without clothes. Around the same year, Margery Dunheved of Dunchurch in Warwickshire presented a petition in which she complained that Sir John Pecche of Hampton-in-Arden broke into her house in the middle of the night to seize and arrest her husband John Dunheved. He was not there, but John Pecche dragged Margery out of bed naked and took her into her hall. See *Calendar of Coroners Rolls of the City of London A. D. 1300–1378*, ed. R. R. Sharpe (1913), p. 126; TNA SC 8/18/863.
3. Burtt, *Account of the Expenses of John of Brabant*, pp. 2-11; Vale, *The Princely Court*, pp. 347-8.
4. Bullock-Davies, *Register of Minstrels*, p. 5.
5. *CCR 1288–96*, pp. 317-18.
6. *Issues of the Exchequer*, p. 110.
7. *CPR 1292–1301*, pp. 9-13, 19, 20, 22-3, 27-8, 30, 31, 36, 39; *CIPM 1300v07*, no. 435, is Joan's inquisition post mortem, mentioning 'Gandin de Clare, brother of the said Gilbert' under Buckinghamshire. He died sometime before Joan's IPM was held, as he is said to have 'died seised' of various tenements Joan had given him after Earl Gilbert's death. The editors of the Patent Rolls transcribed the name as 'Gaudinus'; it is often hard to tell with medieval handwriting whether N or U was meant.

Chapter 21: Eleanor's Wedding and Children

1. *Calendar of Documents Relating to Scotland 1272–1307*, no. 1855; *CPR 1301–7*, p. 386; *CCR 1302–7*, pp. 106, 208, 443, 473, 520.

2. I owe these references to the Medieval Lands project on fmg.ac, accessed 15 June 2020.
3. *CCR 1288–96*, p. 302; *Le Livere de Reis de Brittaniae*, p. 313.
4. Joan and Gilbert were still in Ireland on 14 January 1294: *CPR 1292–1301*, p. 60.
5. Johnstone, *Edward of Carnarvon*, pp. 26-7.
6. *Calendar of Chancery Warrants 1244–1326*, pp. 38, 91; *CPR 1292–1301*, pp. 345, 399, 409.
7. *CPR 1292–1301*, pp. 67-9; *Calendar of Chancery Warrants 1244–1326*, pp. 41-2.
8. TNA SC 8/276/13753.
9. *CPR 1292–1301*, pp. 133, 186.
10. Linehan, 'English Mission of Cardinal Petrus Hispanus', pp. 615-18.
11. Elizabeth's exact date and place of birth are given in *Complete Peerage*, vol. 4, on the 'Addenda & Corrigenda' page near the front of the volume. Unfortunately, no source is cited for the statement, though the *Complete Peerage* can usually be trusted on dates.
12. Gilbert's entry in the *ODNB* gives the place of his death.
13. TNA SC 8/271/13549; *CPR 1307–13*, pp. 256-7.
14. Cockerill, *Eleanor of Castile*, p. 361; G. T. O. Bridgeman, *History of the Princes of South Wales* (1876), p. 240.
15. Cockerill, *Eleanor of Castile*, p. 361. Elizabeth Woodville was also descended from Edward I's cousin Guy de Montfort, count of Nola, one of the killers of their other cousin Henry of Almain in 1271.
16. *Foedera 1272–1307*, p. 838.

Chapter 22: The Count's Murder and Elizabeth's Wedding

1. S. Levelt, *Jan van Naaldwijk's Chronicles of Holland: Continuity and Transformation*, pp. 134, 173; *Vaderlandsche Chronyk, of Jaarboek van Holland, Zeeland en Friesland, van de Vroegste Tijden af tot op 1404*, ed. P. van der Eyk and D. Vygh (1784), pp. 113-14; H. S. Lucas, 'The Problem of the Poems Concerning the Murder of Count Floris V of Holland', *Speculum*, 32 (1958), pp. 283-98.
2. M. Prestwich, *Documents Illustrating the Crisis of 1297-98 in England* (1980), pp. 34, 164-5, and see also Verkaik, *De Moord op Graaf Floris V*, pp. 135-6, 212-13. Renesse witnessed a document

sealed by Count Jan in Ipswich on 8 January 1297: *Foedera 1272–1307*, p. 855.

3. *Foedera 1272–1307*, p. 841. The King of the Romans/Germany was Adolf von Nassau, elected in 1292 as Rudolf von Habsburg's successor. Adolf was succeeded in July 1298 by Rudolf's eldest son Albrecht, older brother of the late Hartmann von Habsburg.
4. J. F. Verbruggen, trans. into English by D. R. Ferguson and ed. K. DeVries, *The Battle of the Golden Spurs (Courtrai, 11 July 1302): A Contribution to the History of Flanders' War of Liberation, 1297–1305*, p. 15, citing H. van Werveke, *Avesnes en Dampierre, Vlaanderens Vrijheidsoorlog 1244–1305*, pp. 322-23.
5. *Foedera 1272–1307*, p. 841.
6. *CPR 1292–1301*, pp. 202-3, 209 *Foedera 1272–1307*, pp. 846-7.
7. *CCR 1296–1302*, p. 75; *Foedera 1272–1307*, pp. 850, 853.
8. Verkaik, *De Moord op Graaf Floris V*, p. 19.
9. Verkaik, *De Moord op Graaf Floris V*, p. 18 note 2; J. Wodderspoon, *Memorials of the Ancient Town of Ipswich in the County of Suffolk* (1850), p. 249.
10. Verkaik, *De Moord*, pp. 18-19 and note 3, citing British Library MS Add.7965, f. 13v; Farris, 'Pious Practices', p. 267; Prestwich, *Edward I*, pp. 128-9; F. Palgrave, ed., *The Antient Kalendars and Inventories of the Treasury of His Majesty's Exchequer*, vol. 1 (1836), pp. 138-9; Green, *Lives of the Princesses*, vol. 3, p. 14.
11. Wodderspoon, *Memorials of the Ancient Town*, pp. 246-7; Gough, *Itinerary of Edward I*, part 2, pp. 148-9.
12. Bullock-Davies, *Register of Minstrels*, p. 108; Wodderspoon, *Ancient Town*, p. 253. Matilda was still active as a tumbler more than fifteen years later in June 1312: Bullock-Davies, *Register of Minstrels*, p. 109. A. Weir's *Isabella, She-Wolf of France, Queen of England* (2005), p. 20, says Matilda's 'name implies she was a prostitute'. It does not, and she was not.
13. Wodderspoon, *Ancient Town*, p. 250; Prestwich, *Edward I*, p. 111.
14. Wodderspoon, *Ancient Town*, p. 251. The countess of Luxembourg presumably means Beatrice of Avesnes, who died in 1321 and was the widow of Henry, count of Luxembourg, killed at the battle of Worringen in 1288. Her brother John married Agnes de Valence, one of the daughters of the earl of Pembroke and a cousin of Edward I.

15. Bullock-Davies, *Register of Minstrels*, pp. 7, 26, 44, 64, 67, 68, 70, 89, 92, 93, 95, 108, 111, 117, 122, 124, 138, 163, 174, 184, 205, 207-8, 210, 214, 216; C. Bullock-Davies, *Menestrellorum Multitudo: Minstrels at a Royal Feast* (1978), pp. 77-9; Wodderspoon, *Ancient Town*, p. 253.
16. *CCR 1296–1302*, p. 75; Bullock-Davies, *Register of Minstrels*, p. 117; *Complete Peerage*, vol. 9, p. 404; Wodderspoon, *Ancient Town*, pp. 247-8, 251-2; Vale, *The Princely Court*, p. 239.
17. *CCR 1296–1302*, p. 10.
18. Wodderspoon, *Ancient Town*, p. 248; Vale, *The Princely Court*, p. 239, and pp. 359-61, which provides the inventory of all the plate in the Latin original.
19. *CPR 1292–1301*, pp. 232-3; *Calendar of Papal Letters 1198–1304*, p. 579. Philippa and Isabella of Flanders were the much younger half-sisters of Margaretha and Beatrijs van Vlaanderen, the mothers of Duke Jan II of Brabant and Count Jan I of Holland.
20. Green, *Lives of the Princesses*, vol. 3, p. 16.

Chapter 23: A Secret Wedding

1. Cited in J. Peltzer, 'The Marriages of the English Earls in the Thirteenth Century: A Social Perspective', *Thirteenth Century England XIV*, ed. J. Burton, P. Schofield and B. Weiler (2013), pp. 73-4.
2. Peltzer, 'Marriages of the English Earls', p. 76.
3. *CCR 1296–1302*, p. 12.
4. *CPR 1292–1301*, p. 243.
5. Cited in *Complete Peerage*, vol 5, pp. 709-10.
6. F. Underhill, *For Her Good Estate: The Life of Elizabeth de Burgh*, p. 6 (Joan's Clare daughters); TNA SC 1/18/161 (Joan's letter to the king).
7. *Annales Londonienses 1195–1330*, in. ed. W. Stubbs, *Chronicles of the Reigns of Edward I and Edward II*, vol. 1 (1882), p. 133; *Complete Peerage*, vol. 9, pp. 140-42. Ralph married his much younger second wife, Isabella, Lady Hastings, née Despenser (b. *c.* 1290/92), in or soon before November 1318.
8. *Complete Peerage*, vol. 9, p. 142, says that Ralph was 63 when he died in April 1325.

9. Woolgar, *Great Household*, pp. 21, 53, 115.
10. *CCR 1296–1302*, pp. 30, 41; *CPR 1292–1301*, p. 288.
11. *Complete Peerage*, vol. 5, pp. 709-10, citing *Parliamentary Writs*, vol. 1, p. 745, though I cannot find the pardon or the homage in this document.
12. *CPR 1292–1301*, pp. 306, 343; *The Parliamentary Writs and Writs of Military Summons*, ed. F. Palgrave, vol. 1 (1827), p. 745.
13. *CPR 1292–1301*, p. 534; TNA SC 8/327/E825.
14. *CCR 1296–1302*, p. 63.
15. *CCR 1296–1302*, p. 72.

Chapter 24: Travelling to the Continent

1. *CPR 1292–1301*, p. 229; *CCR 1296–1302*, pp. 80-81.
2. *CPR 1292–1301*, p. 303.
3. Their paternal grandfather John Brienne of Champagne (d. 1237), who married Berenguela of Leon as his third wife, was king of Jerusalem by his first marriage and claimant to the throne of Armenia by his second, was elected Latin Emperor of Constantinople in 1229, and was also the grandfather of Konrad von Hohenstaufen, king of Germany and Italy (1228–54). The Beaumont siblings' father Louis Brienne, also sometimes known as Louis of Acre, was the youngest child of Emperor John.
4. *Flores Historiarum*, vol. 3, p. 103 ('*Quarto idus Octobris apud Bristolliam obiit domina Alianora, primogenita regis Edwardi, comitissa de Barz; et sepelitur apud Westmonasterium*'); Parsons, 'Year of Birth', p. 260.
5. Gough, *Itinerary of Edward I*, part 2, pp. 156-63.
6. Vale, *Princely Court*, pp. 104-5, 143.
7. Prestwich, *Documents Illustrating the Crisis*, no. 103, pp. 119-20.
8. Vale, *Princely Court*, p. 143; Green, *Lives of the Princesses*, vol. 3, p. 19.
9. Printed in the original French in Prestwich, *Documents Illustrating the Crisis*, no. 148, p. 152, and in English translation in Prestwich, *Edward I*, 128; my translation is a little different. SC 1/18/125 in the National Archives is the original letter.
10. Prestwich, *Documents Illustrating the Crisis*, p. 34, for Elizabeth as a possible hostage. For Jan's charters in Dutch, *Groot Charterboek*

der Graaven van Holland en Zeeland en Heeren van Vriesland*, vol. 1, ed. F. van Mieris (1753), p. 581ff.

11. Printed in the original French in Prestwich, *Documents Illustrating the Crisis*, no. 160, pp. 164-5; the letter intercepted by the duke of Brabant is mentioned in note 2, p. 165. For the 1297 quarrel between Jan of Holland and Jan of Brabant, see *Foedera 1272–1307*, p. 853, and *Groot Charterboek der Graaven van Holland*, vol. 1, pp. 576-7. Jan of Brabant's welcoming two of his uncle-in-law Count Floris's killers, Woerden and Amstel, in his lands is in Lucas, 'Problems of the Poems', p. 296.
12. *Foedera 1307–27*, p. 204; Parsons, 'Year of Birth', p. 260.

Chapter 25: A Royal Death

1. Green, *Lives of the Princesses*, vol. 2, pp. 314-15; for the *Flores*, see Chapter 24, note 4, above.
2. Green, *Lives of the Princesses*, vol. 2, pp. 311-12, 314.
3. Marguerite's older brother Louis (1276–1219) became count of Évreux; her younger sister Blanche, probably born in the early 1280s, was unsuccessfully betrothed to Edward of Caernarfon between 1291 and 1294, and ultimately became duchess of Austria by marriage. Her mother Queen Marie was the sister of Duke Jan I of Brabant, making Marguerite the first cousin of Margaret of Windsor's husband Jan II. Edward I and Marguerite were first cousins once removed (he was the grandson of Ramon-Berenger, count of Provence, and Beatrice of Savoy, and Marguerite was their great-granddaughter), and a papal dispensation for consanguinity was issued in July 1298: *CPL 1198–1304*, pp. 576-7.
4. Vale, *Princely Court*, pp. 351-6.
5. http://members.chello.nl/~a.w.slager/graven/pag/florisV.html, accessed 18 May 2020; *Groot Charterboek der Graaven van Holland*, vol. 1, pp. 611-12. D. E. H. De Boer, E. H. P. Cordfunke, and H, Sarfatij, eds., *1299, Één Graaf, Drie Graafschappen: De Vereniging van Holland, Zeeland en Henegouwen* (2000), p. 15, states that Jan died of dysentery.
6. *CPR 1313–17*, p. 556; *Foedera 1272v1307*, p. 855. Count Jan of Hainault was not, as stated by Mary Anne Everett Green and some

modern writers, Jan of Holland's uncle, but his father's cousin. Jan of Hainault was the son of Adelaide of Holland (d. 1284), sister of Willem, count of Holland and King of the Romans (d. 1256), father of Floris V and grandfather of Jan I. Jan II, count of Hainault and Holland, died in August 1304 and was succeeded by his third but eldest surviving son Willem (*c.* 1286/87–1337). Willem's third daughter Philippa (b. *c.* 1314) would become queen of England in 1328 on marriage to Edward III, Elizabeth of Rhuddlan's nephew.

7. Green, *Lives of the Princesses*, vol. 3, p. 24.
8. *Groot Charterboek der Graaven van Holland*, vol. 1, pp. 603, 612-19; Green, *Lives of the Princesses*, vol. 3, p. 32. Green (*Lives*, vol. 3, p. 30) states that Jan died in Haarlem.
9. *CCR 1296–1302*, pp. 382-3.

Chapter 26: Two Royal Half-Brothers

1. *The Roll of Arms of the Princes, Barons and Knights who Attended King Edward I to the Siege of Caerlaverock, in 1300*, ed. T. Wright (1864), pp. 4, 10, 17-18.
2. *CIPM 1291–1300*, no. 604, 'Edward, king of England, his kinsman, is his next heir and of full age'. Edmund of Cornwall's disastrous marriage to Margaret de Clare (d. 1312), sister of Gilbert 'the Red', was childless, and he had no siblings, nieces or nephews. His and King Edward's fathers Henry III and Richard of Cornwall were brothers, and their mothers Eleanor and Sancha of Provence were sisters.
3. *Foedera 1307–27*, p. 203 ('*de doun Edmon counte de Cornewaile a madame Isabell, la seor*'), in Edward II's possession in 1312/13; Green, *Lives of the Princesses*, vol 3, p. 34.
4. *CChR 1300–26*, p. 31; *CPR 1301–7*, p. 327.
5. *List of Diplomatic Documents, Scottish Documents and Papal Bulls*, p. 6; Burtt, *Account of the Expenses of John of Brabant*, p. ix; TNA E 30/1507.
6. *CCR 1296–1302*, p. 474.
7. *CPR 1292–1301*, p. 587; *CCR 1296–1302*, p. 442.
8. *CPR 1301–7*, pp. 63, 215, 330; TNA E 101/308/27.

9. *CPR 1292–1301*, pp. 592, 606; Lisa Benz St John, *Three Medieval Queens: Queenship and the Crown in Fourteenth-Century England*, p. 119.

Chapter 27: The New Countess of Hereford and Essex

1. *CPR 1301–7*, p. 66; *CCR 1302–7*, pp. 605-7.
2. *CPR 1301–7*, p. 386; *CCR 1302–7*, p. 321.
3. *CPR 1301–7*, pp. 36-8.
4. *CPR 1301–7*, pp. 65, 96.
5. *CIPM 1291–1300*, no. 552; *Annales Paulini*, in Stubbs, *Chronicles of the Reigns of Edward I and Edward II*, p. 129. *Le Livere de Reis de Brittaniae*, pp. 324-5, made a similar error with Margaret of Windsor at the time of her 1290 wedding, calling her 'Beatrice'.
6. Guillaume Fiennes was, via his daughters Marguerite and Jeanne, the grandfather of two important English noblemen of the early fourteenth century: Roger Mortimer (*c.* 1287–1330), lord of Wigmore and first earl of March, and Thomas, Lord Wake (1298–1349), whose heir was his sister Margaret's daughter Joan of Kent, later princess of Wales and the mother of Richard II. Humphrey's father had feuded with Gilbert 'the Red' de Clare, earl of Gloucester, in the early 1290s.
7. *Calendar of Papal Letters 1198–1304*, p. 602. Humphrey's mother Maud Fiennes was the granddaughter of Agnès de Dammartin, sister of Elizabeth's great-grandfather Simon de Dammartin, count of Aumale (d. 1239). Humphrey was slightly more closely related to Elizabeth's first husband Jan of Holland than to Elizabeth herself.
8. *CPR 1301–7*, pp. 101-2; TNA E 101/365/8, E 101/365/19, E 101/367/5.
9. *Calendar of Inquisitions Miscellaneous 1219–1307*, no. 1870.
10. B. Verity, 'The Children of Elizabeth, Countess of Hereford, Daughter of Edward I of England', *Foundations*, vol. 6 (2014), p. 4; Devon, *Issues of the Exchequer*, p. 116.
11. Woolgar, *Great Household*, p. 98; Bullock-Davies, *Register of Minstrels*, p. 118.
12. Verity, 'Children of Elizabeth, Countess of Hereford', pp. 4-5; Woolgar, *Great Household*, p. 100.

13. Farris, 'Pious Practices', pp. 266-7, dating the account to 1303/04 and the purification to 11 October 1303, but this was too soon after the birth of Elizabeth's daughter Margaret in late September 1303. Woolgar, *Great Household*, p. 100, for the shrine.
14. Woolgar, *Great Household*, p. 100; Verity, 'Children of Elizabeth', p. 4. Bullock-Davies, *Register of Minstrels*, p. 118, states that Elizabeth's baby son died in Stony Stratford on 24 October on his way to Windsor Castle to be raised with Elizabeth's little half-brothers Thomas and Edmund, and dates this entry in the royal accounts to 1303/04.
15. TNA SC 1/62/36. Unfortunately, owing to the lockdown in the UK in 2020 and the closure of the National Archives and limitation of their services, I have been unable to access this letter.
16. TNA E 101/366/30, and E 101/365/14 is a membrane of Elizabeth's household expenses from 20 November 1303 to 19 November 1304.
17. M Prestwich, 'Royal Patronage under Edward I', *Thirteenth Century England 1*, p. 44.

Chapter 28: The Prince of Wales and his Sisters

1. H. Johnstone, *Letters of Edward, Prince of Wales, 1304–5*, p. 70.
2. *The War of Saint-Sardos (1323–1325): Gascon Correspondence and Diplomatic Documents*, ed. P. Chaplais (1954), pp. 119-20, is a letter to John Haustede dated *c.* December 1324 from Hugh Despenser the Younger, Edward II's powerful chamberlain and perhaps lover, telling Haustede that *vous estoiez nurri od nostre dit seignur*, 'you were suckled with our said lord', i.e. Edward.
3. Johnstone, *Letters of Edward, Prince of Wales*, pp. 60-61.
4. J. S. Hamilton, 'The Character of Edward II: The Letters of Edward II Reconsidered', *The Reign of Edward II: New Perspectives*, ed. G. Dodd and A. Musson, p. 15; Johnstone, Letters of Edward, p. 15 ('*nostre cher seignur le roy, nostre pere e la* [sic] *vostre*').
5. Hamilton, 'Character of Edward', pp. 9, 16; Johnstone, *Letters of Edward*, pp. 16-17, 106, 108, 114, 115, 124, 134.
6. Hamilton, 'Character of Edward', pp. 7, 8, 12-13; Johnstone, *Letters of Edward,* pp. 14-15, 41, 70, 75, 111, 116, 117, 120, 127, 132-3, 158.

7. Verity, 'Children of Elizabeth, Countess of Hereford', p. 4-5; *CCR 1327–30*, pp. 26, 38, gives the date of John's birth.
8. *CPR 1301–7*, pp. 313, 325, 327, 342, 389; A. Marshall, 'Childhood and Household of Edward II's Half-Brothers', *The Reign of Edward II: New Perspectives,* pp. 198, 202.
9. *CPR 1301–7*, p. 431.
10. *CPR 1301–7*, p. 460. Jeanne of Burgundy became queen-consort of France as the wife of Philip V (r. 1316–22), second son of Philip IV (d. 1314) and Juana I of Navarre (d. 1305).
11. *Foedera 1272–1307*, p. 998.
12. *Foedera 1272-1307*, pp. 986-7. Confusingly, there was a duchy of Burgundy and also a county palatinate of Burgundy.
13. B. Prost and S. Bougenot, eds., *Cartulaire de Hugues de Chalon (1220–1319)* (1904), p. 442 ('*mariaige qui doit estre fait entre notre cher et amé cousin Eduart, de la contée de Barz, et Marie, nostre chiere suer*'). I owe this reference to the Medieval Lands Project on the fmg.ac website; the cartulary is available on the Bibliothèque Nationale de France site, gallica.bnf.fr, accessed 15 June 2020.
14. See the Medieval lands Project on www.fmg.ac, accessed 15 June 2020.
15. See Appendix 2, note 1.

Chapter 29: Three Weddings and a Death

1. Vale, *Princely Court*, pp. 50-1, 349-50. The king provided John with clothes twice a year, two palfrey horses and two men to look after them, three squires who each had a servant and five horses for the squires, three pack-horses, a chamberlain, a cook, officials for his pantry and buttery, three personal attendants, and so on. He was entitled to a pitcher of wine and two pitchers of ale daily for his dinner while eating in the king's hall, and two pitchers of wine and three of ale for his supper.
2. *CPR 1301–7*, p. 308.
3. M. Prestwich, 'Royal Patronage under Edward I', *Thirteenth Century England*, vol. 1, ed. P. R. Coss and S. D. Lloyd (1986), pp. 44-5; Bullock-Davies, *Menestrellorum Multitudo*, pp. 4, 86-7, 133.
4. *CPR 1301–7*, pp. 492, 496-7.

5. *CPR 1307–13*, p. 594.
6. *Calendar of Chancery Warrants 1244–1326*, p. 296; *Calendar of Papal Letters 1342–62*, p. 116; *CPR 1307-13*, p. 330; *CPR 1313–17*, pp. 528-9; *CCR 1339–41*, pp. 18, 82; *Calendar of Inquisitions Miscellaneous 1308–48*, no. 1622. A 1348 petition by John de Warenne's nephew and heir talks of *danz William de Warenn' bastard filtz al count de Warenn'*: TNA SC 8/247/12337.
7. TNA E 101/369/11, folio 96v.
8. *Calendar of Documents Relating to Scotland*, vol. 5, no. 2600, naming him as 'Hugh son of Hugh Despenser'.
9. *The Flowers of History*, p. 585; *Foedera 1272–1307*, pp. 1001-2.
10. *Calendar of Papal Letters 1305–41*, p. 30.
11. *CCR 1302–7*, p. 533, and *Foedera 1272-1307*, p. 1016 (with the 6 May date); *Calendar of Chancery Warrants 1244–1326*, p. 259, and *Foedera 1272–1307*, p. 1013 (with the 1 April date); TNA SC 1/48/158, an order by King Edward to purchase robes for Gilbert de Clare, dated at Carlisle 12 April 1307.
12. *Cartulary of the Augustinian Friars of Clare*, ed. C. Harper-Bill (1991), p. 12 (Joan's burial); L. L. Gee, *Women, Art and Patronage from Henry III to Edward III* (2002), p. 27 (awareness of St Vincent in England); TNA SC 1/30/3 (Bishop Suger's letter to Joan, dated on the National Archives website to *c.* 1276–1284); *Lists and Indexes: Supplementary Series, vol. 15, issue 2: Index to the Ancient Correspondence of the Chancery and the Exchequer, vol. 2, L-Z* (reprinted 1969), p. 437 (identifies Suger). Master Peter Arnaldi de Vico was Edward I's lieutenant in Gascony: *CPR 1292–1301*, p. 357; *CPR 1301–7*, p. 35.
13. *CIPM 1300-07*, no. 435.
14. K. Wilson-Lee, *Daughters of Chivalry: The Forgotten Children of Edward I*, location 3645 states that Joan's brother Edward of Caernarfon represented the family at her funeral, though he was in London on 24 April, in Badlesmere, Kent on 30 April, and in Canterbury on 2 May (see Johnstone, *Edward of Carnarvon*, p. 124). The timing is a little tight, albeit not impossible.
15. Ralph was Isabella Despenser's third husband after Joan of Acre's nephew-in-law Gilbert de Clare of Thomond (d. 1307) and John Hastings (d. 1313). Ralph and Isabella married without Edward II's

permission: *CFR 1307–19*, pp. 380, 388, 394; *CPR 1317–21*, pp. 387, 582. Ralph and Isabella had no children, though Isabella had three from her second marriage. In his will, Ralph called Isabella his 'dearest wife': *Calendar of Wills Proved in the Court of Husting, London*, part 1, 1258–1358 (1889), p. 315. For the grant to Ralph of the earldom of Atholl, see *Calendar of Charter Rolls 1300–26*, p. 72, and *Calendar of Documents Relating to Scotland 1272–1307*, no. 1945.

16. *CPR 1307–13*, pp. 1, 21.
17. TNA SC 8/82/4098.

Chapter 30: Death of the King

1. *A Collection of All the Wills Now Known to be Extant of the Kings and Queens of England, Princes and Princess of Wales, and Every Branch of the Blood Royal, From the Reign of William the Conqueror to That of Henry the Seventh*, ed. J. Nichols (1780), pp. 18-21.
2. Devon, *Issues of the Exchequer*, pp. 119-20; Chaplais, *Piers Gaveston: Edward II's Adoptive Brother* (1994), p. 34; Vale, *The Princely Court*, p. 239.
3. Cited in Verity, 'Children of Elizabeth, Countess of Hereford', p. 6.
4. *CIPM 1336–46*, no. 55. Verity, 'Children of Elizabeth', p. 7, suggests that the date of birth of *c.* 6 December 1309 given to Humphrey by some of the jurors might in fact have been the date of birth of her twins, Edward and William. On the other hand, if Humphrey really was born in 1307 one might expect at least some of the IPM jurors to give his age as 28 or 29 in 1336.
5. *CPR 1330–34*, pp. 12, 14. In 1973, historian K. B. McFarlane stated that Humphrey de Bohun (b. 1307/09) was an invalid: K. B. McFarlane, *The Nobility of Later Medieval England*, p. 161.
6. Verity, 'Children of Elizabeth', pp. 8-9.
7. See Appendix 2.
8. *CCR 1323–27*, pp. 409-10.
9. P. De Ridder, 'Brussel, Residentie der Hertogen van Brabant onder Jan I (1267–1294) en Jan II (1294–1312)', *Revue Belge de Philologie et d'Histoire*, 57 (1979), pp. 332-3, 335-6.

Chapter 31: Coronation

1. *CCR 1307–13*, pp. 8, 113.
2. TNA C 53/94, nos. 11, 12, 15, 16, 19-21, 24, 28, 29, 31, 34.
3. *CPR 1307–13*, pp. 17, 21.
4. Devon, *Issues of the Exchequer*, p. 123.
5. Phillips, *Edward II*, pp. 134-5; Warner, *Edward II: The Unconventional King*, pp. 39-40.
6. *CCR 1307–13*, p. 51; Phillips, *Edward II*, p. 145 note 114.
7. *Annales Paulini*, p. 260; *Adae Murimuth Continuatio Chronicarum*, ed. E. M.Thompson (1889), p. 12; Devon, *Issues of the Exchequer*, pp. 120-22, lists the expenses of the coronation.
8. Phillips, *Edward II*, pp. 143-4, note 108; J. R. S. Phillips, 'Edward II and the Prophets', in ed. W. M. Ormrod, *England in the Century: Proceedings of the 1985 Harlaxton Symposium* (1986), pp. 196-7.
9. Cited in Chaplais, *Piers Gaveston: Edward II's Adoptive Brother*, pp. 61-8, 116.
10. TNA C 53/94, no. 12; C 53/95, no. 51.

Chapter 32: Downfall of a Royal Favourite

1. *CPR 1307–13*, pp. 145-6.
2. Stapleton, 'Brief Summary of the Wardrobe Accounts', p. 338, and see below.
3. *Chancery Warrants 1244–1326*, pp. 286-7; *Letters of Royal and Illustrious Ladies of Great Britain, from the Commencement of the Twelfth Century to the Close of the Reign of Queen Mary*, ed. M. A. E. Wood, vol. 1 (1846), pp. 61-3; *The Victoria History of Wiltshire*, vol. 3, ed. R. B. Pugh (1953), pp. 258, 408.
4. *CPR 1307–13,* p. 131. Sherston lies about 40 miles from Amesbury; Edward I stayed there at the beginning of October 1293 (*CPR 1292–1301*, pp. 36, 39), and in 1332, the year of Mary's death, it was called 'the king's manor of Sherstone', *CPR 1330–34*, p. 304.
5. TNA SC 1/32/73.
6. *Calendar of Chancery Warrants 1244–1326*, p. 357.
7. *Issues of the Exchequer*, ed. Devon, p. 124.
8. *Foedera 1307–27*, p. 144.

9. J. S. Hamilton, *Piers Gaveston, Earl of Cornwall 1307–1312: Politics and Patronage in the Reign of Edward II* (1988), p. 101, citing TNA E 101/325/13, membrane 5.
10. *Flores Historiarum*, ed. H. R. Luard, vol. 3 (1890), p. 335; *Monasticon Anglicanum*, ed. W Dugdale, vol. 2 (new edition, 1819), p. 61.

Chapter 33: The Knight of the Swan

1. N. Orme, *Medieval Children* (2003), p. 291; *A Collection of All the Wills*, pp. 177-85.
2. See V. B. Richmond, *The Legend of Guy of Warwick* (2020), and A. Wiggins and R. Field, *Guy of Warwick: Icon and Ancestor* (2007).
3. *Calendar of Memoranda Rolls (Exchequer): Michaelmas 1326–Michaelmas 1327*, nos. 2270 (ii), p. 373, and no. 2271 (i) and (v), pp. 377-8. Other high-ranking royal squires in 1330 were Giles Badlesmere, born 1314, heir to his father Lord Badlesmere, and John Lovel, also born 1314, heir to his father Lord Lovel.
4. *CIPM 1327–36*, no. 542.
5. De Ridder, 'Brussel, Residentie', pp. 338-9, citing the *Brabantsche Yeesten* ('*Ter Vuren sterf hi in sine zale*'). Jan II's sister Margaretha, born in 1276 and just over a year his junior, had married Henry of Luxembourg (b. *c.* 1275) in 1292. They were the parents of Johann 'the Blind', king of Bohemia by right of his wife, who was killed at the battle of Crécy in 1346, Edward III's great victory over the French. For Margaret's building work, see Green, *Lives of the Princesses*, vol. 2, pp. 389-90.
6. *CPR 1307–13*, p. 510.
7. *CCR 1307–13*, pp. 500-01.
8. TNA C 53/99, no. 47; this was the only charter Humphrey witnessed in Edward II's sixth regnal year, which ran from 8 July 1312 to 7 July 1313.
9. *Vita Edwardi Secundi*, ed. Denholm-Young, p. 36; *Johannis de Trokelowe et Henrici de Blaneforde Chronica et Annales*, ed. H. T. Riley (1866), pp. 79-80.
10. *Foedera 1307–27*, pp. 203-5; *CPR 1307–13*, p. 525; *CPR 1313–17*, pp. 25-6, 34.
11. *CPR 1313–17*, p. 12.

Chapter 34: Defeat in Scotland

1. A. Nusbacher, *Bannockburn 1314*, p. 89.
2. *Calendar of Documents Relating to Scotland*, vol. 5, no. 2964.
3. *Calendar of Chancery Warrants 1244–1326*, p. 404.
4. *CCR 1313–18*, p. 109.
5. TNA E 101/375/14, E 101/376/19, E 101/99/25.
6. *CCR 1313–18*, pp. 153-4.
7. The document is TNA DL 27/13, in French in the original. J. C. Ward, *Women of the English Nobility and Gentry 1066–1500* (1995), pp. 29-30, provides an English translation of the marriage contract.
8. *CPR 1313–17*, p. 278.
9. *CCR 1313–18*, p. 301; *CPR 1313–17*, pp. 332-3; TNA DL 10/221.

Chapter 35: Death in Childbirth

1. *CCR 1313–18*, p. 301.
2. *CPR 1313–17*, p. 577.
3. *CCR 1313–18*, pp. 119, 308.
4. TNA SC 8/30/1499; *Calendar of Chancery Warrants 1244–1326*, pp. 425, 433-4; *Flores Historiarum*, vol. 3, p. 173, for the 'great company' quotation. For more information about the election, see *CPR 1313–17*, pp. 218, 290, and https://www.british-history.ac.uk/vch/beds/vol1/pp353-358, accessed 6 August 2020.
5. Devon, *Issues of the Exchequer*, pp. 128-9.
6. Bullock-Davies, *Register of Royal and Domestic Minstrels*, p. 147; TNA E 101/380/4.
7. *CCR 1313–18*, p. 294; *CPR 1313–17*, pp. 472, 478; TNA C 53/102, nos. 13, 15, 16, 18.
8. Bigelow, 'The Bohun Wills, II', *The American Historical Review*, vol. 1 (1896), p. 637; Woolgar, *Great Household*, p. 167. Humphrey's will is printed in full in *A Collection of All the Wills*, pp. 44-56; the reference to Elizabeth is on p. 51, and he called his sister Eleanor *n're soer countesse Doremant*, 'our sister, countess of Ormond'. A much abridged English translation of the will is in *Testamenta Vetusta*, vol. 1, pp. 66-8.

9. Margaret's cousin Margaret Marshal, countess of Norfolk (born *c.* 1322), eldest child and ultimately the sole heir of Edward I and his second wife Marguerite of France's elder son Thomas, was the only grandchild of Edward I who outlived her, and died in March 1399, well into her seventies.
10. *Annales Paulini*, in ed. Stubbs, *Chronicles of the Reigns of Edward I and Edward II*, vol. 1, p. 279, gives the date and location: '*obiit domina Elysabet comitassa Herfordiae, soror regis Edwardi, et sepulta fuit apud Waldene, x kalendas Junii*'.
11. Hallam, E. M., *The Itinerary of Edward II and his Household, 1307–1327* (1984), p. 140; TNA C 53/102, no. 8.
12. *CCR 1313–18*, p. 454.
13. *Foedera 1307–27*, p. 290; '*Excellentissimae dominae, dominae Elizabethae, Dei gratia Francie & Navarr' Reginae*'. Clemence gave birth on 15 November 1316 to a son who became King John I of France the moment he drew his first breath, but the baby king died five days later. Louis X and Queen Isabella's brother Philip, count of Poitiers, therefore succeeded his infant nephew as Philip V.

Chapter 36: Maud Nerford and the Court Christian

1. TNA SC 1/33/54; *Calendar of Chancery Warrants 1244–1326*, p. 451.
2. T. Stapleton, 'A Brief Summary of the Wardrobe Accounts of the Tenth, Eleventh and Fourteenth years of King Edward the Second', *Archaeologia*, 26 (1836), p. 343.
3. *CIPM 1327–36*, no. 395; Stapelton, 'Brief Summary of the Wardrobe Accounts', p. 338.
4. *CPR 1313–17*, pp. 401, 434, 528-9.
5. Stapleton, 'Brief Summary of the Wardrobe Accounts', p. 341 (Aymon de Jovenzano, who must have been Italian and from the village of Giovenzano between Milan and Pavia); TNA SC 8/87/4348 ('*la dite dame [de Nerforde] par la reson qe le dit counte ad aloigne son quer e ouste de sa companye*'). Maud Nerford, born *c.* 1290/92, was of noble birth; she was the daughter of Sir William Nerford of Norfolk and Pernel or Petronilla Vaux, and the niece by marriage

of William, Lord Ros of Helmsley in Yorkshire. Her family owned lands in Norfolk and Suffolk.

6. TNA E 101/377/2 is the account of their expenses; see also F. Underhill, *For Her Good Estate: The Life of Elizabeth de Burgh*, pp. 18-19, and J. C. Davies, *The Baronial Opposition to Edward II: Its Character and Policy* (1918), pp. 161, 212.
7. *CCR 1313–18*, p. 470.
8. *CPR 1317–21*, pp. 139, 403.
9. Stapleton, 'Brief Summary of the Wardrobe Accounts', p. 337.
10. Hallam, *Itinerary of Edward II*, p. 165

Chapter 37: Holy Oil and Simplicity

1. Green, *Lives of the Princesses*, vol. 2, p. 400, states 'The death of the duchess-dowager took place in the year 1318.' For the erroneous date being copied in modern works, see e.g. A. Weir, *Britain's Royal Families,* pp. 84-5, and R. M. Haines, *King Edward II: His Life, His Reign, and Its Aftermath, 1284–1330* (2003), p. 371 note 45. Parsons, 'Date of Birth', p. 262, corrects the date. Green, *Lives*, vol. 2, p. 390 note 2, even remarks that Margaret granted a forest to one of her husband's illegitimate sons in 1329, but, mystified, adds that the date of this deed is 'certainly wrong'. She also wrongly believed that Duke Jan II was older than his wife and born in 1270 (*Lives*, vol. 2, p. 368). His father Duke Jan I, however, married his first wife Marguerite of France (b. 1254, one of the daughters of Louis IX and Marguerite of Provence) in September 1270; she died after giving birth to a stillborn infant in 1271, and Jan married his second wife Margaretha of Flanders, Jan II's mother, in 1272 or 1273.
2. *CCR 1323–7*, p. 652.
3. *CPR 1313–17*, p. 628; *CPR 1317–21*, p. 69; *Calendar of Papal Letters 1305–41*, pp. 172, 423; J. R. S. Phillips, 'Edward II and the Prophets', in ed. W. M. Ormrod, *England in the Century: Proceedings of the 1985 Harlaxton Symposium* (1986), p. 198; Phillips, *Edward II*, pp. 325-6.
4. *Vita Edwardi Secundi*, ed. Denholm-Young, p. 89.
5. Phillips, *Edward II*, pp. 325-7, 341-2; Phillips, 'Place of the Reign of Edward II in English History', *Reign of Edward II:*

New Perspectives, p. 228; Phillips, 'Edward II and the Prophets', pp. 227-8; Haines, *King Edward II*, pp. 33-5.

6. T. A. Sandquist, 'The Holy Oil of St Thomas of Canterbury', *Essays in Medieval History Presented to Bertie Wilkinson*, ed. T. A. Sandquist and M. R. Powicke (1969), pp. 337-40. Henry IV was the maternal grandson of Henry of Grosmont, who supposedly found the oil in France.
7. M. Andrews-Reading, 'The Will of Humphrey de Bohun, Earl of Hereford and Essex, 1319', *Foundations*, vol. 6 (2014), pp. 11-12; M. M. Bigelow, 'The Bohun Wills', *The American Historical Review*, vol. 1 (1896), pp. 422-26. TNA C 53/106, nos. 21-32, shows that Humphrey was often at court with Edward II in the early autumn of 1319.
8. Robert Haustede's brother John was Edward II's milk-brother; see Chapter 28 and Chapter 28, note 2.

Chapter 38: Mary and the Chronicler

1. *Foedera 1307–27*, p. 392.
2. *CPR 1317–21*, p. 472.
3. L. Barefield, 'Lineage and Women's Patronage: Mary of Woodstock and Nicholas Trevet's *Les Cronicles*', *Medieval Feminist Forum*, 33 (2002), pp. 21, 28 note 8; H. Pagan, 'Trevet's *Les Cronicles*: Manuscripts, Owners and Readers', in ed. J. Rajsic, E. Kooper and D. Hoche, *The Prose Brut and Other Late Medieval Chronicles: Books Have Their Histories. Essays in Honour of Lister M. Matheson* (2016), pp. 150-51, 153 note 16, 154. Edward I was almost always known in his own lifetime and during the reign of his son as 'King Edward, son of King Henry'; Edward II was 'King Edward, son of King Edward'.
4. R. M. Correale, 'Chaucer's Manuscript of Nicholas Trevet's "Les Cronicles"', *The Chaucer Review*, 25 (1991), p. 262. The *Cronicles* of Nicholas Trivet contain a story which was the source of *The Man of Law's Tale*, one of the *Canterbury Tales* written near the end of the fourteenth century by the great poet Geoffrey Chaucer (*c*. 1342–1400).
5. Information from the Medieval Lands project at fmg.ac, accessed 25 August 2020.

6. TNA SC 1/63/159.
7. J. Ward, *Elizabeth de Burgh, Lady of Clare (1295–1360)*, p. 63.
8. *Complete Peerage*, vol. 4, p. 325, gives Hugh's date of birth, though does not cite a source.
9. *Calendar of Papal Letters 1305–41*, p. 242; *CPR 1324–27*, p. 281; *Calendar of Memoranda Rolls (Exchequer): Michaelmas 1326-Michaelmas 1327*, no. 177.

Chapter 39: Estrangement and Invasion

1. Edward's surviving chamber accounts are E 101/380/4 (1324/25) in the National Archives, and Society of Antiquaries of London, manuscript no. 122 (1325/26). His chamber accounts only survive in fragments from 1322/23 and none from before 1322 still exist. There are no references to Mary at all in *CCR 1323–27* or in *CPR 1324–27*, and none in *Calendar of Chancery Warrants 1244–1326* after 1318. There is one reference to her in *CFR 1319–27*, p. 345, dated 6 May 1325: Mary held the church of Tintagel in Cornwall from her superior the abbess of Fontévrault, and Edward had seized it when he went to war against Charles IV of France. He ordered it to be given back to Mary after being informed of an inquisition on the matter by the sheriff of Cornwall.
2. For more information, see my *Edward II's Nieces, the Clare Sisters: Powerful Pawns of the Crown* (2020), and for the 'king and his husband' statement, see Phillips, *Edward II*, p. 98 ('*rex et maritus eius*').
3. Ward, *Elizabeth de Burgh, Lady of Clare*, p. 4. Ward identifies 'Lady Maria' as Elizabeth's friend and cousin Marie de St Pol (*c.* 1303–77), dowager countess of Pembroke and a great-granddaughter of Henry III and Eleanor of Provence, but on every other occasion when she appears in Elizabeth's accounts, Marie was referred to as 'countess of Pembroke' or 'lady countess of Pembroke': see Ward, *Lady of Clare,* pp. 42, 43, 45, 76, 77, 86, 147.
4. *CCR 1323–27*, pp. 647-8, 652.
5. Ward, *Lady of Clare*, p. 4.
6. *CCR 1327–30*, pp. 26, 38 (John); *CPR 1324–27*, p. 336 (Edward).
7. G. A. Holmes, 'The Judgement on the Younger Despenser, 1326', *English Historical Review*, 70 (1955), pp. 264-7, in French;

See my book *Downfall of a King's Favourite: Edward II and Hugh Despenser the Younger*, p. 151, for the English translation.

Chapter 40: Depositions and Deaths

1. *CCR 1327–30*, p. 100.
2. TNA DL 10/253, '*nostre trescher seignur et piere est a dieu comaundez*'.
3. *CPR 1327–30*, pp. 164, 175, 181, 182, 403.
4. *CPR 1327–30*, pp. 230, 340, for Eleanor's marriage, and for the earldom, see the *Parliament Rolls of Medieval England*, ed. C. Given-Wilson et al, under the October 1328 parliament.
5. *CIPM 1336–46*, no. 476.
6. *CCR 1330–33*, p. 14; *Adae Murimuth*, ed. Thompson, pp. 255-7. Edward's older brother Thomas Monthermer had joined a rebellion against Queen Isabella and Roger Mortimer in 1328/29: *CCR 1327–30*, p. 530; *CPR 1327–30*, p. 547. See also my 'The Adherents of Edmund of Woodstock, Earl of Kent, in March 1330', *English Historical Review*, 126 (2011), pp. 779-805.
7. *CPR 1327–30*, p. 534.
8. The date is given in *CCR 1330–33*, p. 511.
9. *Calendar of Papal Letters 1342–62*, pp. 116, 169, 173.
10. Power, *Medieval English Nunneries*, p. 455, states that Mary was 'declared to have been seduced by the rather disreputable earl of Surrey'. For the earl's illegitimate children (Sir William, Prior William, John, Thomas, Edward, Ravlyn or Rawlyn, Joan de Basing, Katherine, and Isabel, nun of Sempringham Priory in Lincolnshire), see my blog post http://edwardthesecond.blogspot.com/2009/09/illegitimate-children-of-john-de.html. Like Surrey's much earlier mistress Maud Nerford, Isabelle Holland was of noble birth. She was the daughter of Sir Robert Holland (d. 1328), and her brother Sir Thomas (b. *c.* 1314/15) married Edward II's niece Joan of Kent; his sons Thomas, earl of Kent, and John, duke of Exeter and earl of Huntingdon, were the older half-brothers of King Richard II.
11. *CCR 1330–33*, p. 396; *CCR 1333–37*, p. 96. 'Hastyng Rope' means the Rape of Hastings, one of the six historical divisions of the county of Sussex, which included the towns of Hastings, Rye and Battle.

12. https://cathedralisbruxellensis.be/en, accessed 19 August 2020. Almost 300 years later in 1617, Margaret and Jan's sepulchre was visited by the then duke and duchess of Brabant, Archduke Albrecht VII of Austria and Isabel Clara Eugenia, infanta of Spain and ruler of the Spanish Netherlands. Green, *Lives of the Princesses*, vol. 2, p. 400.

Appendix 1: Brief Biographical Details of Edward I's Daughters

1. This is taken from J. C. Parsons, 'The Year of Eleanor of Castile's Birth and Her Children by Edward I', pp. 245-65.
2. Parsons, 'Year of Birth', p. 262, gives the location of Margaret's burial.

Appendix 2: The Children of Edward I's Daughters

1. Marie's older sisters who became queens were Marguerite of Burgundy (*c.* 1290–1315), adulterous and imprisoned first wife of Louis X (b. 1289), king of Navarre 1305–16 and king of France 1314-16, who was the mother of Juana II, queen of Navarre (b. 1312, r. 1328–49); and Jeanne 'the Lame' (*la Boiteuse*) of Burgundy (*c.* 1293–1348), queen of the first Valois king of France, Philip VI (b. 1293, r. 1328-50), and the mother of John II (b. 1319, r. 1350–64).
2. Stapleton, 'Brief Summary of the Wardrobe Accounts', p. 338.
3. J. Ward, *Elizabeth de Burgh, Lady of Clare*, p. 147. Jeanne's inquisition post mortem is in *CIPM 1361–65*, no. 215.
4. Stapleton, 'Brief Summary of the Wardrobe Accounts', p. 341.
5. Ward, *Elizabeth de Burgh, Lady of Clare*, p. 43.
6. Marie's younger sister Jeanne (1310–71) married their first cousin Charles IV in July 1324 as his third wife and became queen-consort of France, and her younger brother Philippe of Évreux (1306–43) married their cousin Juana II (1312–49), queen-regnant of Navarre, and was the father of Carlos II 'the Bad', who reigned as king of Navarre from 1349 to 1387.
7. *CIPM 1336–46*, no. 55.

8. *CIPM 1327–36*, no. 626.
9. Verity, 'Children of Elizabeth', p. 8, citing *Rotuli Parliamentorum*, vol. 4 (1783), p. 268, for the petition: 'ye eldre Doughtre was wedded to Courteney Erle of Devenshire and yat oyr to Yerle of Ormond'. The Llanthony Abbey Cartulary, also cited in Verity, 'Children of Elizabeth', p. 8, specifically states that Eleanor was the elder daughter ('*Elianora de Bohun supradicta, senior filii praedicti Humfredi*').
10. Eleanor was still called by her maiden name, de Bohun, on 14 February 1328, and on 21 November that year an entry on the Patent Roll states that she had married James Botiler: *CPR 1327–30*, pp. 230, 340. James' IPM is *CIPM 1336–46*, no. 184.
11. *CPR 1327–30*, pp. 164, 175, 181-2 (Henry de Bohun was killed at Bannockburn in 1314, by Robert Bruce, king of Scotland, wielding a battle-axe). Eleanor's Wikipedia page, accessed 22 May 2020, states that she was born on 17 October 1304, though as her eldest brother Humphrey I was born on 10 September 1304, this is obviously impossible. It is very difficult to establish Eleanor's correct date of birth, however, given that her brother Humphrey II was born either sometime in 1307 or possibly in late 1309, the twins Edward and William probably in 1308/09 or 1312/13 (they were certainly younger than Humphrey), and Margaret on 3 April 1311. Perhaps Eleanor and Margaret were also twins, hence the confusion as to which of them was the elder. Eleanor's will is translated in J. Lutkin and J. Mackman, 'Will of Eleanor, Countess of Ormond, 1363', *Foundations*, 8 (2016), pp. 73-74, and B. Verity, 'Descendants to the Third Generation of Eleanor, Countess of Ormond (*c*. 1310–1363)', *Foundations*, vol. 8 (2016), p. 75, gives the place of her death. Her IPM is *CIPM 1361–65*, no. 483.
12. See Verity, 'Children of Elizabeth', p. 9, for Margaret de Bohun's date of birth, citing the Ford Abbey Cartulary in W. Dugdale, ed., *Monasticon Anglicanum*, vol. 5 (1825), p. 381: '*Haec Margareta matrem habuit ingenuam, dominam Elizabetham illustrissimi principis et regis incliti Edwardi post Conquestum Angliae primi filiam, anno Domini mcccxj. iij. nonas Aprilis nata*'. The date of her wedding to Hugh Courtenay is also given in the Ford Abbey Cartulary.